20274

D1533172

Heart Disease In Christ's Body

Dr. Jack Van Impe

**Library
Oakland S.U.M.**

20274

© 1984 by Jack Van Impe Ministries
Box J, Royal Oak, Michigan 48068
Box 1717, Postal Station A
Windsor, Ontario, N9A 6Y1 Canada

All rights reserved. No part of this book may be reproduced in any form without permission in writing from the publisher, except in the case of brief quotations embodied in critical articles or reviews.

All Scripture quotations are from **The King James Version** of the Bible.

Printed in the United States of America

Library
Oakland S.U.M.

A TRIBUTE

To Dr. Van Impe's New Position on Love

by Dr. Robert Savage
Missionary in St. Croix, Virgin Islands

Back in the 1930's and 1940's, my Dad — H. H. Savage — was known as "Mr. Fundamentalist" for the state of Michigan. He courageously and effectively led in the battle for fundamentalism. But if Dad were alive today, he would be called by many a "compromiser." His guilt would be that he cooperated with pastors and churches of many denominations in Union Lenten services (Detroit), evangelistic campaigns and Bible Conferences. I call these who would discredit Dad by the term "neo-fundamentalists." They are not historic fundamentalists because they have added so much to what was originally the position of fundamentalism.

Jack Van Impe's magnificent article, "That They All May Be One," is in a sense a call to return to historic fundamentalism and be rid of the fighting, the extremism and the misguided views of the "neo-fundamentalists."

Back in the 16th century, Martin Luther was used of God to bring multitudes back to the teaching of the Apostles. I pray that Jack Van Impe might be used in this last part of the 20th century to bring multitudes back to a position of love for each other and oneness in Christ.

i

FOREWORD

Many men of God feel led to ignore their critics. I have done so during the last ten years. Now the hour has arrived for me to state my position for a number of reasons:

1. The leading of the Holy Spirit.
2. To keep a movement from destroying itself. Fundamentalism began as a grand and glorious organization to uplift the Lord Jesus Christ and defend Christological truth centering around His deity, virgin birth, substitutionary atonement and bodily resurrection. Presently, however, many of our leaders have become sidetracked. They now judge men and movements on the basis of a leader's likes and dislikes. These personal preferences are based upon man-made rules and regulations rather than the Word of God. If such prejudices against good and godly men continue, fundamentalism's decline and fall will be swift. Jesus said: "a house divided against itself cannot stand."
3. To save the forthcoming generation of ministerial students (preacher boys) the heartaches and pitfalls I encountered by following fallible men rather than the infallible and inerrant Word of God.
4. To correct the rumors and allegations released by the leaders of neo-fundamentalism against hundreds of precious brothers in Christ who have been misjudged, mislabeled and misunderstood.

— Dr. Jack Van Impe

ii

Introduction

HEART DISEASE IN CHRIST'S BODY

Heart disease is the number one destroyer of human life in the world. Striking unexpectedly, it often leaves a trail of sorrow and tears. All are susceptible to its destructiveness and few escape its deadly ravages when attacked.

This enemy of health and wholesomeness is also existent within Christ's body. However, Christ is not the cause. Christians are. Why?

First Corinthians 12:13 teaches that every "born again" believer is implanted into the body of Christ at conversion. "For by one Spirit are we ALL baptized into one body . . ." This immediately makes us members of His body, of His flesh, and of His bones (Ephesians 5:30). Now Christ, as the head of the body, is sinless (I Peter 2:22), but we as members are not. Our hearts are deceitful and desperately wicked (Jeremiah 17:9).

One of the signs of a sick body is the tongue. Doctors usually examine it for clues of illness. Spiritually this is equally true. James 3:2 states: "If any man offend not in word (tongue), the same is a perfect man . . ."

On the other hand, when the tongue is maliciously used, verse six adds: " . . .it defileth the whole body" (ours and Christ's). The misuse of tongue and pen, then, indicates that heart disease exists in Christ's body, for Jesus said: " . . .out of the heart proceed evil thoughts, murders [hatred — I John 3:15], . . .false witness, blasphemies . . ." (Matthew 15:19).

iii

Tragically, the unity for which the Saviour pleaded is too often abused by those who claim to love Christ the most — the so-called orthodox defenders of the faith. These leaders claim to accept the fact that all brothers are members of the body of Christ, yet they refuse fellowship to any who disagree with them over any issue, however insignificant.

The resulting prejudice, bitterness, envy, and evil thinking are symptoms of the dreadful and destructive disease afflicting the hearts of all those who practice such unloveliness as well as the very heart of Christ.

Our Lord prayed for "UNITY" four times in John chapter seventeen. He desired that every member of His body function in a coordinated and harmonious manner. Today, every member of Christ's body is to "endeavor to keep the unity of the Spirit in the bond of peace" (Ephesians 4:3).

Presently, the multitudinous voices proclaiming and printing bigoted statements against those attempting to obey Christ's command to love and live in unity prove that "heart disease in Christ's body" is out of control. Proverbs 6:14 pictures the condition: "Frowardness is in his heart, he deviseth mischief continually; he soweth discord."

The only solution is the Word of God. Let the Holy Spirit, the Author of this great Book, use His sword and scalpel to perform the greatest bypass surgery ever — changing each and all from walking in the flesh to abiding in the Spirit — from carnality to spirituality. When this operation has been completed, healing will return to Christ's body.

TABLE OF CONTENTS

A Tribute I
Foreword II
Introduction III

Chapter 1
Fundamentalism's Citywide Crusader 1

Chapter 2
The Call of God 9

Chapter 3
Separation Without Sanctification 25

Chapter 4
Children Sitting in the Marketplace 35

Chapter 5
I Am a Fundamentalist 43

Chapter 6
Defending the Faith in Love 67

Chapter 7
A Call for Revival Within
   Fundamentalism 77

Chapter 8
That They All May Be One 95

Chapter 9
Historic Fundamentalism's Roots 107

TABLE OF CONTENTS (continued)

Chapter 10
Neo-Fundamentalism's Errant
Interpretation of the Inerrant Word 127

Chapter 11
The Judgment Seat of the Neo-Fundamentalists
or Heart Disease in Christ's Body 165

Chapter 12
Neo-Fundamentalism's Leadership 211

Chapter 13
Obeying Man or God 255

Chapter 14
God's Leaders Respond 281

Chapter 1

Fundamentalism's Citywide Crusader

This chapter is adapted from my biography, **They Call Him the Walking Bible**, by my longtime friend Roger Campbell.

It is the final night of the crusade, the culmination of months of planning and prayer. The crowd is arriving and the chatter of voices provides cover for the choir to rehearse its selection one more time. Those who have found their places early in order to enjoy the preliminary music strain to hear over the scuffing of feet and the buzz of conversation all around them.

In rooms beneath the stadium bleachers there is another kind of conversation going on as hundreds pray for this closing service. They are the counselors, pastors, committee people, and others who have given of themselves to make all this happen.

Some who are making their way down the crowded aisles searching for seats will never forget this week. Their lives have been changed. They feel as if they have come to the end of a long search. Others are still searching.

A man escorts his wife down the stairs and to the row of chairs nearest the speaker's platform. They have decided to make one last try before divorce. It will be their night.

A teenage boy clutching a new Bible moves up the steps to the top row in the stadium.

Ushers assist an older gentleman in a wheelchair.

He has been bitter about life since the accident that caused his paralysis. He had been on his way to a dance, hoping for some vicarious enjoyment in seeing others move about so freely, when the stadium sign attracted his attention and caused him to have his driver bring him to hear "The Walking Bible."

As pastors and workers emerge from the prayer rooms, there is a quieting of the crowd. Eyes follow Dr. Van Impe and Rexella, his wife, as they join others who have platform responsibilities in this crusade finale.

Tonight's message will be prophetic, and everything in the service builds toward it. There is an expectant air in the crowd. They have been looking forward all week to this explanation of Bible prophecy as it relates to world events. Many have brought friends and relatives whose curiosity has been aroused by the timely topic.

First nighters eye the evangelist as the service develops. They see a man who has a burden, yet is human enough for a quick smile. He seems both distant and approachable. Immersed in thought, yet alert to everything around him.

Dr. Van Impe's part in the musical portion of the meeting provides many in the audience their first opportunity to hear the accorgan, an instrument that blends the benefits of both the accordion and the organ. His ability as a musician is established quickly. He is totally involved. A perfectionist.

The bond between this husband-wife team is too strong to be hidden. While Rexella is communicating with the crowd in testimony and song, the man in her life beams approval. And well he might. He knows her ministry in music is no performance, and he respects the work of God through this lady so loved by crusade congregations around the world.

When the evangelist rises to preach there are mixed feelings throughout the stadium. There is anticipation of hearing the awaited prophetic message, but it is accompanied by a touch of sadness at this being the last message Dr. Van Impe will deliver to this audience.

Regular attenders are not surprised at the army of Bible verses marshalled to explain and prove each point of the sermon; they've come to expect it. Many feel as if they have been bathed in the Bible during these meetings, and the cleansing effect is showing in their lives. Old wrongs have been made right. Bills paid. Questionable practices dropped. Dedication renewed.

Newcomers are overwhelmed by the avalanche of inspiration. They have never heard this much Bible in so short a time. They are amazed at the evangelist's ability to quote the written Word of God. It is evident that his aim is to place his own personality in the background and to confront his hearers with an ultimatum from the Almighty. He seems to desire to be only a voice, forcing his audience to grapple with the Word.

In this setting and atmosphere, the results are predictable. Conviction grows. Sin seems more sinful. The cross and resurrection appear in their proper Biblical perspective. Conversions take place. Backsliders return. The faithful are refueled. The fire spreads. Blessings abound. The following reports highlight the excitement of the crusades as crowds build and souls are saved.

In Indianapolis, 12,000 gathered for the closing service of the crusade. Hundreds were converted. It was a cold week for outdoor meetings, yet thousands gathered nightly wrapped in blankets to hear "The Walking Bible."

Over 10,000 attended the final night in Dayton, Ohio. It was a week of great spiritual victories with many decisions for Christ.

"Crusade Crowds Larger Than Any Sports Gathering in the History of Hershey, PA." was the headline in the news release reporting that great crusade. The attendance set a record for any religious gathering in that part of the state.

Portsmouth, Virginia responded so well that closed-circuit TV was used to accommodate the crowds. There were 600 conversions.

In Syracuse, New York, 1,000 came forward at the invitation. The Scranton, Pennsylvania Crusade resulted in the largest attendance since the days of Billy Sunday.

In Honolulu, Hawaii, thousands attended the service at the internationally famous Waikiki Shell and 500 were converted, along with thousands of restorations and rededications of life. In the Panama Canal Zone, the crowds were so large that it was necessary to move the meetings outdoors.

Churches in the Philippines hosted a crusade in January 1975. One of the high points of this effort was the response of the pastors. Special seminars on soulwinning were scheduled for them by Dr. Van Impe, and resulted in a pledge to try to win 10,000 souls during that year. Decisions for Christ totaled 6,514, and the ministers won the additional

10,000, making it one of the most fruitful of Dr. Van Impe's ministry.

Ten million people attended the mass citywide endeavors, and 500,000 decisions for Christ were registered.

All Dr. Van Impe's crusades were sponsored exclusively by great Bible-believing ministers and churches and these stalwarts of the faith made the following comments about Dr. Van Impe's ministry.

Dr. Joseph M. Stowell, D.D. (former national representative of The General Association of Regular Baptist Churches): "I have known Jack Van Impe for a number of years and have been privileged to work with him in evangelistic campaigns. He is true to the Bible, has a burning zeal for the lost, and is fearless in his presentation of divine truth. He sees the issue of apostasy and is obedient to the Bible teaching concerning separation from it. He not only believes in and preaches ecclesiastical separation, but he believes in and practices personal separation. He and his wife Rexella are a wonderful team."

Dr. Lee Roberson (pastor of Highland Park Baptist Church, Chattanooga, Tennessee, and president of Tennessee Temple Schools): "Dr. Van Impe has conducted a number of successful revivals in our church. In the course of these meetings hundreds have been saved and even thousands have responded to the invitation for salvation and dedication of life. He has been a favorite at the Highland Park Baptist Church and Tennessee Temple Schools through the years."

Dr. John R. Rice (editor of **The Sword of the Lord**): "Dr. Jack Van Impe is a good friend. He is a fine gospel preacher. He is separated and stands true, does

5

not have any fellowship with modernists and unbelievers, but in his campaign enlists those who are of like precious faith who hold to the great essentials of the faith. God bless him."

Dr. Jerry Falwell (pastor of Thomas Road Baptist Church, Lynchburg, Virginia): "Dr. Jack Van Impe has conducted several highly successful crusades in the Thomas Road Baptist Church. I consider Dr. Van Impe one of the most dynamic and powerful Bible preachers in the land today. My wife and I are happy to own Jack and Rexella as dear and personal friends.

"Dr. Van Impe also has the distinction of being the only preacher in this generation who has been able to rally the fundamentalist churches into successful cooperative evangelism."

Dr. Jack Hyles (pastor of First Baptist Church of Hammond, Indiana): "Dr. Jack Van Impe has been the answer to the prayers of thousands of fundamentalist people across America. His message has been clear; his convictions have been firm; his zeal has been a pattern and his love for Christ, for souls and for the brethren has never wavered in the years I have followed his ministry. Many of us have prayed for an evangelist who in every sense of the word is a fundamentalist, and is happy and not ashamed to bear the stigma involved. Here is a man who has sacrificed for his convictions and who has been honored for it. America had to have him. I am pleased God has given him to us."

Presently, the mass citywide endeavors in stadiums, coliseums and ball parks have ceased. Sad, but true. Nevertheless, historians will one day record that Dr. Jack Van Impe conducted the most fundamentalist-sponsored crusades of the twentieth century.

Who or what caused the disintegration and demise of such dynamic, Spirit-empowered crusades producing tens of thousands of decisions for Christ?

In the chapters that follow, Dr. Van Impe shares firsthand his call to the ministry and personal experiences in citywide crusades—including the opposition and pressure brought to bear upon him by the leaders of the so-called "neo-fundamentalist" movement (a term coined by Dr. Carl McIntyre). It is a story of heartache and pain inflicted by those who are driven by a spirit of inquisition against all who fail to conform to their narrow and rigid obsessions. In the tradition of the self-righteous, hell-raising Pharisees (the term used by Dr. John R. Rice), this group has ridden roughshod over all other believers in vengeful fury, wrapping themselves in a soiled and tattered banner of Christian separatism.

Chapter 2

The Call of God

My Belgian parents arrived in America in 1929, the time of the Great Depression. They came seeking fame and fortune, but ended up in the deepest of poverty for the first five years of their lives as immigrants in this great land.

Since my father Oscar Van Impe was a talented accordionist, he sought employment as an entertainer in order to supplement his income as an automobile factory worker. Before long, he became a nightclub favorite among the 40,000 Belgians who lived in the city of Detroit. Soon, he had me appearing before the same crowds with a miniature accordion when I was but eight years of age.

As a result of his constant nightclub associations, Dad started to drink heavily and the years that followed became a nightmare in our home. Then, after ten years of a living hell upon the earth, the Spirit of God began to do a deep work within the hearts of my parents.

One holiday weekend, I decided not to accompany Mom and Dad to the nightspots to entertain. I promised them that I would be home by 9 p.m., but decided to stay out as long as I desired thinking that they would never know. At 11 p.m., a car traveling at a tremendous rate of speed struck me as I was crossing an intersection. My body was thrown thirty-five feet through the air. Immediately, the half-drunken occupants of the speeding vehicle stopped, looked at me and decided to stuff my body into the trunk. Fortunately, a detective who was passing by saw what was occurring, stopped the proceedings and arrested the culprits.

Though my body was badly bruised, there were no serious complications. God, however, used this accident to open the minds and hearts of my parents to the reality of death and eternity.

Soon afterward, my father trusted Jesus Christ as his personal Saviour. Then Mom made the same commitment. I was shocked. God had given me a new father and mother. They were born again, and completely changed by His mighty power. At that point, II Corinthians 5:17 became a living reality in our home: "Therefore if any man be in Christ, he is a new creature: old things are passed away; behold, all things are become new."

My heart was so overwhelmed by the change in my parents that I, too, wanted to be saved. We had lived across the street from a small, gospel-preaching church for years. In fact, I had often raided this godly group of people with rotten tomatoes in earlier days. The following Sunday morning, I boldly walked into the church, announced my need of the Saviour and was led to Christ before Sunday school even began. What joy filled my entire being as I became a new creation in Christ Jesus. I made my public profession of faith at the end of the morning service and a few months later submitted to baptism, publicly declaring my faith in the Lord Jesus Christ.

My conversion took place during my high school days, and as a teenager I had but one desire — to follow Christ wholeheartedly. I wanted to go to Bible college so badly that I could hardly wait for graduation day. I longed to begin devouring God's Word.

At the time of my salvation I was such a raw pagan that I did not even know the story of Jonah and the whale. I had never heard John 3:16. In fact, my ignorance of God's Word was so great that I thought an apostle and epistle were husband and wife!

Bible College Days

Imagine my shock when I arrived at Detroit Bible College and heard such mind-boggling terms as "theology," "hermeneutics," "exegesis," "apologetics" and "Greek." I was petrified. I did not know the meaning of "soteriology," "pneumatology," or even such simple phrases as "the deity of Christ," and "the substitutionary atonement." Nevertheless, I was determined to know Christ in a greater way through His blessed Word, and study I did — settling only for an "A" average.

Shortly after beginning college, I began appearing on television with Dr. Robert Parr and "The America Back To God Hour." I also traveled extensively as a musician with the Voice of Christian Youth (Youth for Christ in Detroit). These activities kept me busy in the service of the King until my graduation from college.

Just prior to graduation, I was ordained to the gospel ministry at the Christian Fellowship Tabernacle in Marine City, Michigan. The examining council was composed of eleven ministers: Dr. A.G. Kruschwitz, Rev. Earl Linderholm, Dr. W.S. Hottel, Rev. L.P. Buroker, Rev. Albert Ludwig, Rev. John Pinches, Rev. Harrey E. Cochenour, Rev. Orrin Van Loon, Sr., Rev. Orrin Van Loon, Jr., Rev. Harold

Moran and Rev. William Reiter. The council chairman was Dr. W.S. Hottel, a noted Bible scholar and writer.

I had prepared diligently for the great night when I would be questioned orally for two hours by this panel of godly brethren. For weeks, I had tucked 500 Bible verses into my head and heart through memorization. When I gave my doctrinal statement, I quoted verses in machine-gun fashion to back up each point. I actually used the majority of the memorized portions in my presentation. Upon finishing the task, Dr. W.S. Hottel commended my usage of God's Word.

The Fundamental Fellowship, a Michigan religious periodical, reported my ordination under the heading: "Jack Van Impe Ordained to Ministry Following Unusual Ordination Council." The subtitle read: "Only One Question Asked Following Doctrinal Statement." What was that question? Dr. Hottel, the chairman of the council, voiced it: "Jack, do you really believe what you have just told us you believe?" I replied, "Yes, sir, I certainly do, with all my heart." Dr. Hottel responded by saying, "Gentlemen, we have another Martin Luther on our hands. Let's ordain him."

I can only praise God for His goodness in helping a lost young pagan (who had never heard John 3:16 prior to his salvation) to reach this point in his Christian life in just five short years. After observing the power of God through His Word during this ordination council, I determined that I would complete my memorization program by storing every verse of the New Testament in my head and heart.

The project took seventeen years to complete, but I reached the goal that the Spirit of God had burdened me to attain.

Now, I was on my own, conducting rallies and concerts for Youth for Christ. One night in Pontiac, Michigan, I met a young lady named Rexella Shelton. She was to sing on the same program where I was speaking. When I saw her, it was love at first sight. Then, as she gave her testimony and mentioned that God had called her into evangelism, I knew this was it. Six months later, I asked, "Wilt thou?" It was a hot, summery night and Rexella wilted. Praise God!

The Lord certainly knew what He was doing when He joined in holy matrimony two individuals who would conduct 800 full-length, local church crusades and 253 mass, citywide endeavors over a period of 32 years. Because we were faithful in the smallest churches in earlier days, God gave Rexella and me the largest crusades ever conducted under the banner of fundamentalism.

Today, I am as committed to affirming and upholding the position of historic, biblical fundamentalism as I have ever been. Still, I am deeply burdened over the divisiveness espoused by those who call themselves "militant fundamentalists." As I deal with this issue and tell my story in the remaining pages of this book, I shall do so honestly and factually. Because 10,000 fundamentalist pastors have sponsored my citywide crusades, I know this movement as well as any human being alive.

May I say at the outset that the majority of our fundamentalist leaders are great men of God whose hearts are filled with a love for others. They would gladly lay down their lives to lift the fallen and bring sinners to Christ. Most of them love their brothers in Christ as well, and are as broken over the present infighting as I am. Hundreds of letters which have come to me tell of the heartaches, frustrations and disappointments these men are presently experiencing because of a small, vocal minority who believe that one is compromising if he is not constantly attacking others. Unless this group, which I call "neo-fundamentalists," is labeling and mislabeling others in the most crude language, they feel they are not defending the faith. How wrong when men feel that there is inherent virtue in conflict, criticism, ostracism and suspicion. How wicked when men believe that they constitute a very exclusive group which holds a monopoly on truth and righteousness and constantly adds new names to its "blacklist" as others fail to meet their qualifications and standards. I thank God for the silent majority who believe that Christianity is still based on the premise of love and who attempt to practice and preach it as God's norm for believers. In earlier days, this spirit of inquisition was not present. How joyous it was to serve the Lord in the local churches and citywide endeavors at that time.

Years of Blessing

Because of the love between brethren, the blessing of God overflowed in our crusade services. During more than 800 local church revivals, Rexella and I saw every attendance record shattered in all but ten of our meetings. God mightily was upon the scene, visiting us with genuine revival week after week.

In one church where an invitation had never been given and where the pastor had never pushed for conversion, the entire church membership walked the aisle for salvation or a public profession of their faith. The situation was startling, to say the least.

During our meetings in both Warren and Detroit, Michigan, God visited us with such Holy Spirit conviction that the membership stayed to pray and confess their sins until 4 p.m. on the Lord's Day. They hardly had time to get home and return for the evening service. Hundreds were saved.

Repeatedly, we saw the power of God unleashed in 800 local church crusades conducted from 1948 to 1969. At that point in time, we were faced with an important decision in our expanding ministry. Rexella and I had received over 1,500 invitations to conduct local church endeavors. Were we to give each of them an eight-day meeting, we would be scheduled for the next sixty years!

Because of this situation, as well as the opportunity to reach multitudes more for Christ, we made the decision to begin conducting mass, citywide crusades in 1970. These powerful meetings united local, Bible-believing churches for great outreaches which took place in arenas, ball parks and coliseums. God again smiled upon our decision to unite believers and reach the lost. The doors began opening faster than we had anticipated, and we were faced with many exciting challenges.

The results of these crusades, reported in the opening chapter, tell the story of some of the most thrilling days Rexella and I have ever experienced in our service for the King.

Threats

In the midst of such blessing, of course, Satan was displeased. He wanted to end this ministry. Often, he used threats of death to try to disrupt the joy and blessing we experienced as thousands were saved and revived.

We went to the Panama Canal Zone just after revolutionaries had taken over the University there. The threats by Communist sympathizers were many, the climate was electric and tension was at an all-time high. Still, the response to our crusade was tremendous. In fact, the crowd grew to such proportions that we were forced to meet outdoors. There were hills all around me, and yet I stood in the open, preaching on Ezekiel 38,39 — the great prophecy of a cataclysmic war between Russia and Israel! A sniper on a hillside could easily have shot me, but God gave me the confidence to preach with conviction and power and I was not afraid.

It was the closing Friday night of our Kansas City, Missouri Crusade when I discovered that my life was in jeopardy. As I was announcing the subjects for the final two evenings, I saw a dozen policemen enter the building. One of the officers walked to the platform and whispered, "We have every exit covered because we have received official reports that there is a plot to kill you." For the next forty-eight hours, Rexella and I were unable to travel without armed guards. Neither handshaking nor Bible signing was allowed until the final night of the crusade, and even then only with officers present.

I recall that before the police came on the scene,

just preceding the service, a man had rushed up to me asking for help in the prayer room immediately. Since there were only four minutes remaining before the start of the service, I told him he would have to wait until after the message. He walked away cursing. Perhaps this was the key move in the planned assassination. Only God knows, and He is always on time in protecting His own.

We later learned that three men were involved in the plot. Because a number of drug pushers had been converted, the narcotics traffic was disrupted. Therefore, three ringleaders decided that the "troublemaker" had to go. Fortunately, they did not succeed in their murderous venture. Rexella and I arrived home safely, and still continue to give thanks to God for His protection.

Hershey, Pennsylvania was another danger spot. The crusade crowds were especially responsive and the attendance soon built up to 10,500. Revival was in the air! Then, in the midst of this blessing, a note threatening my life was discovered in the offering plate. The writer promised to kill me if I preached my announced message topic, "A Politician's Greatest Blunder," the following evening. That night, the phone in our motel room rang incessantly throughout the night. To make matters worse, the calls were not coming through the switchboard, but were being dialed from other rooms. Masked men attended the meeting the next evening, yet once again the providence of God kept us from harm.

An additional deliverance from death came during our Bicentennial Crusade in Philadelphia in 1976. I shared the experience with our friends and supporters via the Bicentennial/Anniversary issue of our **Jack Van Impe Crusade Newsletter**:

Praise God, from Whom all blessings flow! God graciously protected the city of Philadelphia, America's 200th birthday celebration, the Bicentennial Crusade and my life. Instead of violence, blessing occurred the week of July 4 through 11.

The Congressional Record, F.B.I. files, Reader's Digest and the Herald Tribune (international English newspaper), had all carried warnings concerning the planned violence which might have destroyed Philadelphia and the Bicentennial activities. Communists and militant supporters had mapped out a program in Chicago January 30 through February 1, 1976, to bring "fireworks" to the "City of Brotherly Love" July 4.

In addition to these reports, I had personally received warnings. I was told that militants wanted Dr. Jack Hyles and myself "out of the way."

July 2, Rexella and I left home for Philadelphia. As we stood in the foyer of our home praying, my heart was heavy. I felt that I might not return. I had said nothing to Rexella about the mail I had received.

That same morning, my staff had given me a note. It said: "We are praying that God will bring you back to us safely." Every staff member had signed it. Being a man, I fought my emotions, but was deeply moved. I knew

God had a plan, and all I wanted was His will.

The evening of July 2 was spent in Philadelphia. Three truckloads of militants arrived in front of our hotel and marched past with the clenched fist salute of the Communist movement. On television, radicals were being interviewed. They boldly boasted of the way they would dynamite the city July 4. I wondered how the TV media could be so calloused as to allow these revolutionaries thousands of dollars worth of air time.

The fear could be felt in the air. Millions who had planned to come to Philadelphia stayed away. The downtown hotels were forty to fifty percent vacant, although they had been completely booked months in advance.

On our opening night, fifty of the sponsoring churches believed it best to conduct their own services in order to avoid any violence. Police filled the city, and I was told that the militants were under complete surveillance as plainclothesmen infiltrated their ranks. Six guards were assigned to the crusade platform. My personal bodyguards (one of whom had been personal bodyguard to Mayor Rizzo for three and one-half years) demanded that I wear a bulletproof vest. I tried it the first night and felt handicapped. The next day I said: "Men, I have spent the night in prayer and feel it is a lack of faith to wear this vest for the entire crusade." From that moment onward, perfect peace filled my soul.

Heart Disease in Christ's Body

The 500,000 who came to Christ during our years of citywide evangelism made all the heartaches and threats worthwhile. Yet, in the midst of the blessedness of serving the Lord and seeing all that He was doing through the crusades, my heart began — slowly and almost imperceptibly at first — to be deeply troubled at the inconsistences and injustices I saw. Often, for example, the basic values of honesty and integrity seemed to be lacking in those who thought themselves to be the most committed to righteousness. The threats of death I could take. Dishonesty and hypocrisy I could not.

In Flint, Michigan, a pastor called me several weeks before our citywide crusade and said he would like to have us speak at some special services in his church. "It will give our people enthusiasm for your coming in June," he said. "We will pack the church to the hilt, and it will be a great blessing in preparation for your crusade."

Although I was at that time conducting only citywide crusades, I held a special series of services for that pastor in his church. During the four-day period, more than one hundred people were saved. However, when I went to Flint for the citywide crusade, the same pastor informed me that because I had so recently been in his church, they did not feel it was necessary to support our citywide endeavor. A similar situation also occurred in Tuscon, Arizona.

In Tennessee, the local ministers asked that our meetings not carry over for a second Sunday. They did not want to have to cancel two successive Sunday evening services. Consequently, we decided to close our crusade on Wednesday evening with the videotaping of a nationwide television special. The ministers, in turn, promised that they would cancel their Wednesday evening services so their congregations could be present at the taping. Very few of the pastors kept their promise. However, visitors from non-sponsoring churches filled the building.

In a Florida city, the envelopes we used for our love offerings were sent by mail. When I arrived, they could not be found. The chairman of the crusade acted very concerned and even prayed with me that the envelopes would be located. Later, the wife of one of his associates came to me and said, "It's very hypocritical that he would pray with you about those envelopes. He ordered that they be thrown away. If you'll go over to the city dump, you'll find them." We checked, and that's where they were.

Several months after the close of a crusade in South Carolina, I learned that the crusade chairman — a local pastor — had diverted funds from our meeting to pay the bills of his own church. As a result, some in this city believed that we had defaulted on our payments. Rather than make an issue, we paid the bills.

Similar situations took place in other cities. Our standard agreement was that our organization would pay all the travel expenses and other bills incurred during the preliminary meetings to organize a crusade in a given community. Then, if the local pastors agreed to organize a crusade committee to actually plan a crusade, they were to assume responsibility for all expenses from that point onward. If, for any reason beyond our control, they decided to cancel the crusade, they would remain responsible to pay any bills incurred. Many times, however, crusade committees canceled planned crusades — usually because they were not unified — and left us holding the bag for expenses.

It is amazing to me that men who pride themselves for being men of strong convictions and firm principles can be so insensitive to what is truly righteous. In Florida, the local pastors organized a committee and elected a chairman. He was a godly man, committed to fundamentalism. However, he had been in an accident several years earlier, and had a disfigured ear. For cosmetic reasons, he allowed his hair to grow long enough to cover the deformed ear. His hair wasn't long, but it did cover his ear. Consequently, several of the crusade participants felt that this brother's hair was a sign of compromise. As a result, they withdrew from the crusade, thereby forcing its cancellation. They also refused to pay the substantial bills they had already incurred, though they previously agreed to honorably meet their commitments. Ultimately, our organization absorbed these costs. Sad, isn't it? The men who had canceled the crusade because of their so-called "convictions" about hair conveniently overlooked the principle of honesty concerning their bills. They also lost an opportunity to reach thousands of lost souls in their area for the Lord.

I confess that I do not understand the mentality that permits a person to rationalize away what is clearly sin in the name of avoiding that which is questionably "compromise." These men were like the Pharisees of Christ's time who strained at gnats and swallowed camels (Matthew 23:24). During the decade I spent in citywide crusades, I saw so much of this kind of behavior that I came to expect it. Yet I never ceased to be saddened by it, and I began to wonder how long I could continue working in such an environment and still expect God to bless my labors.

Chapter 3

Separation Without Sanctification

In 1973, we conducted a citywide crusade in Chicago's McCormick Place. I had a new car with only five hundred miles on it, and since I did not need it for the week, I left it parked in the lot. When I picked it up at the end of the week, I gave my claim check to the parking attendant, and off he went to get the car. While I was waiting for him to return, I became engaged in conversation and did not notice the vehicle when the attendant drove up in it. He got out, handed me the key and said, "Have a nice day."

When I entered my automobile, I was startled. The windshield was gone and the entire front end was smashed. The man who had parked it earlier in the week was a drug user. Knowing that I would not return for a week, he had used my car, gotten into an accident and demolished the front end. Then, the attendant who returned my car to me had the audacity to act as if nothing had happened, even to the point of telling me to have a nice day!

The latter attendant's total disregard for what was so obvious reminds me of the attitude of many neo-fundamentalists. In fact, from this point onward, I will use the term "neo-fundamentalist" to designate an unscriptural movement within true fundamentalism that would rather fight than switch.

Neo-fundamentalists seemingly ignore what the Scriptures say about love and unity among Christians and present a lopsided view of what constitutes orthodoxy. They preach and teach a misinterpreted message on separation, and then view themselves as the only ones who understand such truth. They are like the parking lot attendant who handed me the keys to a demolished car and nonchalantly said, "Have a nice day."

Perhaps the single most significant element of neo-fundamentalism is the emphasis given to ecclesi-astical separation. Militant separatists go to unbe-lievable extremes to ensure that their associations are "pure." Some are so consumed with a passion to separate from others who differ with them over non-important issues that it becomes an obsession with them. I have known more than one man who broke fellowship with so many others that, ultimately, he was left completed isolated, feeling that he was God's sole spokesman in the city where he minis-tered. Neo-fundamentalism is filled with this kind of Pharisaism. Elijah in his day told God that he stood alone. God rebuked his foolish servant by stating in I Kings 19:18, "Yet I have left me seven thousand in Israel, all the knees which have not bowed unto Baal, and every mouth which hath not kissed him." Today there are tens of thousands who stand for historic fundamentalism's principles but who are, never-theless, rejected simply because they do not dot their "I's" or cross their "T's" in accordance with a self-appointed leader's inconsequential regulations.

Holy Blackmail

This passion of neo-fundamentalists that drives them into isolationism and demands the same of their followers has led to a climate of fear, suspicion and underhandedness as they attempt to force others into their unscriptural mold.

In fact, neo-fundamentalists frequently use threats and blackmail to accomplish their wishes in manipulating others. This happened to me on a number of occasions. The method of operation is disgustingly simple. It begins as leaders turn brothers against one another by mislabeling them under various titles as compromisers. Then those suspected of fellowship with the alleged compromisers also become guilty. The suspected are then warned by telephone or letter to immediately break fellowship with such tainted brothers or suffer the humiliation and agony of being publicly exposed as defectors. Imagine the mentality involved in such reasoning and also the fear it induces as men, to save their ministries, succumb to such pressure tactics.

To further describe the terror of such un-Christlike methods, the system seems to reach everywhere. There is a sort of unofficial "K.G.B." spy system within neo-fundamentalism. It is composed of students and pastors who seek to please the leadership by serving as informers within the system. They scrutinize pastors, evangelists and teachers as to their religious affiliations and then notify headquarters. Those fellowshipping with disapproved brethren are sternly rebuked or excommunicated by the leadership sitting on the sidelines "calling the shots." If all this suspicion is based on misinformation or misinterpretation, it doesn't matter. The rules and regulations of the party must triumph. Justice is meaningless. Except for the few who are members of the cabal that passes down edicts upon others, anyone and everyone is fair game for criticism.

Believe me when I say that there is no place for

liberty in the Lord under this biased system. Am I talking about a Russian or a Cuban organization? No, I am describing a group of Christians in America who use such procedures. Let me give you an example. A loved one had the privacy of his dormitory room invaded at 10 p.m. After a search they confiscated all Van Impe albums, including Rexella's musical renditions. That such proceedings should occur on the campus of a Christian university seems appalling and shocking to many. Still, it is common within this group.

Then, when one is caught compromising on a local or a national level according to their interpretation, that person is roasted at "open forums." These inquisitions, however, are not really "open." Why? The accused is never asked to be present to defend himself. Instead, at such gatherings neo-fundamentalist leaders flown in from other states as well as local pastors compose a panel which answers questions about alleged defectors. The castigation and backbiting that results is appalling. Chapters eleven and twelve of this book describe the proceedings and document my allegations.

The other method of public exposure involves the neo-fundamentalist scandal sheets which usually copy one another's rumors about brothers in Christ. These small papers are nothing more than gossip columns produced under the guise of "defending the faith." They contain the latest "uncovered compromise" of alleged pseudo-fundamentalists (fakes) or supposed new-evangelicals, who are one rung down the ladder. Since Christians are forbidden to go to law against believers, the slander is never retracted via an apology if proven wrong.

Do such inquisitions and scandal sheets hurt the reputations of God's servants? Unfortunately, yes. Some Christians are ready to believe virtually anything they hear or read. Few bother to investigate or write the accused for verification of the innuendos and rumors slandering him.

On Trial

During my latter years in citywide endeavors, pastors who had heard such allegations often questioned me at the inception of a crusade. I would usually meet with them on Monday afternoon to answer the numerous charges about my fellowship with some good brothers in Christ who had also been mislabeled. At times the sessions would last three or four hours before the men were convinced that the religious gazettes were erroneous in the presentation of the facts or that they had purposely stacked the evidence against solid men of God. Frequently, the same question resurfaced years after an issue had been settled. Needless to say, the hours of questioning were exasperating and emotionally draining. By crusade time I had neither the enthusiasm nor the joy necessary to do my best service for Christ under such judgmental circumstances.

Why did I allow such trials to occur? Simply because I wanted to be a staunch fundamentalist. Consequently, I did everything within my power to correct any misunderstanding created by the neo-fundamentalist media machine. As a result, I continued bowing to men, thinking this was the way to please God, but also growing exceedingly frustrated in my attempts to please men with such condemnatory mentalities. My spirit became grieved at being forced to break fellowship with accused brothers in Christ I loved dearly in the Lord. They were giants for God holding to the principles of historic fundamentalism. Nevertheless, I was forbidden fellowship because an autocratic leader disliked them.

My Holy Spirit-directed conscience would not allow me to continue under such unscriptural practices. A burden to air a declaration of my views of love for all the brotherhood began building in me. I knew that I must one day reveal publicly what God's Spirit was creating in my heart.

Senseless Criticism

The attitudes held by many people we met seemed to be senseless in the light of the Saviour's command to love one another. For instance, Rexella and I conducted a crusade in Honolulu, Hawaii, in 1980. We decided to combine a tour group from the states for the event. Tours are open to the general public. As a result, many of God's dear people from numerous denominations went with us. A militant fundamentalist pastor in Hawaii discovered this and, on the final evening of the crusade, was backstage at the famous Waikiki Shell. Victory abounded as scores came forward for salvation. We were so short on counselors that I began dealing with the souls personally. This was difficult in that I had just taped a one-hour television special and had additional items that still had needed to be taped. The crew was waiting. Nevertheless, souls came first. While dealing with a broken sinner, I heard shouting. Guess what! I had an angry pastor on my hands. He discovered that one of the tour group members was a Pentecostal. Thus, he could be heard ranting, "This ministry has compromised by allowing a Pentecostal to join the tour group." Imagine the confusion generated as precious souls were turning to Christ. This temper tantrum was certainly out of harmony with the command of Jesus who said in John 13:35, "By this shall all men know that ye are my disciples, if ye have love one for another." Again my spirit and conscience informed me that there had to be something wrong with such prejudiced thinking. This was not historic fundamentalism which originated among brothers of multiplied denominations. This was something new and wrong. It was the seed of neo-fundamentalism beginning to sprout and flourish.

Runaway Separation

There was more to separation than ecclesiastical isolationism. Neo-fundamentalism also practiced racial separation. They went hand in hand. Blacks were usually conveniently excluded by simply stating, "Blacks are not fundamentalists." How well I remember the heartache I experienced when in Maryland two black pastors came to me in tears saying, "Do you really expect God to bless this lily white crusade?" That statement took root and I never forgot it. How hypocritical we are when we send missionaries to Africa and then refuse to fellowship with black brothers in Christ in America.

In all my years of evangelism, I had two integrated campaigns. On the final night of the Philadelphia Bicentennial Crusade, a neo-fundamentalist leader came from out of state to see for himself if I were guilty of all the compromise reported to him by informers. The local crusade leaders, fearful that they too might be labeled as compromisers, told the black sponsoring ministers that they would not be seated on the platform or be recognized as on previous nights. I knew nothing about the situation until black leaders shared the information with me recently. Imagine such bigotry in the name of the God of love. Forgive us, Lord, for our hypocrisy.

Denominational separatism also became popular. Although historic fundamentalism had always been interdenominational, many of today's fundamentalists excluded other fundamentalists who had different denominational tags. As a case in point, two precious men of God whom I met and with whom I fellowshipped at the interdenominational World Congress of Fundamentalists in Scotland were excluded from my crusade in Tennessee a few months later. Why? They were not Baptists. Had I insisted that they be included, the sponsoring pastors would have canceled the crusade. Still, two godly brothers were grieved that one group of fundamentalists accepted them while another group rejected them.

By the mid 1970's I began growing weary of trying to please the militant factions within our movement. Then an event occurred in 1976 that helped me see the futility and hopelessness of future united mass campaigns.

We were chosen to conduct the Bicentennial

Crusade in Philadelphia. At approximately the same time,
Campus Crusade for Christ was planning its "Here's Life" outreach in the area. Bill Bright had contacted a number of local fundamentalist pastors to inquire if they would be willing to nurture precious souls who came to Christ through the "Here's Life" campaign. Since critics of Dr. Bright had already branded Campus Crusade as a "neo-evangelical" organization, anyone who accepted their converts also became tainted. Thus, the problem began when some of the local pastors who attended a preliminary session of a "Here's Life" meeting also participated in an early briefing meeting of our crusade. A Bob Jones University graduate made it his duty to attend our session, taking the names of all those present and sending them to Dr. Bob Jones, Jr.

Immediately, Dr. Jones notified me that I had to either cast out of the Philadelphia crusade fifteen compromisers or consider my speaking engagement in Scotland canceled. Naturally, if I did not appear as a guest speaker, I would be labeled to the attending crowd as an alleged compromiser or defector. My grieved spirit and conscience had enough. I had bowed to the threats of men far too long. I would now obey God exclusively. I canceled.

Later, Dr. Jones reneged on his threat to me. In Christian love I went to Scotland. I still wanted to be part of this group which included the friendships of a lifetime. I soon discovered how fleeting friendship is and how quickly one becomes an object of scorn among those he thought loved him the most.

By 1977, I was consciously grappling with the question of whether or not I wanted to continue being identified with the judgmental mentality of neo-fundamentalism — not historic fundamentalism, but radicalism. Thus, I preached a message of unity at the Sword of the Lord Conference on Soulwinning and Revival at Cobo Hall in Detroit. Repeatedly in the sermon I stated that I could no longer conduct citywide crusades in an atmosphere of suspicion, disunity and hatred. I pled for a new love among the brethren. Did it work? Following my message the rumor sheets announced that I had "renounced fundamentalism" at Cobo Hall. This was totally untrue.

Soon there was little hope of ever seeing another crusade where love abounded. The bitterness grew, fighting flourished, and suspicion reigned. No one would again be able to make a move of any kind without being accused. Informers increased. New victims were added to the blacklist. In spite of this situation, I continued citywide crusades for another three years. The meetings, however, began to deteriorate noticeably. The rumor mill was succeeding. The infighting it caused robbed us of former blessings. Whereas hundreds had been saved in each meeting during previous years, we were now fortunate to see a handful of converts. Without the manifestation of love visible among the brethren, what could we expect?

Chapter 4

Children Sitting in the Marketplace

In one church where Rexella and I conducted a crusade, the pastor's three-year-old son was present in all the meetings. He especially liked the music, and had never seen an accordion before. It so fascinated him when I did the bellows shake on this instrument that he went home and tried to imitate me. His father told me about it, and I related the story to the congregation. The little fellow, after hearing me discuss him, said to his father, "If that evangelist makes one more remark about me, I'm quitting the church."

Such an incident is humorous when a three-year-old child is involved. It is not so funny when a grown man acts this way. How interesting is the fact that Jesus compared the Pharisees to children:

> But whereunto shall I liken this generation? It is like unto children sitting in the market, and calling unto their fellows, and saying, "We have piped unto you and you have not danced; we have mourned unto you, and ye have not lamented" (Matthew 11:17).

I have often discovered neo-fundamentalists to be similar to this biblical description. They are like children who throw temper tantrums when they do not get their way.

In North Carolina, for example, the pastors of the two largest churches involved in my crusade were at each other's throats the entire week. One even came to me and said that he was actually praying for the death of the other. If God answered, the work of the Lord would then be done properly throughout the area. What a climate for revival!

Similar attitudes among ministers would either make or break a crusade. If the men were unified, loving and supportive, the blessings of God were innumerable as multitudes flocked to the Saviour. If, on the other hand, the pastors were fighting and fussing, the crusade was drastically hindered.

The problem was usually jealousy, not doctrinal purity. When we were considering a crusade in Lynchburg, Virginia, a group of local pastors informed me that the campaign would not be considered unless Jerry Falwell was excluded. Their motivation was the green-eyed monster of envy. Because I felt that such pettiness could not be honored, I refused their request and the plans to reach this area with a great unified effort were canceled.

A tragic spirit of divisiveness also occurred in Pennsylvania. A local pastor chosen as the publicity agent became extremely embittered at the crusade's success. He said to me: "I preach better than you do —still I can't fill my church. Why do these people want to come and listen to you? Why do they fill this huge auditorium nightly?" Needless to say, Satan had won the victory. Demonic power took over. Three times during the week, people were removed from the auditorium bodily, screaming obscenities. What I felt was frightening and the meeting ended as a disastrous reproach to the cause of Christ.

In Alabama, we were looking forward with expectation to a wonderful crusade. Upon arrival at the auditorium, a pastor met me, threw his arms around me and tearfully said, "This is a victory. For years I have prayed for a Jack Van Impe crusade in our city." By Tuesday night, however, he had become involved in a ruckus with another pastor and childishly cried: "If I can't have it my way, I'll take my buses and go home." He did. I never saw him again. I wonder what he told his members.

On other occasions, I actually observed ministers fighting publicly backstage over decision cards. How often leading preachers, looked up to by thousands, became like children. That God blessed some of these meetings at all is solely because of His abounding grace.

Small-Minded Legalism

One of the most troubling aspects of neo-fundamentalism was the extremes of legalism that were often espoused. One crusade sponsor refused to support the endeavor unless I submitted a written statement that none of my employees wore wire-rimmed glasses. He felt they were an indication of "hippyism." Other standards were set for choir members, counselors and ushers. Rules governing makeup, hair styles, clothing fashions and accessories were among the regulations demanded by some of the legalists. Pastors not in agreement usually remained silent so as to keep peace.

The tragedy of the situation was that those who practiced the enforcement of such standards oftentimes overlooked gross sins committed by leaders of fundamentalism or by members within their own churches. First Timothy 5:19-20 states: "Against an

37

elder [minister] receive not an accusation, but before two or three witnesses. Them that sin rebuke before all, that others also may fear." Instead of practicing this biblical injunction, Christian leaders at times aided and abetted the transgressors by covering up or attempting to get church boards to overlook the wicked offense. Though the sins included adultery, homosexuality, possession of sex magazines, lying, cheating and numerous other forms of wickedness scripturally condemned, still these iniquities by religious leaders were overlooked. At the same time, men who winked at such sin broke fellowship with brothers who held different views concerning hair, sideburns, pantsuits, bell-bottom trousers and music.

How wrong such unscriptural separation is. There isn't a verse in God's Book that commands us to separate from a brother over hair length or clothing fashion. There are, however, scores of texts that order us to break fellowship with anyone practicing immorality in thought, word and deed (study I Corinthians 5:9-11, Ephesians 5:3-12). If we based our separatist stance on God's Word, a lot of childish isolationism would cease.

I was guilty of childish attitudes myself. As I look back on things that I said and did — often publicly — there is much about which I am embarrassed. From the earliest days of my ministry, I was proud of my fighting spirit. I did not mind confrontation, and I thought I was at my best as God's messenger when I was "riled up" about non-important issues.

In the late 1960's, we conducted a crusade in Ann Arbor, Michigan, one of the hotbeds of revolutionaries in those days. We met in the auditorium at the university. One night a group of radical students came in without shirts or shoes and tried to disrupt the meeting. I seized the opportunity to respond to them in the only way I knew — blunt confrontation. I told them I would throw them out bodily if they didn't sit down and "fermez le bouche" — that's French for "shut up!" Fortunately, they did. If they hadn't, we might have had a riot.

I regret many things I did. If someone did not understand my position on separation and questioned me, I took it as a challenge to "let them have it" with both barrels. At McCormick Place in Chicago, Illinois, I told one individual that if one more word were uttered to me concerning my views on separation I would throw him out.

At another crusade, I was preaching against long hair on men when I heard a stir in the audience. I looked and saw a young man with modestly long hair getting up to leave. "There goes one now!" I said. Everyone applauded. I now grieve as I remember such incidents, for that young man might have been leaving for reasons completely unrelated to what I was saying. He might have been an unbeliever, and an incident like that could have turned him against Christ forever.

If I ever noticed people leaving the auditorium early, I would think of something to say to attack them. If I was preaching about some particular sin, I would say, "There they go! You know what sins they've committed. They can't sit here and listen to the exposure of their lifestyle." Yet, for all I knew, such persons might have simply been stepping out to the restroom. Looking back, I know that my attitude must have grieved the Spirit of God.

I also criticized leading Christians publicly. I recently apologized by letter or telephone for such ungraciousness, and asked many of God's people for forgiveness. Truly I regret with sorrow many of the things I said and did in the past.

In bygone days this was called revival; now it is labeled compromise. Let's get back to scriptural terminology and practice the confession of our sins both privately and publicly when a brother or sister has been hurt.

What was behind my actions in former days? To be perfectly truthful, the fighting spirit was considered essential if one was to be accepted as a militant fundamentalist. I always felt that my best preaching took place when I was stirred to "righteous indignation," and I often ended up tearing people to shreds in ungracious tones and with unkind words. When I blasted alleged compromisers by name publicly, those steeped in neo-fundamentalism responded with enthusiasm because it was negative and inflammatory. Forgive me, dear Lord, for all those I hurt with my cursory ways.

Preaching on the crucifixion, the precious blood of Christ, assurance of salvation or other edifying topics produced a few, rare "amens." Conversely, preaching against rock music, dancing, hair length or pantsuits created deafening applause.

I was recently made startlingly aware of this fact when I listened to a taped message I preached several years ago. As I spoke against other denominations and named names in a vitriolic manner, the audience cheered and applauded with a standing ovation. Then when I got into the body of my message — presenting information which was biblical, doctrinal and edifying — the crowd was silent for more than 30 minutes. I sensed that their enthusiasm was waning and, responding to my desire to get them stirred again, I went back to attacking others. The applause and amens became deafening a second time. Surely there is something wrong when negativism is applauded and love is looked upon with suspicion and contempt. There is equally something wrong when a man preaches to the prejudices of men. God forgive me.

In Green Bay, Wisconsin, we were closing our crusade on Sunday afternoon. The arena we were using featured wrestling on Sunday night, and then Rex Humbard was scheduled to begin a meeting on Monday. Humorously, the marquee outside the facility read:

Jack Van Impe
Wrestling
Rex Humbard

That might have been true of Jack Van Impe at one time. However, during my remaining years in the ministry, I want to glorify God by being an example of His love — striving to promote true Christian unity among all members of His body.

I regret the years I spent bowing to the wishes of a few judgmental men. By accepting the platform of militant neo-fundamentalism, I consigned myself to their disgruntled ranks and forfeited fellowship with some wonderful men of God. Now when I fellowship with men of like precious faith whom, through fear, I had kept at arm's length, I find that they are brothers deeply committed to God. They love the same Lord and preach the same message. Most of all, while holding to the true fundamentals of faith, they are not afraid to practice biblical love and unity.

In coming to the end of the line with militant radicalism — not historic fundamentalism but the hate movement I mentioned at the 1977 Sword of the Lord Conference — I have found a freedom in the Spirit that I had forgotten was possible.

Several months ago, I spoke with the pastor of a large church in Michigan. This pastor is a great historic fundamentalist who, like myself, has recently come out of the militantism. As we spoke, his comment to me was, "Jack, do you know what it is like to be **free**?"

I knew exactly what he meant.

Chapter 5

I Am A Fundamentalist*

Rexella and I are grateful for fundamentalist friends following a time of sorrow. 1977 has been a year of testing in our lives, physically. We have experienced many attacks of Satan — even upon our lives — within the last year. However, the last eight weeks have been unbelieveable as a few brothers in Christ have even tried to destroy our ministry.

In August, I preached a message at the Sword of the Lord Conference at Cobo Hall in Detroit. In the message, I called upon my fundamentalist brothers to love one another, to stop "nit-picking" on minor, nonessentials, and to move together in a spirit of unity in winning a lost world to Christ. The message had been embedded in my heart by the Holy Spirit at 6 a.m. that very morning. Unable to sleep, I had gone outside to plead with God for the message HE wanted me to deliver. He gave it to me.

In the message, I mentioned some of the faults among the brethren. I did not attack the movement I have always loved, but rather issued a call for "a revival of love among fundamentalists." This is the method I have followed ever since God called me to preach twenty-nine years ago. This is God's method. Isaiah 58:1 states: "Cry aloud, spare not, lift up thy voice like a trumpet, and shew my people their transgressions." Second Timothy 4:2 echoes the refrain: "Preach the word; be instant in season, out of

*This chapter is taken from an article that appeared in the December 1977 issue of our **Newsletter**. Chapters 5-8 show a progressive growth in my quest for love and unity. They also describe my seven-year spiritual struggle as I felt compelled by God to rebuke the errors of neo-fundamentalism, without naming its leaders.

season: reprove, rebuke, exhort with all long-suffering and doctrine."

Was my mention of some common faults wrong? Did not God write His Word "...for reproof, for correction, for instruction in righteousness?" (II Timothy 3:16). This has always been my manner of preaching. I did so in other years at nationwide ministerial conferences in Charlotte, North Carolina; Lynchburg, Virginia; and Chattanooga, Tennessee. My sermon, "Preachers, America Needs You," delivered a few years ago, was probably the strongest denunciation of sin I ever proclaimed at nationwide conferences. At the World Congress of Fundamentalists in Edinburgh, Scotland, as well as at the 1976 Sword of the Lord Conference in Atlanta, Georgia, point number three of my message, "Dangerous Evangelism," dealt with sins many fundamentalists sweep under the carpet. I did not change my approach at the Sword of the Lord Conference this year.

After mentioning the many side issues that currently divide our fundamentalist ranks, I stated that I would not continue to conduct citywide meetings in areas which were being torn asunder by strife and division because of a few of the brethren. I went on to say I would no longer work under this system. My clearly stated intention was that I would not conduct any future citywide crusades in any areas where there was division among the brethren. I would go only where there was a spirit of love and unity. The audience — wearied with all the name-calling, mudslinging and muckraking that is taking place publicly and through religious "scandal sheets" — signified their approval by an ovation when this statement was made. Surely this nationwide gathering of 5,000 fundamentalists on Tuesday evening — and 2,500 on Friday morning — did not misunderstand what I was attempting to say. Their hearts were crying along with mine saying: "Let's stop fighting among ourselves and, unitedly in love, go out to win a lost and dying world to the Lord Jesus Christ."

Immediately following the message, staunch fundamentalists such as Dr. Al Janney and Dr. Robert Sumner commended me for "having the courage to say what had to be said." Obviously, the message of "uncompromising love" had been used of God.

Then, on August 22, clouds of darkness appeared. A letter from a well-known Christian educator arrived at our headquarters. It was followed by a second letter on September 2. In the harshest of language, the man and his group accused me of renouncing fundamentalism at the Sword of the Lord Conference. I was shocked. I did not reply because the second letter stated: "I told you when I had opportunity to hear the tape of the message you delivered at the Detroit debacle [Sword Conference] I would write you further....Now, Jack, I am going to be perfectly honest with you. That sermon is the most perfect example I have ever heard of grandstanding, playing up to the weak crowd [thousands of fundamentalists at a Sword of the Lord Conference on Soulwinning and Revival...]" Weak? He continued: "...we have only now been forced to break with you." Again: "...after that message in Detroit, I think you will find that other men will do what _____ and _____ are doing; that is, give up on you..." This last statement seemed so final that I did not bother to answer at that time. I have since.

This letter, filled with name-calling, brought sadness to both Rexella and me because we had always admired the writer of the letters. The situation worsened. Soon, copies of the second letter were sent to scores of preachers and even read publicly to 500 preacher boys. Calls began coming to my office concerning my position. At this writing, we have received letters and telephone calls from nine states asking the question, "Have you renounced fundamentalism?"

Rexella and I are broken to think that this could have happened to us after we so faithfully served the Lord Jesus Christ all these years. In our devotions together, we questioned why such an attack had happened. We wondered how this would "work together for good" according to Romans 8:28. What good could come out of all this? Would God's people, my friends, my converts and my preacher brethren believe the accusation? The very fault I had agonizingly pointed out at the Sword Conference — please stop calling good fundamentalist "neo-evangelicals" — was now happening to me!

Men are mislabeled today by others who dislike them or wish to "even" a score. The best method of turning one brother against another is to call him a "compromiser." **Please do not misunderstand me.** I am **against** compromise in every way, shape and form! However, this is **not** the major problem presently existing among fundamentalists. The problem **is** that scores of good fundamentalists are being

falsely branded. THEN, anyone who is sponsored by these **mislabeled, misrepresented** fundamentalists becomes a "neo-evangelical." A perfect example is what just happened to me! All I did was call for "uncompromising love" among **all** fundamentalists. If this does not occur, our camp will soon consist only of the "me and thee, and I'm not so sure about thee" proponents!

God says: "Yet have I left me seven thousand Israel all the knees which have not bowed unto Baal..." (I Kings 19:18). **America is still full of solid fundamentalists** — though often mislabeled. Don't be so quick to pick up all the latest gossip about the servants of God. Don't pass on rumors so easily. Instead, thank God for Dr. Lee Roberson, Dr. Jack Hyles, Dr. Jerry Falwell, Dr. John R. Rice and others. A Christian educator came to Flint, Michigan recently and attacked all these giants of the faith, after trying to divide the pastors who will be sponsoring my citywide crusade in 1978. Think how this must grieve the Holy Spirit. Ephesians 4:30,31 states: "And grieve not the Holy Spirit of God, whereby ye are sealed unto the day of redemption. Let all bitterness, and wrath, and anger, and clamour, and evil speaking, be put away from you, with all malice." Remember, one of the sins God hates is sowing discord among the brethren (Proverbs 6:19).

In the light of what has happened, may I again state:

1. I would live and die for Christ and fundamentalism.
2. If I were going to renounce my position, I would have more sense than to do it at a fundamentalist gathering.

3. The fundamentalists, gathered from all over the United States did not misinterpret my statement for there was a tremendous round of applause when it was made. We fundamentalists should be given credit for having more intelligence than this. We do not normally applaud one of our defectors!

The situation is tragic. We have come to a day within our ranks when if a man is unable to excommunicate a brother out of a movement because of his lack of power, he must seek to destroy him some other way. I have news for the few who would try to make me a new-evangelical: "The fundamentalists are stuck with me till Jesus comes!"

May I say that although the clouds were dark for two months, the sun is shining now. Rexella and I again see how "...all things work together for good to them that love God..." My heart is filled with thanksgiving because calls and letters have now come to us from FUNDAMENTALIST LEADERS throughout the nation. They have encouraged us, prayed with us, wept with us and counseled us. We are so grateful for their expressions of love and understanding, and for their desire to stand with us in praying for and working toward an attitude of unity and love among all fundamentalists.

I am printing excerpts from many of the letters received. Our friends will rejoice after reading the statements made by America's fundamentalist leaders. These are the men who head up most of the fundamentalist organizations and schools in America. The majority of them have listened to and analyzed the message under discussion. I believe you

will see that our united cry is: "Contend for the faith,
but don't be contentious; defend the faith, but don't
destroy the faithful!" Shocking as it may seem, even
defending and dying for the faith is meaningless if
love is missing: "...though I give my body to be
burned, and have not charity [love], it profiteth me
nothing" (I Corinthians 13:3).

I have purposely omitted the names of accusers. I
have never attacked a Christian brother in this **Newsletter** during its eight years of publication. I do not
want to harm any servant of God. Nevertheless, it has
become obvious that I must release a statement concerning my position — without name-calling. I ask
you now to share with Rexella and me the letters from
America's fundamentalist leaders. Thank God for
friends!

Dear Jack:

I understand accusations are springing from
sundry sources, accusing you of compromise, neo-
evangelicalism and selling the cause of Fundamentalism down the river. The charge is so ridiculous it possibly should be ignored, but since error
still goes around the world while truth is getting her
boots on, I am delighted to say a word in your
defense.

I have known and appreciated you and your ministry in a personal way now for about 15 years. As a
local church evangelist, you were fearless, hard-
hitting and bold in denunciation of evil in every form.
I listened to you with deep gratitude on numerous
occasions as you preached plainly and powerfully
against booze, Hollywood, false cults, liberalism and

many other of today's deadly isms. In your meetings you distributed, personally, many hundreds of my huge expose, HOLLYWOOD CESSPOOL, as I recall.

However, I have been even more grateful that your message has not toned down one iota since the Lord began opening the door of citywide crusades for you and Rexella. You have hit worldliness, modernism and the cults just as hard as before. In fact, if there is an evangelist anywhere — local church or citywide — who preaches stronger against the world, the flesh and the devil, I do not know who he is.

This is what makes the current charges against you so ludicrous.

And unfair!

Since my understanding is that these claims relate to your message at the Detroit Sword of the Lord Conference, let me offer a specific word about it. I was there; I heard it. In fact, I dropped you a note afterward, commending your main thesis. (One of our leading failings as Fundamentalists has been our lack of charity toward one another!) At any rate, I got the tape of your message and listened to it again this morning, paying close attention to what you said. I am at a loss to understand how anyone could listen to it, hear the sob in your throat as you poured out your heart in a plea for a return to "discipleship love" among Fundamentalists, then accuse you of compromise or new-evangelicalism.

You may quote me as being one who has complete confidence in you and your ministry, one who endeavors to take you and your work to the Throne daily, and one who rejoices in every advance God

gives you in getting out the blessed Word of God.
Dr. Robert L. Sumner
President & Director "Biblical Evangelism"
(Affliated with General Association of
Regular Baptist Churches)

Dear Jack & Rexella:
DON'T get upset at this vicious and slanderous attack. I have had the same thing — and even worse — happen to me by the same party some years ago. This is a good sign. The Devil is mad and is using these tactics.

I have complete confidence and trust in you and Rexella. I will recommend you any time to anybody, anywhere. Keep on preaching and praying and plugging away. He is coming soon. God bless you both.
Dr. David Otis Fuller
General Association of Regular
Baptist Churches, Leader and member of the
original Council of 14, Author of **Valiant For the Faith**

To Whom It May Concern:
I have known Dr. Van Impe for over 25 years and have found him to be true to the Word, believing its absolute and unqualified authority. He has maintained a clear-cut, separated stand, coupled with an exemplary evangelistic fervor for the lost. He in no way reflects a new-evangelical spirit and he is welcome to my pulpit and Seminary, of which I am the President, at any time. I support his methods and message without qualification.

51

Dr. Charles Wagner
President, Northwest Baptist Seminary Pastor,
Temple Baptist Church of Tacoma, Washington
(Affliated with General Association of Regular
Baptist Churches)

Dear Jack:

I had the privilege of introducing you to the Baptist
Bible Fellowship, and praise God for your consistent
stand for fundamentalism. You are not only a staunch
fundamentalist, but right wing as far as one can go!

Dr. John W. Rawlings
(Co-founder, Baptist Bible Fellowship
International and Baptist Bible College
Former BBC Vice-President and 3-year
President, BBFI) Pastor, Landmark Baptist
Temple, Cincinnati, Ohio

Dear Dr. Van Impe,

I have just finished reading a letter being circulated
by concerning a message you preached in Detroit. I
have listened to the tape referred to in the letter. This
last week I also had the privilege of hearing you
preach again in the area meeting in Aurora sponsored
by our Fellowship churches. I think the accusations
made in the letter are totally unfounded and without
reason. I have personally seen no change in your
position. I am glad to count you as a Brother in Christ
and a fellow soldier in the battle for truth.

May God richly bless you is my prayer.

Dr. David A. Cavin
President, Baptist Bible Fellowship
International Pastor, High Street Baptist Church
Springfield, Missouri

Dear Brother Van Impe:

Don't worry about these people and their attacks, as they will come to naught.

I listened to your tape along with Don Price. We both agreed that we would take the same position if we were in citywide campaigns.

May the Lord bless you and your work.

Dr. Greg Dixon
Pastor, Indianapolis Baptist Temple
Indianapolis, Indiana (Affiliated with
Baptist Bible Fellowship International)

Dear Dr. Van Impe:

Your message, preached at the Sword of the Lord Conference in Detroit, was a classic. I had the privilege of speaking in that same conference and, therefore, have a good understanding of what you were trying to say. It seems that the Lord is directing the leaders in fundamentalism today to call the brethren to a scriptural unity. In my opinion, easily 95 percent of all fundamentalist brethren will say a loud "Amen" to every comment in your great sermon.

At the same time, as an evangelist, I am sure you need to be very sensitive to what the other 5 percent (I believe it is even less than this) are also saying. There are those divisive brethren who seem to be committed to building their own "bastion of fundamentalism" to the exclusion of most of the good men in the vineyard of the Lord today. Paul reminded Titus that a Bishop must be "a lover of good men." I am sorry that some of our dear brethren have never read this, or at least they are not willing to heed it.

No fair, honest and objective person could ever

find fault with your message or your method. It has been our privilege at Thomas Road Baptist to have your ministry in our midst many times. Your preaching has always been dynamic. I personally feel that God has raised you up as the voice of cooperative evangelism among fundamentalists for this day. Every outstanding man of God that I know personally agrees with me in this statement.

Presently, most of us are being attacked by the same sources who are attacking you at this time. I have read carefully the letter which was directed to you from one of the leading fundamentalists of our day. The same letter took a very cheap swipe at dear Dr. John Rice, Dr. Lee Roberson and myself. When I read such unfounded and unloving comments from one who is supposed to represent our Lord, I am reminded that "those who live godly in Christ Jesus shall suffer persecution." I think our reaction must be one of love toward our enemies. We must be careful not to launch offensive attacks against those who are attempting to hurt us. I have asked the members of Thomas Road Baptist Church and the students of Liberty Baptist Schools to pray for these men, that God will deliver them from the gall of bitterness and help them to love one another.

If ever fundamentalists needed to come together and to unify time, talents and resources, it is now. We must learn who the enemy is. We must stop fighting ourselves. We must stop attacking each other. This certainly must cause Satan to laugh up his sleeve. May God help us to have such a Holy Spirit revival among all the brethren that this kind of pettiness will cease forever.

I simply want to reassure you of our confidence in you. We have never believed that you were anything but a fundamentalist and a separatist. I join with men like Dr. Jack Hyles, Dr. W.E. Dowell, Dr. John Rawlings, Dr. John R. Rice and other great giants who say, "God bless you and continue to use you!"

Dr. Jerry Falwell
President, Liberty Baptist College
Pastor, Thomas Road Baptist Church
Lynchburg, Virginia

To Whom It May Concern:

Dr. Jack Van Impe has recently been accused of being a new-evangelical and publicly breaking with the fundamentalists. These charges were based upon a sermon he preached at a John R. Rice Conference.

However, after hearing the tape of his sermon, I can see that these charges were not actually based upon what he said, but that his statements were taken out of context.

I have just participated in an area-wide revival with Dr. Van Impe and I listened very carefully to his preaching. In my estimation — both from the taped Sword of the Lord sermon and the sermons I heard in the revival — I do not believe there is a stronger fundamentalist in America than Jack Van Impe. He is sound in doctrine and fearless in his preaching. Again and again he disassociates himself from modernists and new-evangelicals.

In my opinion, all true fundamentalists should back him in his world-wide evangelism efforts.

Dr. W.E. Dowell
President, Baptist Bible College
Pastor, Baptist Temple, Springfield, Missouri

Heart Disease in Christ's Body

To Whom It May Concern:

I have known Dr. Jack Van Impe for the past ten years. He is a fundamentalist in his local church preaching and in his citywide crusades. He has done much to strengthen the fundamentalist position in the city of Savannah.

I wholeheartedly endorse Dr. Van Impe as a true fundamentalist and see nothing in his ministry that would lead me to believe that he is departing from this position. May God give us more evangelists like Dr. Jack Van Impe.

Dr. Cecil Hodges
President, Baptist University of America
Decatur, Georgia Pastor, Bible Baptist Church,
Savannah Georgia

Dear Dr. Van Impe:

As your pastor, I follow your ministry closely and I see no indication that you are weakening your position as a preacher of the fundamentals of the faith.

Those of us who work with people will always be plagued with people problems. Encourage yourself in the Lord and continue the good fight of faith.

Dr. A.V. Henderson
President, Baptist Bible College East Peekskill,
New York Pastor, Temple Baptist Church,
Detroit, Michigan

Dear Jack:

I received your letter of October 15th concerning the ____ attack on your ministry. I think you did the right thing in bringing the message you did at Detroit and that you should not allow these threats to hinder you in preaching the Gospel and winning souls.

Everyone that I have talked to feels that message was outstanding and that it was needed because of the continuous threats and striking at everyone if they do not "hue the line" according to ____'s thinking.

I have always tried to be a friend to ____, however, I am greatly concerned that godly men that stand for the faith are being attacked constantly, and it does not appear to be in the spirit of love, but in a very harmful manner. I believe God will vindicate you...

We are looking forward to the Washington Crusade and doing what we can to make it go.

> Dr. R. Herbert Fitzpatrick
> Pastor, First Baptist Church of Riverdale
> Riverdale, Maryland (Affiliated with Baptist
> Bible Fellowship International)

Dear Brethren:

In every generation a man of God is unusual among men, and as such he is observed and criticized from every quarter. He and his convictions must be anchored to the Rock amid the surging and receeding tides of human issues.

Dr. Jack Van Impe has consistently declared his uncompromising devotion to the Bible and fundamental Christianity. Voluminous scripture quotations in personal use support his unqualified stand on the Bible while he accepts no sponsoring pastor or church which has not likewise declared full allegiance to the Word with all its precepts.

In all the personal experiences I have witnessed or

have heard reported, Dr. Van Impe has refused to be identified with or sponsored by men who deny any of the tenets of the faith.

While the campaign audiences who hear his Bible-saturated messages are composed of persons of every form of religious conviction (and those who have no convictions at all), his sponsoring and identifying base of support encompasses only those who "earnestly contend for the faith."

We are happy to walk with him.

Rev. Carl E. Baugh
Pastor, Calvary Heights Baptist Temple,
St. Louis, Missouri (Affiliated with Baptist
Bible Fellowship International)

To Whom It May Concern:

Dr. Jack Van Impe has conducted five evangelistic campaigns in the Highland Park Baptist Church and Tennessee Temple Schools. In addition to his meetings with us, I have heard him on a number of occasions in other cities.

I know Dr. Van Impe as a strong fundamentalist and a fervent soul winner. He is uncompromising in his proclamation of the Word of God. He has memorized literally thousands of verses of the Bible, and every sermon is saturated with the Word of God.

It is a joy to give our commendation of his evangelistic ministry. We shall continue to pray that God will use him mightily from place to place.

Dr. Lee Roberson
President, Tennessee Temple Schools
Pastor Highland Park Baptist Church
Chattanooga, Tennessee

Dear Dr. Van Impe:

...it was my joy to be present in Detroit and hear your message. I thought it was exactly what needed to be said. I admired and appreciated your courage. I did not consider it an attack on anybody. I considered it to be an honest evaluation and appraisal of the situation-on-hand in our day, and I hollered "Amen" at every point!

I want you to know that we have been praying for you in these days. All of us have been feeling a lot of pressure from this conflict and the trend of these days. I'm greatly burdened about it.

It might be that God would have you to publish a message on the issue, similar to the one you delivered at Detroit. The country needs to face these issues.

> Dr. Tom Wallace
> Pastor, Beth Haven Baptist Church
> Louisville, Kentucky (President of Southside Baptist Fellowship 1973-74)

Dear Brother Van Impe:

To me, you are a fundamentalist out and out, and I have never heard you say one word, whether in televised messages, in print or in person, that would give any indication of any shadow of turning.

The term, "Mr. Fundamentalist," is Jack Van Impe.

> Dr. Gerald O. Fleming
> Pastor, Dayton Baptist Temple,
> Dayton, Ohio (Affiliated with
> World Baptist Fellowship)

My Dear Brother:

I want you to know that I love you and have great confidence in you and your ministry. May God bless you and give you grace for the load you carry. I believe your name will go down as one of the great giants of the faith.

Dr. Jack Hyles
President, Hyles-Anderson College Pastor,
First Baptist Church, Hammond, Indiana

Brethren:

I was glad to have the splendid message by Dr. Jack Van Impe at the August Sword of the Lord Conference nationwide at Cobo Hall in Detroit. We agree with his stand that Christians should not yoke up with unbelievers, nor support them, nor sponsor them, but should work with out-and-out Bible-believing, devoted Christians whenever possible, even though we reserve the right to disagree on some minor differences in doctrine.

That position is the fundamentalist position written out and adopted at the Hamilton Hotel in Chicago, Illinois, in a meeting of evangelists called by Dr. Bob Jones, Sr. on January 6, 1958. It was signed by some 34 Christian leaders. The first two to sign it were Dr. John R. Rice and Dr. Bob Jones, Sr. The name of Dr. Bob Jones, Jr. was not on the published list.

We rejoice in the ministry of Dr. Jack Van Impe.

Dr. John R. Rice President and Editor
Sword of the Lord Murfreesboro, Tennessee

Dear Dr. Van Impe:

My staff and I heard the tape of the message you

gave for our dear Brother John Rice during the Detroit convention. We thought it was so good that, with your permission, we are duplicating it and will be sending it out to our staff and network on six continents plus our five Bible institutes overseas and one in America.

I hope you will soon put this message into print so that it can be translated and multiplied world-wide and given out to the entire body of Christ. We pray constantly for you and rejoice in what God is doing with you and through you in citywide evangelism. Keep at it on the victory side!

Dr. Jack Wyrtzen
President, Word of Life International
Schroon Lake, New York

Dear Dr. Van Impe:

In my estimation, you are a fundamentalist in your message and in your ecclesiastical separation from apostasy. It is my prayer, Dr. Van Impe, that you will not be swayed, but will continue your God-blessed, Biblical ministry of evangelism.

Dr. Robert L. Gray
Pastor, Westchester Bible Church Westchester, Illinois (President, Independent Fundamental Churches of America, 1972-1975)

Dear Jack:

Below is my statement concerning your person and ministry:

I heartily endorse Dr. Jack Van Impe as a Biblical fundamentalist and separatist. His Crusades in our area have reinforced fundamentalism. America desperately needs his type of evangelism.

Rev. Emmett Pope
Pastor, Mayfair Bible Church Flint,
Michigan (Member, Executive Council,
Independent Fundamental Churches of
America)

To Whom It May Concern:

I thank God for Dr. Jack Van Impe and his outreach for Christ. I believe Dr. Van Impe is a fundamentalist. He has stated this privately and publicly, and his ministry reflects this.

Dr. Clinton Branine
President, Indiana Baptist College
Indianapolis, Indiana Pastor, Suburban Baptist
Church Greenwood, Indiana (Leader in the
Indiana Fundamental Baptist Fellowship)

Here is a letter from Dr. Myron Cedarholm, President of Maranatha Baptist Bible College, to Dr. Bob Jones, Jr. commenting on the men who had endorsed me in this message.

Dear Dr. Bob, Jr. and Dr. Bob, III,

I have Jack Van Impe's November 1977 Newsletter before me in which he professes to be a fundamentalist and then quotes portions of several letters from "Fundamentalists" across America who defend him. I am sure that you have seen this issue.

I just cannot believe what I read! If these men who defend Jack Van Impe are fundamentalists, there are not many real fundamentalists left. We really are at a low spiritual plane in the U.S.A. This defense of Jack Van Impe is the harvest of compromise, emphasis on "Bigness" at any cost, cheap music, quick "conversions," deficit financing and all the other foolishness and unscriptural practices that have been allowed by preachers in the churches for the last thirty years. Billy Graham's compromise and inclusivism have done more to drag down and lower the cause of Christ than we probably realize. God help us!

Satan is certainly having a field day in deceiving men that we thought had scriptural discernment and would stand by God's Word when the battle waxed hot rather than by men who compromise.

Dr. Rodney Bell, President of Fundamental Baptist Fellowship of America, also sent a response to my message.

Dear Jack:

There comes a time in every's man life when his real character shows. Without a doubt in your address at Cobo Hall and your November newsletter, the real Jack Van Impe manifested himself.

I would like to set the record straight. First of all, you said that you gave your message at Cobo Hall in Detroit, before America's greatest and most solid fundamentalists. I want to say that most of these men are good men but are ignorant of the position of historical fundamentalism. There is a nation of ignorance concerning Biblical Fundamentalism and Scriptural Separation. They are misguided pseudo-fundamentalists and you have proven to be "pseudo" yourself. Pseudo means something that looks genuine, appears to be genuine, but is not. It is a substitute or a phony. You know that John R. Rice, Lee Roberson, Jerry Falwell and others have always been soft when it comes to new-evangelicalism and they have practiced their inclusivism without even blushing.

You brought your message in the presence of Dr. John R. Rice, who is the father and prophet of so called second-degree separation, the super agressive church building, baptize three hundred or you're not spiritual club, the side show gimmickery, the ring master circus, and the softness toward Southern Baptists and new-evangelicals. I do not believe that you fell into this trap. I believe you went into it with your eyes open, knowing on which side your bread is buttered. When you have to identify yourself and say "I am a fundamentalist," it is evident that you have compromised. You should stand so clearly that no one would ever question your stand on the fundamentals of the Faith. Fundamentalism is not only a doctrine, but also a position. It is not what you say, but what you do that counts. "Birds of a feather flock together." No one has ever accused me of not being a fundamentalist. Nor has anyone ever accused Bob Jones University of not being a fundamentalist institution, because their mouth and their feet line up together.

The frightening thing about your newsletter is that fifteen "so-called" fundamental Baptists agreed with John R. Rice's soft position. It is frightening to me that the fundamental Baptist movement is in far more trouble than some of its leaders care to admit. You have done some asinine things, Brother Jack, but without a doubt this is the most asinine thing you have ever done, sending your newsletter into the homes of my people, forcing me to get into the pulpit and explain.

Jack, you turned your newsletter into a "scandal sheet" for the enemies of Bob Jones University to sink their poisonous fangs into its Chancellor, Dr. Bob Jones.

My prayer is that you will see what great heartache you are causing true fundamentalists and the cause of Christ and make restitution. I would start by apologizing to Dr. Bob Jones, Chancellor of Bob Jones University.

Chapter 6

Defending the Faith in Love*

GOD IS LOVE (I John 4:8).

This is the message of Christianity.

LOVE brought Christ to earth. Jesus said: "I am come that they might have life, and that they might have it more abundantly" (John 10:10).

LOVE sent Him to the cross. "Hereby perceive we the love of God, because he laid down his life for us" (I John 3:16).

LOVE made Him willing to die a sacrificial death by the shedding of His blood: "Unto Christ that loved us, and washed us from our sins in his own blood" (Revelation 1:5).

THIS LOVE WAS FOR THE UNLOVELY — you and me. " . . . Christ died for the ungodly" (Romans 5:6). Because of His love for us, we can gratefully say with Paul, "Thanks be unto God for his unspeakable gift" (II Corinthians 9:15).

Has His Love Touched You?

Again, I say, GOD IS LOVE. It is part of His

---

*This chapter is taken from an article in the 1980 November/December issue of **Perhaps Today,** the Jack Van Impe Ministries newsletter.

67

nature; one of His attributes. This nature becomes ours when the new birth occurs. When one becomes a new creation in Christ Jesus (II Corinthians 5:17), he partakes of the DIVINE NATURE (II Peter 1:4). LOVE, then, is the hallmark, the evidence, the proof of a genuine salvation experience.

John 13:35: "By this shall all men know that ye are my disciples, if ye have LOVE one to another."

"He that saith he is in the light, and hateth his brother, is in darkness even until now. He that loveth his brother abideth in the light, and there is none occasion of stumbling in him. But he that hateth his brother is in darkness, and walketh in darkness, and knoweth not whither he goeth, because that darkness hath blinded his eyes" (I John 2:9-11).

"Beloved, let us love one another: for love is of God; and every one that loveth is born of God, and knoweth God. He that loveth not knoweth not God; for God is love" (I John 4:7,8).

"If we love one another, God dwelleth in us . . . " (I John 4:12). "If a man say, I love God, and hateth his brother, he is a liar" (I John 4:20).

As one grows in grace, walks in the light and seeks the filling of the Spirit, the intensity and immensity of love increases. When the Spirit of God is in control, one can begin to understand and practice the command of Jesus in Luke 6:27,28: " . . . LOVE your enemies, do good to them which hate you, bless them that curse you, and pray for them which despitefully use you."

No one can do this apart from the Holy Spirit. That's why there is so little love evidenced among brethren these days! You see, it is not difficult to fake spiritual gifts, **but the fruit cannot be imitated**: ". . . love, joy, peace, longsuffering, gentleness, goodness, faith, meekness, temperance" (Galatians 5:22,23). What a revival would break forth if men could see real Spirit-empowered Christianity in action! Instead, they see or hear about our "religious scandal sheets" which tear good Christians to shreds through articles by little men with big, jealous hearts.

Beloved, this is not the work of the Holy Spirit but rather of another spirit — the same spirit that made Cain envious to the point of slaying his brother; the spirit which entered into Saul and caused him to seek David's life. Yes, it is the spirit of him known as the "the accuser of the brethren" (Revelation 12:10). Paul felt his attacks often. Sad to say, the attacks came through "ministers of Christ" — Paul's brothers in the faith who allowed themselves to be so used (II Corinthians 11:23).

John, the disciple closest to the heart of Jesus, also knew the bitter pangs his brethren could inflict. He said: "I wrote unto the church: but Diotrephes, who loveth to have the preeminence [be number one] among them, receiveth us not. Wherefore, if I come, I will remember his deeds which he doeth, prating against us with malicious words: and not content therewith, neither doth he himself receive the brethren, and forbiddeth them that would, and casteth them out of the church" (III John 9,10).

Sound familiar? Diotrephes is still present in the form of those who excommunicate, or attempt to destroy by written or spoken slander, fellowship with any brother who has shaken hands with the third cousin of an imagined compromiser. It's a good thing the original Diotrephes did not possess a printing press and mailing list, or he would have smeared Christ's favorite apostle in his "religious gazette!"

Beloved, don't follow this type of leadership. It bears all the earmarks of carnality. Galatians 5:19-21 lists the works of the flesh. Among them are: " . . . hatred, variance, emulations, wrath, strife, seditions . . . envyings, [and] murders . . . " All these terms are related to fighting. Immediately following this listing, verse 22 says that there is a BETTER way — the FRUIT OF THE SPIRIT, which is " . . . love, joy, peace, longsuffering, gentleness, goodness, faith, meekness [and] temperance." Follow the leader who follows Christ (I Corinthians 11:1). Look to the man who possesses love, gentleness and meekness of spirit. He will be easy to find. His life and ministry are ones of reconciliation. He obeys all the Book, including Galatians 6:1: "BRETHREN, if a man be overtaken in a fault, ye which are spiritual, restore such an one in the spirit of meekness; considering thyself, lest thou also be tempted."

As a layman, where do you stand? Do you look to men? Do you argue with your friends as to which leader is the greatest "saber rattler" of the faith? Are you, in effect, saying, "I am of Paul," or "I am of Apollos?" If so, you are carnal (I Corinthians 3:4). Do you rejoice when one of God's servants is defamed by another? Do you eagerly await the next edition of "Religious Rumors" to read the latest "scoop" on some brother in Christ? Do you delight in a brother or sister's heart being crushed through the poison pen of a carnal leader? The Spirit-filled believer " . . . [weeps] with them that weep"

(Romans 12:15).

Every born-again Christian, within many denominations, is a member of the BODY of Christ (I Corinthians 12:13). When one member of that body is injured, the true Christian feels the hurt. "Bear ye one another's burdens, and so fulfil the law of Christ" (Galatians 6:2).

I can identify with many of my brothers who have felt the pangs of being publicly roasted by militant warriors. Three years ago, I preached a message on LOVE at a Sword of the Lord Conference on Soul-winning and Revival. Never did I realize what problems a message on love could create. If you want to avoid being labeled a "pseudo [fake] fundamentalist" or a "compromiser," don't preach on love. This automatically brands one!

Since that day, article after article has attacked both my position and my character. **My position is: "I will love all of God's blood-bought children. I will refuse to accept the false labels placed upon good, godly men by those who, like Diotrephes, want preeminence and glory, and who try to force their unscriptural convictions upon all believers under the threat of expulsion."**

Don't accept the man-made labels placed upon good and godly men simply because an envious leader misbrands them.

My experience has been a blessed one. It made a new man out of me. I, too, lived in a state of negativism. I also found fault and wrote hard letters. Then, three months ago, after reading about myself in a 35-page release that could be purchased for $5.00 (to support a ministry of defamation), I sat back and

for the first time in my life said: "Thank you, Lord."
Why? First, because I could rest in Christ, even under
attack. Secondly, because I had no desire to defend
myself against the petty allegations concerning "secondary separation."

It was charged that I should not use a particular
broadcasting company to get my message to the
world because two good brothers whom the militants
had labeled as "neo-evangelicals" also used the
company. (I wonder what I would have had to do if
we shopped at the same supermarket?)

Finally, I said, "Thank you, Lord" because He
had delivered me from being like these embittered
men whose entire ministries are based upon spying
out the liberty which we have in Christ Jesus
(Galatians 2:4). It must be a horrible experience to
spend one's life in such unprofitable pursuits.
Romans 14:10 states: "But why dost thou judge thy
brother? or why dost thou set at nought thy brother?
for we shall all stand before the judgment seat of
Christ."

All of us hold certain men in admiration. First, I
desire to be like JESUS, "Who, when he was reviled,
reviled not again; when he suffered, he threatened
not . . ." (I Peter 2:23). Yea, I long to be like
Spirit-filled Stephen, who, when he was being
crushed to death by angry mobs, cried: ". . . Lord, lay
not this sin to their charge" (Acts 7:60).

My former pastor, Dr. G.B. Vick, was undoubtedly one of the greatest leaders of fundamentalism in the twentieth century. I dined with him
on numerous occasions, became his friend and had
one of the greatest crusades of my entire ministry

under his sponsorship. Still, in all our time together, I never heard him utter an unkind word about another brother in Christ. Dr. Vick is now with the Lord. How I miss his love, his counsel and his example.

I also conducted four individual full-length crusades under the direction of Dr. Lee Roberson. Though I spent hours in his presence, I never heard criticism emanate from his lips. Once I saw him get up and walk away from a table where several ministers were slandering another brother. He said: "I don't have to listen to this." Thank you, Dr. Roberson, for the example you have set. I have never read a negative word about any man in your weekly paper. May the Lord raise up 10,000 fundamentalist leaders like you.

I have also observed this same godliness in Dr. Jack Hyles. In fact, if any of his students are caught criticizing any man of God, they are first warned, and then expelled from school. God bless you, Dr. Hyles, for training young people to refrain from gossip (James 3:2).

Defending The Faith In Love

Defending the faith in an unloving, vitriolic manner does not please God. Paul said: ". . . and though I give my body to be burned [as a martyr], and have not charity [LOVE], it profiteth me nothing" (I Corinthians 13:3).

Many of the warriors are going to be shocked when they stand before Christ at the Judgment Seat. Think of it! They will receive no rewards though they DIED in defense of the faith. That's right, defending the faith in a vengeful manner produces no crowns because hatred, variance, wrath, strife and envyings are of the flesh (Galatians 5:19-21).

Love is so important.

LOVE COVERS A MULTITUDE OF SINS (I Peter 4:8).

LOVE MAKES US TO FORBEAR ONE AN-OTHER, "Endeavoring to keep the unity of the Spirit in the bond of peace" (Ephesians 4:3).

LOVE CONSTRAINS US (II Corinthians 5:14).

LOVE IS OF GOD, FOR GOD IS LOVE.

Strife, envy and hatred are not Spirit-instilled qualities. Let God himself speak: ". . . for whereas there is among you envying, and strife, and divisions, are ye not carnal, and walk as men? (I Corinthians 3:3). "From whence come wars and fighting among you? come they not hence, even of your lusts that war in your members?" (James 4:1).

"For where envying and strife is, there is confusion and every evil work. But the wisdom that is from above [from God] is first pure, then peaceable, gentle, and easy to be entreated, full of mercy and good fruits, without partiality, and without hypocrisy. And the fruit of righteousness is sown in peace of them that make peace" (James 3:16-18).

For weeks, this message has been heavy upon my heart. I can no longer remain silent. I must preach on the grievous issues that are causing heartache in the body of Christ. Remember that love and all the verses in this message are also part of the Scriptures and doctrine which must be defended (II Timothy 4:1,2). If the angels aren't weeping over the present situation, the saints should!

Let's follow the footsteps of Jesus, our Saviour. Then let's follow leaders who live and act as though the love of God has been shed abroad in their hearts by the Holy Ghost (Romans 5:8).

"LOVE THE BROTHERHOOD" (I Peter 2:17).

Chapter 7

A Call For Revival
Within Fundamentalism*

Multitudes within the ranks of fundamentalism feel there is something drastically wrong with the attitude of many present-day leaders.

Doctrine vs. Attitudes

Dr. Truman Dollar states:

"A disquieting unrest and discouragement plagues fundamentalism today. It is not discussed publicly. As with an embarrassing family secret, there seems to be a conspiracy of silence. But, then, we rarely discuss the real issues publicly.

"Fundamentalism is doctrinally sound, but its members display a lot of un-Christlike attitudes. While loudly defending the Bible, precious few seem to practice what it says and even fewer seem to know what it says. It discourages me when my heroes fight eternally. One could almost regret that the liberals have lost all their influence. Since it's hardly worth it to fight them because they have no power, we fight each other.

"There is something inherently a part of the sep-

*This chapter is taken from an article in the 1981 November/December issue of Perhaps Today, the Jack Van Impe Ministries newsletter.

aratist fundamentalist that compels him to battle all the time. If he can't find an enemy to fight, he will fight a friend. In this generation, one needs the armor of Ephesians 6 to guard against the attacks of other fundamentalists. What is even more disturbing is that the issues about which they fight do not involve what old Bob Ketcham called the 'irreducible minimum.' Not a single one of these men has ever been accused of denying biblical inerrancy, the deity of Christ, the bodily resurrection, the literal second coming or even a literal seven-day creation. The honest truth is that the issues that separate these men are not essentially doctrinal. I have read all their statements to the contrary. Their differences are so minute that they sound like theologians of the Middle Ages debating on how many angels can stand on the head of a pin. There is not a single, substantive, cardinal doctrine involved.

"I fear that ego and parochial interest are the overriding concerns. We need some strong leadership now — leadership that is not hesitant to talk about the real issues."

Spiritual Insurrection

Dr. Thomas E. Berry says:
"General T.J. 'Stonewall' Jackson was perhaps the most brilliant 'attack' strategist in the Confederate army. It was on the evening of his last victory that he was fired on and fatally wounded by a patrol party of his own men who mistook him and his staff for a detachment of Union cavalry. Unfortunately, this is also a common occurrence for those in the Lord's

army who turn their guns on one another and blast each other to the ground. As in the case of General 'Stonewall' Jackson, the results are often tragic.

"Many of us can remember how great leaders in the army of Christ achieved great victories against the real enemy until they turned their mighty guns on one another and blasted each other into ineffectiveness. They fell into the error of mistaking a soldier in their own army for the enemy. It is good to remember who the real enemy is. The Lord's army appears to have insurrection within its ranks. Instead of leveling their guns on the enemy, they have turned them on one another and the soldiers of Christ are in a battle royal among themselves. While they blast one another to pieces, the enemy laughs and has a field day."

Del Fehsenfeld of Life Action Ministries asks: "Have you ever wondered why there is conflict among people who believe the same Bible and preach the same salvation message? The dilemma is puzzling to many of God's people. In some cases, conflicts happen because Bible convictions draw the lines of distinction (Philippians 3:17-19). In other situations, however, division is a result of failing to understand our purpose for being alive from a Bible perspective. God's men who have the same Bible convictions need desperately to have one heart if our nation is to know the reality of our message.

"We need a good old-fashioned house cleaning, a Holy Spirit shake-up, a complete overhaul starting at the grass roots level. That kind of sin-erasing, saint-edifying, Saviour-exalting, Spirit-empowered revival will only come as we meet God's conditions — one of which is a total abandonment to the will of God with a willingness to pay any price. Part of that price means crucifixion to our pride, death to our traditions, sacred cows, pet phrases and philosophies and an end to our 'position-oriented' politics and all of the 'pulpit pablum' for the sake of prestige and convenience.''

What's In A Name?

The **Journal Champion** newspaper, published by Dr. Jerry Falwell, states:

"Name-calling seems to be one of the pastimes of many in today's churches. With name-calling is the process of labeling, which implies that people are good or bad. Christians give negative names to those they do not admire and positive names to themselves."

Dr. Richard Clearwaters, the great fundamentalist leader, has used the term "biblicist" to characterize his ministry. He states that amid the present-day plethora of labels such as Calvinist, non-Calvinist, hyper-Calvinist, fundamentalist, new-fundamentalist, pseudo-fundamentalist, militant fundamentalist, moderate fundamentalist, modified fundamentalist, evangelical, new-evangelical, etc., the word "biblicist" calls attention to the one and only authority for faith and practice — the Bible!

God help us to become Spirit-filled biblicist fundamentalists. This will do away with much of the name-calling because the Bible says that the fruit of the Spirit is love, joy, peace, longsuffering, gentleness, goodness, faith, meekness and temperance (Galatians 5:22,23).

Honesty And Godliness

The Spirit-controlled fundamentalist is also an honest fundamentalist. Is it not sad that in a major **Detroit News** release Howard Rosenburg, a secular reporter, states: "There are many leaders among the fundamentalists who are willing to lie, cheat, and do anything they have to in dealing with their enemies."

How true! Just read some of the scandal sheets in existence today within our movement. This is why Dr. Paul Tassel's article on godly gentlemen is so needful during this hour when our ranks are filled with rude, crude, deceitful and even lying leaders.

Dr. Tassel is the national representative of the General Association of Regular Baptist Churches. He states: "I believe that the [GARBC], moving into the 1980's, needs to lead the fundamental Baptist world in being gladiators for the truth. And I believe we can be scriptural, gentlemanly gladiators. I believe we can lead the fundamentalists into the 1980's as men of God. But we can do so as scriptural, mannerly men.

"As I have studied this word **gentleness** in the New Testament, I have concluded that godly gentlemen are men of Christian character, Christian conviction and Christian courtesy. And we need to be men who bear all three of those characteristics. We need to have godly character; we need to have scriptural conviction; and we need to be men of spiritual courtesy as we serve the Lord Jesus Christ. As we move into the 1980's, let's do it in a spiritual sense. It's possible, you know, to carry a big stick and speak softly, spiritually. In order to be true to Christ, you don't have to be mean; we can be mannerly. We don't have to be cranks and cantankerous; we can be courteous. We can be gentlemen and gladiators both . . . In short, let's be godly gentlemen. Our churches need it, our association needs it, our country needs it.''

Grace And Humility

Do you feel the heartbeat of these leaders, dear reader? Dr. John Waters, in **The Bible Trumpet**, declares: ''While one says I am of Paul, I am of Apollos, are ye not carnal? (I Corinthians 3:4). We submit that we as fundamentalist Baptists should follow Christ and the Bible and not be divided over men . . . It's 'what think ye of Christ' that makes you a fundamentalist. Otherwise revival will be hindered in our midst and in our churches.''

Again, Dr. Waters states: ''Baptists have always resisted anything savoring of popery. Because of it, several fundamental leaders have consented to a top level meeting to hammer out a united fundamental front.''

[NOTE: I was one of these men. However, the idea of such a meeting has since died.]

Dr. Waters continues: ''My paper, **The Bible Trumpet**, has encouraged this and we urge it even further. Do our big fundamental leaders have the grace and humility to do this, or will they destroy themselves? It seems to us that definitions acceptable to a wider range of fundamental leaders would provide a safer course than that chosen by one or two which could have a tendency of exclusivism or legalism which is just as deadly as liberalism.''

I like what the great GARBC leader, Dr. Ernest Pickering, said in his book entitled, **Biblical Separation**: "Some separatists see a new-evangelical under every bush and a compromiser in every pulpit. They are constantly uncovering the dirt about other brethren. Separatist leaders must guard against an insatiable desire to dominate everyone and everything. If someone disagrees with us on some minor issue, we brand the offenders as new-evangelicals and ostracize them from our fellowship.''

[**NOTE**: The Ayatollah Khomeini, leader of Mohammedan fundamentalism, executes them. Our leaders excommunicate them. They make us pseudo or new-evangelicals, which we are not.]

Dr. Pickering also states: "Some separatists take to the printed page with barbs, innuendos and castigations of their brethren without ever checking privately to see if they have the facts straight.''

Don't believe everything you hear, beloved. Ask the blessed Holy Spirit of God to begin giving you sanctified ears so you won't listen to trash. Then, when there is something wrong, obey Galatians 6:1: "Brethren, if a man be overtaken in a fault, ye which are spiritual, restore such an one in the spirit of meekness; considering thyself, lest thou also be tempted.''

Christian Liberty

In his book, **I Am a Fundamentalist**, the late Dr. John R. Rice states: "There must be room for Christian liberty and the leading of the Holy Spirit among good Christians. We do not need a pope to decide what everybody else must do on some matters not clearly outlined in the Scriptures.

"Are you convinced that you must not have fellowship with some other brother who perhaps is associated with someone with whom you do not have fellowship? Then you must decide that for yourself. Why must you decide it for others? Should my beloved friend, Dr. Falwell, have on his platform a man whom I would not have on my program? Then let him decide that. God will give him wisdom. I had rather Jerry had the liberty to make a mistake than to have no liberty of the direct leading of the Holy Spirit.

"Does Dr. Lee Roberson have a chapel speaker about whom I might doubt? Who am I to say? He is God's man and must have the freedom to do what God leads him to do."

In his book, **Come Out Or Stay In**, Dr. Rice says: " 'I am a companion of all them that fear thee, and of all them that keep thy precepts' (Psalm 119:63). This verse is very sweet to me. On the authority of that verse I decided not to be just a Baptist evangelist, though I am a Baptist, but to be an evangelist to all God's people. I determined I would say what John Wesley said, 'The world is my parish,' and that I would be for the man who is for Christ and the Bible. So, I work with all the people of God who are born again and live like it and believe the Bible and who are willing to work with other Christians. Minor differences should not prevent cooperation of brotherly Christians. 'Him that is weak in the faith receive ye, but not to doubtful disputations' (Romans 14:1).

"Again, let me say it plainly. I am against the devil's crowd and I am for the Lord's people. Those who are out and out for Christ and the Bible and say so and seek to please Him are my people."

Is it any wonder that Dr. Tom Malone said in the April 10, 1981, issue of **The Sword of The Lord**: "It would be impossible to describe what **The Sword of The Lord** has meant to me during these past forty years. It led me to meet Dr. John R. Rice about thirty-six years ago. When I read the first small issues of the **Sword**, I said, 'If someday I can meet that preacher and hear him preach, I will be forever grateful.' Not only was that aspiration fulfilled, but we became good friends and loved one another and conducted scores of conferences all over America.

"Thank God for **The Sword of The Lord**! I am somewhat familiar with the fundamental publications of the past 75 years in America. Many of them are no longer extant. I think the **Sword** is the greatest Christian publication in the history of Christianity in America. The **Sword** is the greatest compilation of biblical sermons there is in existence. **The Sword of The Lord** has led us into the heart and soul of the greatest Christian I ever knew — John R. Rice. Dr. Rice's position as a fundamentalist **in the middle of the right road** has been constantly pictured in the periodical. I tremble to think of the spiritual vacuum that might have been in America in recent years had it not been for **The Sword of the Lord**."

A Cause For Concern

Are our fundamentalist leaders justified in their

concern? Definitely! The present situation is absolutely heartbreaking. My purpose in printing these reports is not to cause greater friction among the brethren, but rather to make all of God's people realize the carnality of the present situation (I Corinthians 3:3,4). Beloved, unless we have an old-fashioned, Holy Spirit-empowered revival, "ruination" may become fundamentalism's epithet.

In order to make Christians aware of the seriousness of the situation — and still do this in the spirit of love — I purposely avoid the names of those individuals or organizations making the following statements. However, I have two hours' worth of tapes documenting what I am about to say. They were recorded during one of this particular fellowship's gatherings.

The following scenario takes place in many statewide meetings of this militant group: First, a number of ministers come to the platform. Then, names are presented to these "ecclesiastical judges" by the audience. In turn, each minister has an opportunity to critically denounce good men of God. Shockingly, the tape which I have in my possession indicates that scores of grade school children were present to hear top fundamentalist leaders denounced by these militant fundamentalists.

During this particular meeting, the General Association of Regular Baptist Churches, as well as the Baptist Bible Fellowship International, was derogatorily attacked. The following colleges (or their presidents) were also maligned: Hyles-Anderson College, Dr. Jack Hyles; Liberty Baptist College, Dr. Jerry Falwell; Baptist Bible College, Dr. Bill Dowell;

Baptist Bible Institute East, Dr. A.V. Henderson; Midwestern Baptist College, Dr. Tom Malone; and the GARBC schools.

Other great men of God were also ridiculed, including Dr. Hyman Appleman, Dr. Bill Gothard, Dr. Theodore Epp, Dr. John Rawlings, Dr. Wendell Zimmerman and Dr. Greg Dixon.

A Call For Revival

Beloved, which spirit produces such an attitude? Galatians 5:19-21 answers the question plainly: "Now the works of the flesh are manifest . . . [among them are:] hatred, variance, emulations, wrath, strife, seditions . . . envyings [and] murders . . . " Each of these terms is related to fighting. Is this wrong in the eyes of God? Is it sin? The answer is dogmatically, "YES!" In fact, such dissonance is one of the sins God hates the most — Proverbs 6:16-19: "These six things doth the Lord hate: yea, seven are an abomination unto him: A proud look, a lying tongue, and hands that shed innocent blood, An heart that deviseth wicked imaginations, feet that be swift in running to mischief, A false witness that speaketh lies, **and he that soweth discord among brethren.**"

The great need of the present hour in fundamentalism is for LOVE — not a sentimental, compromising love, but a Spirit-produced affection for all God's blood-bought children!

Please begin to pray with me for a revival that will change many of our leaders. My position is and always will be the one declared in the November/

December 1980 issue of **Perhaps Today** magazine:
**"I will love all of God's blood-bought children.
I will refuse to accept the false labels placed upon
good, godly men by those who, like Diotrephes,
want preeminence and glory, and who try to force
their unscriptural convictions upon all believers
under the threat of expulsion."**

Beloved, don't accept the man-made labels placed
upon good and godly brethren simply because another leader misbrands them. Don't follow men
whose ministries revolve largely around spying out
the liberty which we have been granted in Christ
Jesus (Galatians 2:4).

Let's follow the footsteps of Jesus, our Saviour.
Then let's follow leaders who live and act as though
the love of God has been shed abroad in their hearts
by the Holy Ghost (Romans 5:5).

"LOVE THE BROTHERHOOD" (I Peter 2:17).

The following letters indicate that many of our
fundamentalist brethren agree that a Holy Spirit- em-
powered revival is necessary within fundamentalism.

> Pastor Robert L. Weiss
> Calvary Baptist Church
> Jefferson, Wisconsin

Dear Brother Van Impe:

Your article, "A Call For Revival Within Fundamentalism" is excellent. This has been my concern
for some time.

I would be interested in 50 reprints of the article.
Could you quote us a price?

* * *

A Call for Revival Within Fundamentalism

Rev. Keith O. Gingrich,
    Pastor, Calvary Independent Bible Church
Clearfield, Pennsylvania

Dear Brother Van Impe:

Recently I read the November/December issue of "Perhaps Today" prophetic magazine, and praised the Lord that somebody finally called attention to a very real problem within the fundamental camp called, "sowing discord among the brethren." There were other articles that were a blessing to my heart. I would like for our people to be able to read these articles. What would be the cost of ordering 20 copies?

* * *

Rev. Larry E. Schwarck, Vice President
I.F.C.A. of Michigan
Pastor, Dayton Center Church
Silverwood, Michigan

Dear Brother Van Impe:
Greetings in the name of our Wonderful Lord.

I want to thank you for the excellent article, "A Call For Revival Within Fundamentalism," in the Nov./Dec. "Perhaps Today." My heart was encouraged with this scriptural challenge both as a pastor and leader in the I.F.C.A. in Michigan.

In a recent meeting of the I.F.C.A. brethren there were encouraged to secure copies of the publication and read the article. Many had already read it and added a hearty Amen!

I have been called a compromiser by some and a

hyper-fundamentalist by others. So the labels fly. Oh, how I pray as fundamentalists, we will begin to experience the heaven sent revival in our midst that is so badly needed.

Again thank you dear brother for that much needed challenge from the Word.

* * *

Dr. Ron Adrian, Pastor
First Baptist Church
New Castle, Delaware

Dear Dr. & Mrs. Van Impe:

Please let me express to you how much I appreciated your recent article "A CALL FOR REVIVAL WITHIN FUNDAMENTALISM." I believe you properly addressed the issue as it is . . . I appreciated your position and stand with you.

There is a great need for God's men to demonstrate our fellowship with one another through Christ. " . . . we were called unto the fellowship of his Son Jesus Christ our Lord" (I Corinthians 1:9). May God give us a unity, a healing in the land among the brethren "that the world may know."

As a pastor, I worked on the committees that brought you to Wichita, Kansas, for three crusades.

I have been pastor here for nearly two years. We have averaged 1,852 in Sunday School for the past five weeks.

* * *

A Call for Revival Within Fundamentalism

Dr. Paul N. Tassell, National Representative
General Association of
Regular Baptist Churches
Schaumburg, Illinois

Dear Brother Van Impe:

Just a note to thank you for your letter of October 13 and also for a copy of the prophetic news magazine containing your excellent article entitled, "A Call For Revival Within Fundamentalism." I am happy that some of my material was helpful to you.

In the event you have not seen my latest Information Bulletin on the subject of New Evangelicalism, I am enclosing one for your personal purusal. I trust that it will be of blessing to you also.

Please give my greetings to your good wife.

* * *

Pastor J.L. Garland
Grace Bible Church
Rialto, California

Dear Brother:

I want to thank you and commend you for your "Call for Revival Within Fundamentalism" in your recent Prophetic Magazine.

You have written with sincere passion, and with knowledge that your position has support from other Christian leaders. I trust what you have written will be seriously considered by many who are so often guilty of judgmental and condemning spirits, which are so condemned by the Word of God.

Heart Disease in Christ's Body

The spirits which are manifested by leaders of many of our groups are so distressing that it makes one feel he wants to just stay to himself. This is not the answer to the problem, nor does it please the Lord. We need so much to be a part of each other.

God bless you in this effort, and I pray it may spread to the pleasure and glory of God.

* * *

Dr. Robert C. Savage, Pastor
Haslett Baptist Church
Haslett, Michigan

Dear Jack:

It has been several years since we've had any fellowship but often you come into our home via T.V.

I'm writing simply to say "Praise the Lord for your new emphasis on love rather than negativism and fighting." I rejoice in your position: "I will love all of God's blood-bought children. I will refuse to accept the false labels placed upon good, godly men."

My Dad was perhaps the #1 leader of Fundamentalism in Michigan back in the 1920s and 1930s. But if he were alive today many would label him as a "neo-evangelical" or maybe even "modernist."

Personally I like the term "historic fundamentalist" which simply means I want to stand for the same principles that the fundamentalists of the 20s and 30s stood for and assiduously avoid the fighting, criticising, legalistic attitude of so many fellows in our day.

A Call for Revival Within Fundamentalism

May the Lord's richest blessing be HEAPED upon you, Jack. Warmest greetings to Rexella.

* * *

Rev. Jim W. Baize, Pastor
Midway Baptist Church
San Diego, California

Dear Brother Van Impe:

I recently received the November/December issue of your "Perhaps Today" magazine and was really pleased to have read the article "A Call for Revival Within Fundamentalism."

The article really impressed me and I was glad to see it in the magazine. It was very refreshing and I hope that as others read the article that they too will see the need for a revival within fundamentalism.

As a pastor, I try to keep the philosophy of Dr. Jack Hyles. That is of keeping quiet when it comes to other Christian leaders who are winning souls. I make it a policy to not say anything bad about other Christians who are doing all that they can to lead others to Christ even if they do differ with me on some minor issue. Our major concern is for winning souls to Christ and I feel that we should not argue or speak badly of anyone if they are leading others to a saving knowledge of Jesus Christ.

My thoughts and prayers are with you and your ministry and may the Lord continue to bless and guide you abundantly!

* * *

Heart Disease in Christ's Body

Rev. Robert Benefield, Pastor
Sequoia Baptist Church
Visalia, California

Dear Brother Van Impe:

I just received your magazine for Nov/Dec. I appreciate your article and think you hit the nail on the head. The magazine sparked my memory and it seems as though some months ago I received a letter from you asking if we were in agreement with your doctrine and philosophy. You were looking for local churches to which you could send referrals and contacts for follow-up and for local church and personal work. I fully intended to return that letter but it somehow got misplaced.

In times past I have received numerous referrals from your office and faithfully followed up on each one with, of course, varying results. We have a fundamental, growing, soul-winning church here in Visalia and I would be more than happy to receive your local referrals on people who have responded to your ministry. I would promise you that I would promptly and efficiently follow-up on each soul in our area.

May God bless your labor for Him.

* * *

94

Chapter 8

That They All May Be One *

— Why I Discontinued
Citywide Crusades —

The Lord Jesus, in His high priestly prayer, said: "[Father], as thou hast sent me into the world, even so have I also sent them into the world. Neither pray I for these alone [my sent ones], but for them also which shall believe on me [converts of future generations] through their word; THAT THEY ALL MAY BE ONE; as thou, Father, art in me, and I in thee, that they also may be one in us: that the world may believe that thou hast sent me" (John 17:18,20,21).

The unity or oneness of the family of God is the purpose of the Lord's prayer. Imagine, God in the flesh prayed that all Christians in all eras of time might have love for one another as a sign that the Father really sent the Son and that Christianity is genuine. Is it any wonder that Jesus said in John 13:35:" By this shall all men know that ye are my disciples, if ye have love one to another."

---

*This chapter is taken from my address to the delegates attending the International Christian Educator's Conference in Detroit, Michigan, October 22, 1982, and printed in my November/December, 1982, **Perhaps Today** magazine. There I pleaded, especially with young ministers, to avoid the pitfalls I encountered.

We fundamentalists have often shied away from this text on oneness because of its constant use by the perpetrators of the one-world church — but should we discard the baby with the bath water simply because an opponent has used it? Never. Such a position is woefully wrong when one considers that the desire of the Saviour's heart is that all genuine believers — past, present and future — be united in love. Since we are to be "doers of the word, and not hearers only" (James 1:22), we sooth our consciences by convincing ourselves that the oneness for which Jesus prayed is realized and fulfilled solely through loving believers within our own denominational affiliation. How wrong! This is only the tip of the iceberg.

First Corinthians 12:13 declares: "For by one Spirit are we all baptized into one body." This is not a Baptist, Nazarene, Pentecostal, Wesleyan Methodist, Christian and Missionary Alliance or Evangelical Free Church body. Rather, it is the one body of Jesus Christ composed of all born-again believers found in numerous denominations. Oh, if the Church of Jesus Christ would quit sporting its labels and begin exalting the Saviour, calling themselves by His name — Christ or Christians — then love for one another would become the effectual force it was meant to be within the evangelical scene. It's too bad that God, who chose us and called us to salvation (Ephesians 1:4) did not do it through one denomination. This would have made unity much simpler.

Do you really think that denominational tags are that important to God? In approximately 950-1100 A.D., the following evangelical groups existed: the

Petrobrusians, Henricians, Arnoldists, Humiliati, Waldenses, Taborites, Lollards and Bohemians. Where are they today, denominationally? Extinct! No one even recognizes their names unless he is a church history buff. Nevertheless, they were all powerful groups similar to our modern-day denominations. Often, they ostracized and broke fellowship over secondary differences — just as denominationalists do today.

Picture a future scene mentally with me, if you will — the entrance of believers into glory at the Rapture. Can you envision them running to those who have been there for centuries and inquiring: "Were you a Henrician? An Arnoldist? Would you tell me if the Waldenses were greater separatists than the Lollards? What am I saying? Simply that the only meaningful label in eternity will be 'Christian'." If Christ tarries another 500 years, the majority of today's labels will also pass away — but Christ and Christianity will live eternally!

Don't misunderstand. We may each have our personal convictions and hold to our doctrinal distinctives. I do, as a Baptist. Still, should we shun other brothers in Christ who disagree with our position? Could it be that most of us follow at least one man-made teaching within each of our denominations that could prove to be wrong, and scorn all brothers who disagree with us? Remember that no man is right on every issue, be he Calvin, Luther, Zwingli, Wesley or the leader upon whom your denomination was founded or for whom it is named.

Let's go one step farther. Not only do we break communion with other members of the body of Christ because of denominational distinctives, but we often break fellowship with brothers in our own denomination because of misguided views on secondary separation. Don't misunderstand me. I am a Baptist, a fundamentalist and a separatist, and practice Romans 16:17 and II John 7-11. However, separation in these texts is based exclusively on the doctrine of Christ — His deity, virgin birth, blood atonement, bodily resurrection and return — not one's personal standards or rules based on a misinterpretation of these texts.

Scores who hold to these Christological truths have nevertheless been "disfellowshipped" because of their refusal to bow to man-made principles of separation. Further, they are roasted in print and mislabeled as "pseudo-fundamentalists" (fakes) or "neo-evangelicals." The situation is heartbreaking as an ungodly world mocks this brand of Christianity.

Dr. Paul E. Billheimer states: "I believe personally that the main thing hindering the return of the Lord is the disunity of the Body. This is the greatest sin in the Church because it is the real cause of more souls being lost than any other sin. Born-again believers should be united on the basis of a common origin, a common fatherhood, a common parenthood, a common relationship rather than a common opinion on non-essentials. We will never agree theologically. It is my position that if we're born again, we're members of the same family and that is the basis of fellowship, love, and union rather than agreement on the non-essentials."

On August 23, 1981, the **Knight News Service** released a report from Chicago, Illinois, entitled:

That They All May Be One

"FUNDAMENTALISTS AT WAR WITHIN CHRISTIAN RANKS." Multiplied national news agencies carried the article. My heart literally ached as I read it and saw our famous leaders malign, vilify and slander one another publicly by name!

What did You say in Your compassionate prayer, Lord Jesus? You want us to be one in order that the world may believe that the Father truly sent You and that Christianity is real? Oh, if we could have an old-fashioned, Holy Spirit-empowered revival! Then the "warriors" of the faith would beat their swords into plowshares and their spears into pruning hooks. Until such a time occurs, however, the world will laugh at our great "defenders of the faith" who use unethical tactics to crush their brothers.

Am I being condemnatory? By no means. In fact, I, too, was guilty. In my mass, areawide crusades, dating from 1969 to 1980, many good brothers in Christ were barred from participation because I allowed "militant" leaders in numerous cities to establish false standards of separation. Consequently, men who dearly loved God were often banned because they did not bear the same denominational tag. Later, even those within the same group were at one another's throats — each classifying the other as a "pseudo-fundamentalist" or "neo-evangelical" solely on the biased views of a vocal minority. As a result, many good men were deeply hurt. Yet, I remained silent.

During the last five years, my spirit grew progressively troubled and many decisions were made. Consequently, I am now able to fulfill the promise I made at the 1977 Sword of The Lord Conference in

Detroit. At that time I stated: "I can no longer tolerate the dissention and division occurring among the brethren. It hinders genuine revival and makes a mocking world reject the message of Christ. I will no longer go into areas for future evangelistic campaigns unless there is a new spirit of love and unity among our leaders."

Unfortunately, the love and unity for which my soul cried out did not occur. In fact, the divisiveness became worse. In earlier days, the first 60 of my 253 united crusades to audiences totaling more than 10,000,000 persons were sponsored by scores of solid, evangelical denominations. Before long, however, various exclusions took place, depending on local preferences:

(1) All non-Baptistic groups, such as the Nazarenes, Wesleyan Methodists, Free Methodists, Missionary churches, Mennonites and numerous others — including Dr. A.W. Tozer's great fellowship of Christian and Missionary Alliance churches — were banned. I remember with gratitude the love these brethren in Christ manifested toward me even though they knew they were sponsoring a Baptist evangelist. D.L. Moody, Billy Sunday, Dr. John R. Rice and Dr. Bob Jones, Sr., had always included such groups. Thus, a **new** separatist position was instituted.

(2) The next move was to eliminate the Grace Brethren fellowship of churches, headquartered at Winona Lake, Indiana. In addition, depending on geographical location, the Independent Fundamental Churches of America (the group who ordained me) plus other Bible and Community churches were also

barred from participation. Extremists would not recognize these brethren because the Baptist label was not above the entrance of their church buildings. Though they were doctrinally sound, as well as Baptistic in practice, they were still banned because they were not considered part of the "Baptist Bride" — a position held by some ultra-denominationalists.

(3) Later in my ministry, all Conservative Baptists of America (CBA), along with all Baptist General Conference churches (Swedish), North American German Baptists, Free Will Baptists and the majority of the remaining Baptist groups were excluded. While they were considered part of the "Baptist Bride," they were shunned on the basis of a "soiled wedding garment." In other words, the "ecclesiastical judges" decided that these brethren had fellowshipped with those whom they had "disfellowshipped," and thus were tainted. At this point practically everyone had been eliminated.

(4) Finally, the "super-separatist society" was reduced to a handful of independents who accused and eliminated one another from participations in united (?) crusades for the souls of men.

Men were now divided over institutions and personalities. Schools such as Asbury College, Biola, Cedarville (GARBC), Calvary Bible College, Dallas Bible College, Dallas Theological Seminary, Detroit Bible College (now William Tyndale College), Florida Bible College, Grace College and Seminary, Grand Rapids Baptist Seminary (GARBC), Grand Rapids School of the Bible (IFCA), John Brown University, Liberty Baptist Seminary, Moody Bible Institute, Tennessee Temple Schools and scores of others were now classified as "moderate fundamentalist institutions who were willing to compromise with neo-evangelicals." (For documentation, see Dr. George Dollar's book, **The History of Fundamentalism.**)

Soon, all pastors who claimed one of these schools as their alma mater were suspect as "pseudofundamentalists," "modified fundamentalists" (compromisers) or "neo-evangelicals." On one occasion, I was told by extremist leaders that my appearance at a Moody Founder's Week Conference would result in the cancellation of one or more of my forthcoming citywide endeavors. Under pressure, I yielded. I have since asked God's forgiveness, as well as Dr. George Sweeting's (president of Moody Bible Institute), for cancelling my appearance at this great event. As a matter of fact, I have had to write many letters of apology in recent days under the leadership of the Holy Spirit.

Men were also divided over pantsuits, hair-covered ears and, on one occasion, wire-rimmed glasses. Now, while I believe that every pastor and church has the privilege of setting individual standards, a problem arises when they attempt to force their rules upon others as a basis for fellowship or the sponsorship of crusades. The heartbreaking fact was that those who were so judgmental on these issues involving secondary separation were often lenient concerning sexual promiscuity, smutty jokes and slander within their personal associations and churches. Hypocrisy abounded, and my heart was crushed.

I have lived with this heartache long enough. Now

it is finished, and my only desire is to love all the family of God and proclaim the message of reconciliation until I go home. How else can I expect to hear my Lord say, "Well done, thou good and faithful servant"?

Prejudice and hatred are never God's will for defenders of the faith. Paul said in I Corinthians 13:3: " . . . though I give my body to be burned, and have not charity [love], it profiteth me nothing." Oh, let's get filled with the Spirit! When that happens, love will dominate our beings and we will share that love with all members of the body of Christ: "For the fruit of the Spirit is love, joy, peace, longsuffering, gentleness, goodness, faith, meekness, temperance" (Galatians 5:22,23).

Because the situation concerning my areawide crusades became seemingly hopeless, I realized the futility of attempting to reach a world of lost men under these heartbreaking conditions. Thus, I ended this aspect of my ministry, fulfilling my promise made at the Sword of The Lord Conference in 1977. My experience has made me realize how true the following statement, taken from **The Herald of His Coming,** really is:

"Satan is a keen fighter against the body as a whole. The main thing he is driving at on earth is to divide the body. He is adept at divisive tactics. Under one cover or another, he aims to separate one member of the body from another. He knows the tremendous power there is in unity. He knows so well the resistless power against his person when there is united prayer and united action coming from a united body. He will do his utmost to kill that spirit of unity. So anything that divides the body or splits up any group of Christ's followers suits his purpose.''

My Personal Apology To The Body of Christ

Beloved brothers in Christ, I reach out to you with open arms of love. If you were ostracized and banned from my crusades, I apologize. I also ask forgiveness for injuring you — a true member of the body of Christ. I promise both my God and you that the rest of my years will be spent proclaiming the message of reconciliation and love for **all** the brotherhood (I Peter 2:17). I cannot do otherwise, for we are all one body in Christ Jesus (I Corinthians 12:13), and the Holy Spirit adds in verses 25 and 26 that ''there should be no schism [or division] in the body'' because it inflicts agonizing pain upon all of us. Yes, ''[if] one member suffers, all the members suffer with it.''

Brothers and sisters, since I have caused some of this pain in the body of Christ, I ask once again for your forgiveness. I truly love each of you who are members of the family of God, and never want to knowingly hurt anyone again.

May I conclude by asking all ministers and laymen the following question: ''When did you last exemplify the love of Christ to a brother or sister within another denomination — or even within your own if they are of another association or affiliation? If not, why not? Since we are all members of the one body, are we not ''fingers on the same hand'' as it were?

What a shame, then, that religious leaders will not allow these fingers — representing various denominational brothers — to touch one another until we reach heaven's golden shores! God forgive all of us. We have been wrong . . . so drastically wrong . . . so scripturally wrong!

SHOW LOVE . . .

to manifest to an unbelieving world that we all **are** one, and that the Father **hath** sent the Son!

*   *   *

Is love for one another regardless of denominational affiliation a scriptural principle? Were our founding fathers right, or were they wrong? You be the judge.

Chapter 9

Historic Fundamentalism's Roots

Forty years ago, I met Jesus and was gloriously saved. I shall never forget my newly found joy in the Lord. The experience took place in a small church established by the North American (German) Baptist Conference directly across from my home. As I mentioned in chapter two, often in my pagan state, I had raided this group with rotten tomatoes little realizing that I would one day be led to Jesus Christ by those I had persecuted.

One thing these precious Christians taught me was a love for all of God's people. They were Christians first — then Baptists. Because of it, I soon shared both my testimony and my talents as an accordionist within numerous denominations. This was an era of interdenominational fellowship, and no one was criticized, stigmatized or ostracized because of his love for all members of the family of God.

In the '40s, I often heard messages that incorporated the following truth: "When one is a Christian, he can travel anywhere globally and experience intimate fellowship with brethren of like precious faith." How true it was. These were happy days of loving the people of God, regardless of their denominational affiliation.

Fundamentalism's Roots

The harmony I experienced and enjoyed was the natural outgrowth of fundamentalism's roots. Separatist denominationalists should sit up and take notice at this point. Apparently they know little about their heritage. Dr. George Dollar, in his book, **A History of Fundamentalism in America**, reports that the who's who of first-generation fundamentalists consisted of leaders identified with the following denominations: Presbyterian, Reformed, Reformed Episcopal, Methodist, Anglican, Baptist, Lutheran, Wesleyan (holiness) and Congregational. By the way, Billy Sunday was a Presbyterian and the revered D.L. Moody a Congregationalist, as was C.I. Scofield.

What do our roots teach us? Simply that the amalgamated mixture of first-generation fundamentalists included numerous groups composed of Calvinists and Arminians, eternal security advocates and "falling from grace" proponents, pre-millennialists and a-millennialists, sprinklers and immersionists, sacramentalists and the non-sacramentalists who opted for ordinances. Nevertheless, all were rooted in one heart and spirit around the five points of historic fundamentalism:

1. The inspiration and inerrancy of Scripture.
2. The deity of Jesus Christ.
3. The virgin birth of Christ.
4. The substitutionary, atoning work of Christ on the cross.
5. The physical resurrection and the personal, bodily return of Christ to earth.

These five points constituted the basis for withdrawal from liberalism and apostasy, and men from all backgrounds took their stand on these issues — nothing additional.

Today, the waters have become muddied and bloodied by militant leadership. In fact, one may no longer be considered a genuine fundamentalist even though he is so devoted to these five points that he would gladly give his life for his beliefs.

How has all this confusion, bigotry, prejudice and lovelessness become so pervasive and predominant in a good and God-honoring movement that had such a grand beginning? It happened simply because men whose hearts brimmed with love toward others — men who were basically shy and unassuming — sat idly by and never protested the creation of neo-fundamentalism — a movement that continually added rules, regulations and resolutions to the five original points at their conferences, convocations and congress of fundamentalism.

Dr. Truman Dollar, a prominent leader in the Baptist Bible Fellowship movement of Springfield, Missouri, writes: "The men who contributed to The Fundamentals had widely diverse backgrounds. They were united by their common commitment to the basics ("fundamentals") of the Christian faith. In their defense of the faith, they . . . **refused** to be divided over denominational distinctives or personal biases.

"Since that early coalition, the situation has dramatically changed. There are those within the Fundamentalist movement who want to add their own beliefs and practices to the five fundamentals. Their list continually expands until it eventually excludes everyone who disagrees with any position they represent. The issue is no longer a commitment to the five fundamentals but rather allegiance to what they claim are the 7 fundamentals, the 10 fundamentals, the 20 fundamentals, the 50 fundamentals, and so on."

Dr. Dollar adds: "Who are the real pseudo-fundamentalists? [I prefer the term, "neo-fundamentalists" — JVI.] From a historical perspective they are those who have added their personal preferences to the fundamentals and have demanded allegiance to every jot and tittle of THEIR LAW. Within fundamentalism are those who want to saturate the movement with their own brand of additives dangerous to the health of the movement and, unrestrained, may produce a cancer that will destroy its life and vitality. Perhaps the time has come to perform major surgery in order to deal with the cancer."

God bless you, Dr. Dollar. You have expressed my sentiments precisely! Since I released my article entitled "That They All May Be One," I have discovered that there are hundreds in our ranks who are heartsick over the bitterness, prejudice and name-calling that abounds. These fundamentalists have hearts filled with love, and want change. God help us to "walk tall" at such an hour as this, and protest whatever the cost. Let's oppose the man-made labels placed upon good and godly men whose only crime is that they will not bow to man as they reject the 7, 10, 20 or 50 points contrary to historic fundamentalism's roots.

Let's also reject the harsh, crude and intemperate language neo-fundamentalists use in describing others. Recently, the World Congress of Fundamentalists met under the co-chairmanship of Dr. Bob Jones, Jr., and Dr. Ian Paisley. Concerning this meeting, **The Detroit News,** Saturday, August 20, 1983, reported that Rev. Paisley "called down the wrath of God on 'the papist rats and murdering scum'." What a shame to label Catholics or any other religious group in such vitriolic terms! I, for one, protest. I have Catholic relatives I love dearly. More importantly, God commands that we "speak evil of no man" (Titus 3:2), that we "do good unto all men" (Galatians 6:10), that our speech "be always with grace" (Colossians 4:6), and that "all [our] things be done with [love]" (I Corinthians 16:14).

Then again, in the Resolutions section, concerning the charismatic movement, the delegates to this Congress used language unbecoming to the cause of Christ, His Church, and fundamentalism. After de-

111

nouncing the charismatics, they stated: "Therefore, we call upon all born-again believers to come out from this Satanic charismatic movement and we denounce this wicked hell-inspired charismatic movement as the devil's masterpiece of camouflage to deceive and destroy the very elect."

How ungracious and condemnatory. Surely every reasonable and rational fundamentalist must understand that there are scores of believers in this movement also trusting in the precious blood of Jesus for salvation. How wrong, then, to coin or condone such abusive and judgmental rhetoric against any segment of Christ's body (I Corinthians 12:13). A disagreement over the interpretation of chapters 12 and 14 of I Corinthians is one thing, but a resolution damning an entire movement as a Satanic and hell-inspired masterpiece of the devil is quite another matter. Again, I protest such abusive language as a fundamentalist. You must also. The silent majority — numbering millions — within our ranks must not allow one small but vocal segment to speak so derogatorily of others in our behalf. The number of commands to "love one another" listed in chapter thirteen demands this conclusion. Let's obey God instead of man.

There was a period of time in my life when I, too, thought that God was pleased with such abusive verbal assaults on other men and movements in my crusades attended by thousands. Then the Holy Spirit began to do a deep work within my being, convicting me of my ungraciousness. I now know that "the servant of the Lord must not strive, **but be gentle unto all men**" (II Timothy 2:24). If God could do this work of grace in my heart, I'm certain He can do it for others.

In the flesh, this is an impossibility. However, through the infilling of the Holy Spirit, it becomes a reality. Then "love, joy, peace, longsuffering, gentleness, goodness, faith, meekness, [and] temperance" (Galatians 5:22,23) will become evident. When the Spirit controls men and movements, we will "be kindly affectioned one to another" (Romans 12:10) and will "do good unto all men, especially unto them who are of the household of faith" (Galatians 6:10). Then we will "increase and abound in love one toward another" (I Thessalonians 3:12) and overlook the faults of others as love covers a multitude of sins (I Peter 4:8) — and perhaps a few mistakes as well. Then love will no longer be thought of as a sentimental sickness inherent in compromisers, but a healthy wholesomeness within Spirit-controlled brethren.

Fundamentalism's Silent Majority
Men of Love and Compassion

I have read many fundamentalist publications and heard numerous innuendos concerning my new position. One stated that I was attempting to unite cultists and evangelicals! Another said that I had renounced my relationship with the Baptist Bible Fellowship International. This was announced to thousands at a gathering. I have a tape recording of the event.

None of the statements and accusations are true. Some of my friends have encouraged me to retaliate. I will not. I rest upon the promise of my heavenly Father who said, "Be still, and know that I am God" (Psalm 46:10). Time heals all wounds. I will wait.

At this point, may I simply say that I am a historic fundamentalist who would lay down his life for the five foundational points because they center around my wonderful Lord and the Book so precious to me. As such, I will love all blood-bought members of God's family because this is a scriptural principle preached and practiced by historic fundamentalists. I stand where the late Dr. John R. Rice stood when he so often stated with great dogmatism in **The Sword of The Lord**, "I am a companion of all them that fear thee" (Psalm 119:63).

One year ago, Rexella and I vowed before the Lord that LOVE FOR ALL THE FAMILY OF GOD would be our new position until Christ calls us home. We agreed that if this conviction cost us the loss of numerous supporters, or even the dissolution of our national television ministry, we would gladly pay the price. In fact, we prepared the following letter for the great number we thought would cancel their prayer and financial support.

Dear Brother:

With respect to your concern about the direction I am taking, may I immediately state that the only change is that the sweet Spirit of the Lord has broadened my convictions to practice all of God's Word, including John 13:35 and I John 4:7,8,12,20.

In my article entitled, "That They All May Be One," I said: "I promise God and all members of His family that the remainder of my life will be spent proclaiming the message of reconciliation and love for ALL the brotherhood" (I Peter 2:17). I meant this. I will live and die for this biblical principle called love.

If my position causes you to withdraw your church's prayer and financial support, that must be your decision before God. Even if all men follow your example and I become financially unable to continue my ministry, I will know that I have obeyed God and His commandment to love one another — and nothing else matters.

Sincerely in Christ,
Jack Van Impe

Instead of having had to use this letter often, hundreds wrote to say, "Brother Van Impe, we, too, are fundamentalists standing where you do on this matter of love. We also are grieved by the rampant divisiveness within our movement, and thank God for the breath of fresh air the Spirit of God is sending our way through your new position of love."

Some 2,100 of the churches supporting our ministry are in my denomination, and I praise God for the vision of love they, too, hold in their hearts for other brothers and sisters in Jesus Christ. Join their ranks. It's mandatory, for "If a man say, I love God, and hateth his brother, he is a liar" (I John 4:20).

Fundamentalism's Marching Orders

Is love for one another regardless of denominational affiliation a scriptural principle? Were our founding fathers right, or were they wrong? You be the judge.

ORDER #1: Every born-again believer is a member in the body of Christ.

In Christ's great priestly prayer, recorded in John 17:11,21-23, He prayed for unity four times. Dr. Lewis Sperry Chafer says: "With all these requests in view, it must be conceded that few, if any, truths are so emphasized in the Word of God as the unity of the believers. Now this prayer began to be answered on the Day of Pentecost when those then saved were fused into one body. The prayer has also been answered continuously as all those at the moment of believing were added to Christ's body by the operation of the Holy Spirit (I Corinthians 12:13). This marvelous unity between believers then becomes the logical ground for all Christian action [namely, love (JVI)] one toward another."

Presently, it is the duty of every Christian to keep the unity the Holy Spirit has already begun and continued for 20 centuries (Ephesians 4:1-3). This is God's commandment, and no set of resolutions adopted at a fundamentalist congress can alter God's marching orders.

ORDER #2: Every born-again believer is a member of the family of God.

Ephesians 3:15 speaks of the family as being "in heaven and [upon] earth." What does the verse mean? Those who have died in Jesus are already present in glory, "absent from the body . . . present with the Lord" (II Corinthians 5:8). Hence, all fam-

116

ily members — spanning 2,000 years of Christendom
— now in heaven await the homecoming of family
members still upon earth. Now get it, this is important: These believers in heaven and upon earth got
there by being saved in thousands of denominations
in which they were members during their lifetime.
Since there is no way one can get rid of his spiritual
relatives in heaven or upon earth (the saved from
thousands of denominations covering 20 centuries),
let's LOVE THEM — especially the ones still
breathing!

ORDER #3: **Every born-again believer is a son or daughter of God.**

"As many as received him, to them gave he power
to become the sons of God" (John 1:12). Since none
of us has the right to eliminate or ignore our brothers
or sisters within the family, I suggest that we begin to
"LOVE THE BROTHERHOOD" (I Peter 2:17).

ORDER #4: **Every born-again believer is the Lord's by adoption (Ephesians 1:5).**

Scriptural adoption means that the new "babe in
Christ" is placed into the family as an adult son or
daughter with all the rights and privileges of one who
has reached legal age (21 in America). These rights
make every child an heir of God and "joint heirs with
Jesus Christ" (Romans 8:17).

117

ORDER #5: **Every born-again believer has been cleansed by the blood of Jesus (I John 1:7).**

And "what God hath cleansed, that call not thou common [or unclean]" (Acts 11:9).

ORDER #6: **Every born-again believer has been forgiven.**

"In [Christ] we have redemption through his blood, the forgiveness of sins, according to the riches of his grace" (Ephesians 1:7).

ORDER #7: **Every born-again believer has been redeemed or bought back from the slave market of sin and set free through the precious blood of Jesus (I Peter 1:19).**

This includes every child of God saved in every gospel-preaching denomination.

ORDER #8: **Every born-again believer has been reconciled (II Corinthians 5:19,20).**

This means that every brother in Christ is eternally at peace with God. Since God has been so gracious to us, we, in turn, should practice Hebrews 12:14 which commands us to "follow peace with all men and holiness, without which no man shall see the Lord."

118

ORDER #9: **Every born-again believer has been regenerated (Titus 3:5), meaning that life and the divine nature have been imparted to him (II Peter 1:4).**

This includes every child of God who ever got it, gets it or ever will get it in the years ahead as Jesus tarries. Sad, is it not, that many Christians are forbidden to fellowship with believers who have God's own nature. No wonder new converts are confused.

ORDER #10: **Every born-again believer has been "made nigh" or close to God by the blood of Jesus (Ephesians 2:13).**

No one is any closer to God than another on the basis of denominational merit. Instead, this nearness is based on a blood relationship — that of the Lamb of God. Thank God this is so, for there are presently 20,780 distinct Christian denominations now locatable in Christian atlases internationally — and a great percentage of them uplift Jesus.

ORDER #11: **Every born-again believer has been "accepted in the beloved [Jesus]" (Ephesians 1:6).**

Our acceptance is on the basis that we have become "the righteousness of God in Christ" (II Corinthians 5:21). This includes all "relatives" found in all Bible-believing churches. Don't forget it. If every child of God is "accepted in the beloved," perhaps we should show a little more kindness to all of our relatives in Christ Jesus.

ORDER #12: **Every born-again believer is a citizen of heaven.**

Philippians 3:20 declares: "For our conversation [citizenship] is in heaven." Because of it, "we are no more strangers and foreigners, but fellow-citizens with the saints and the household of God" (Ephesians 2:19). This citizenship is bestowed upon red, yellow, black and white, completed Jews and Gentiles, Calvinists and Arminians, pre-Tribulationists and post-Tribulationists, pre-millennialists and a-millennialists. Many of our founding fathers were a-millennialists! Anyone who has put his faith and trust in Christ has a passport for heaven, and no militant group passing resolutions making good men "pseudo-fundamentalists" or "neo-evangelicals" can change that.

ORDER #13: **Every born-again believer has been "justified" or declared absolutely righteous — just as if he had never sinned.**

This is because of the merits of the shed blood of Jesus (Romans 5:9). If this be true — and it is — I find it ridiculous that most of us are forbidden fellowship with other brothers and sisters of like precious faith who have been declared absolutely righteous in Jesus. What bigots we denominationalists and separatists often are.

120

ORDER #14: **Every born-again believer is a member of the "royal priesthood" (I Peter 2:9).**

Even this status symbol is ignored in our separatist "caste system."

ORDER #15: **Every born-again believer (you Calvinists will love this) has been:**

A. Chosen in Him before the foundation of the world (Ephesians 1:4).

B. Elected (Romans 8:33).

C. Called with an holy calling (II Timothy 1:9; Hebrews 1:14).

D. Drawn by the Father (John 6:44).

E. Given to Christ by the Father (John 6:37).

F. Predestined to be conformed to the image of His Son (Romans 8:29).

Imagine! The omniscient, all-knowing God planned in centuries past to save His children in thousands of denominations spanning a period of approximately 2,000 years. He placed the first convert into the "body" of Christ at Pentecost, and will continue the process until the final member completes the one body. Just think — if the Father had not

121

bungled the job (according to some denominationalists), the situation might have been so different. If
He had planned to save all His chosen in one group,
we would not have had to make as many resolutions
against others.

Well, since the all-wise God did it His way, and
since this includes every saved person in Baptist,
Presbyterian, Methodist, Episcopalian, Lutheran,
Reformed, Wesleyan, Free Methodist, Pilgrim
Holiness, Nazarene and Pentecostal churches —
recognize that God did it and accept His eternal plan.
Then decide to love and accept all those HE included.
He made no mistakes. You do when you reject His
foreordained plan.

Finally . . .

ORDER #16: **Every born-again believer is
already seated "in heavenly
places in Christ Jesus"
(Ephesians 2:6).**

Theologically and biblically, this is acceptable.
However, let's not practice this truth until we get
there. Presently, let's not even sit with them in a
restaurant — we might be suspected of compromise!

Have I made the scriptural position clear? I am not
talking about anyone's forfeiting his denominational
distinctives or giving up his doctrinal position. However, I **am** saying that because of our unity as members of the "one body," we must love one another.

Someone may be asking, "What about the verses
that command us to 'avoid them,' 'come out from
among them,' 'judge them,' 'reprove them,' 'mark

them,' 'identify them,' 'withdraw from them,' 'turn away from them,' 'reject them,' 'keep not company with them' and 'note them?'" In the next chapter, I will deal with the meaning of the term "them," proving that the World Congress of Fundamentalists has misapplied a number of texts as they, through a resolution, declared Drs. W.A. Criswell, Jerry Falwell, George Sweeting and Jack Van Impe "fake," "false" and "counterfeit" fundamentalists, charging us as fellow travelers with apostates.

In conclusion, if I have gotten through to your mind and heart via these tremendous scriptural truths, would you pray and ask forgiveness for your hardness of heart and prejudices? I came to this point, and asked forgiveness of both God and men. My article entitled, "That They All May Be One," reprinted in chapter eight, tells of my seven-year battle with the truths presented in this article. The Scriptures were plain, and I had to obey. Will you?

Don't let carnal leaders misguide you so that you lose your rewards (I Corinthians 13:4). Remember: "And now abideth faith, hope, charity [or love]; these three, but the greatest of these is love" (I Corinthians 13:13). So, "let brotherly love continue" (Hebrews 13:1).

In addition to the 16 marching orders contained in the message itself, I include the following commands for your further consideration and blessing.

17. **EVERY BORN-AGAIN BELIEVER is the salt of the earth (Matthew 5:13).**
18. **EVERY BORN-AGAIN BELIEVER is the light of the world (Matthew 5:14).**

19. **EVERY BORN-AGAIN BELIEVER possesses everlasting life (John 3:36).**

20. **EVERY BORN-AGAIN BELIEVER is one of God's sheep (John 10:27).**

21. **EVERY BORN-AGAIN BELIEVER is a saint (Romans 1:7).**

22. **EVERY BORN-AGAIN BELIEVER has been baptized into Christ (Romans 6:3-5).**

23. **EVERY BORN-AGAIN BELIEVER is free from condemnation (Romans 8:1).**

24. **EVERY BORN-AGAIN BELIEVER is inseparable from the love of God (Romans 8:38-39).**

25. **EVERY BORN-AGAIN BELIEVER is sanctified (I Corinthians 1:2).**

26. **EVERY BORN-AGAIN BELIEVER is a partaker of God's grace (I Corinthians 1:4).**

27. **EVERY BORN-AGAIN BELIEVER is confirmed to the end (I Corinthians 1:8).**

28. **EVERY BORN-AGAIN BELIEVER is called into the fellowship of His Son (I Corinthians 1:9).**

29. **EVERY BORN-AGAIN BELIEVER is a part of God's building (I Corinthians 3:9).**

30. **EVERY BORN-AGAIN BELIEVER is the temple of God (I Corinthians 3:16).**

31. **EVERY BORN-AGAIN BELIEVER is the temple of the Holy Spirit (I Corinthians 6:19).**

32. **EVERY BORN-AGAIN BELIEVER drinks the same spiritual drink (I Corinthians 10:4).**

33. **EVERY BORN-AGAIN BELIEVER partakes of one bread (I Corinthians 10:17).**

34. **EVERY BORN-AGAIN BELIEVER is gifted (I Corinthians 12:7).**

35. **EVERY BORN-AGAIN BELIEVER is sealed (II Corinthians 1:22).**

36. **EVERY BORN-AGAIN BELIEVER is a sweet savour of Christ (II Corinthians 2:15).**

37. **EVERY BORN-AGAIN BELIEVER has a new house or bodily covering awaiting him in heaven (II Corinthians 5:1).**

38. **EVERY BORN-AGAIN BELIEVER is a new creation (II Corinthians 5:17).**

39. **EVERY BORN-AGAIN BELIEVER is an ambassador for Christ (II Corinthians 5:20).**

40. **EVERY BORN-AGAIN BELIEVER is one of God's people (II Corinthians 6:16).**

41. **EVERY BORN-AGAIN BELIEVER is a child of Abraham spiritually (Galatians 3:7).**

42. **EVERY BORN-AGAIN BELIEVER has been redeemed from the curse of the law (Galatians 3:13).**

43. **EVERY BORN-AGAIN BELIEVER is Christ's purchased possession (Ephesians 1:13, 14).**

44. **EVERY BORN-AGAIN BELIEVER is saved by grace (Ephesians 2:8,9).**

45. **EVERY BORN-AGAIN BELIEVER is God's workmanship (Ephesians 2:10).**

46. **EVERY BORN-AGAIN BELIEVER is a child of light (Ephesians 5:8).**

47. **EVERY BORN-AGAIN BELIEVER has been delivered from darkness (Colossians 1:13).**

48. **EVERY BORN-AGAIN BELIEVER has an eternal inheritance (Hebrews 9:15).**

49. **EVERY BORN-AGAIN BELIEVER is already perfected in Christ (Hebrews 10:14).**

50. **EVERY BORN-AGAIN BELIEVER is a king (Revelation 5:9).**

After studying this tremendous additional listing as to what every child of God is or shall be, don't you agree it is sad that we are often asked to reject brothers and sisters in whom God has performed such mighty works?

* * *

Two misinterpreted biblical texts have been used to create the greatest mistrust of brothers in the history of Christendom.

Chapter 10

Neo-Fundamentalism's Errant Interpretation of the Inerrant Word

The twentieth century began with a tumultuous conservative uproar over the infiltration of numerous denominations by liberalism. The severity of the situation demanded immediate action. Heretical teachings were captivating and corrupting entire churches, schools and related organizations within multiplied denominations. Therefore, a coalition of interdenominational brethren, following a number of conferences, united around the five "fundamentals" of the faith. They were:

1. The inspiration and inerrancy of Scripture
2. The deity of Jesus Christ
3. The virgin birth of Christ

4. The substitutionary, atoning work of Christ on the cross
5. The physical resurrection and the personal, bodily return of Christ to the earth.

The adherents to these five "fundamental" truths were naturally labeled "fundamentalists." Those opposing them were called "liberals."

The men joining together around these five points (commonly called "the doctrine of Christ") were from varied and diversified religious backgrounds. Thus, this amalgamation of "first generation fundamentalists" included Presbyterians, Baptists, Reformers, Reformed Episcopalians, Lutherans, Methodists, Anglicans, Congregationalists, and Wesleyan Holiness brothers. The astounding thing about the members of this interdenominational movement was their love for one another. All secondary differences concerning personal preferences and denominational distinctives were laid aside. Their only burden and goal was to glorify the Lord Jesus Christ. They were "warriors" in a battle against liberalism and they knew who the "enemies of the cross of Christ" were (Philippians 3:18).

Historians inform us that all conferences leading up to the formation of this glorious and biblically oriented movement were non-sectarian. Denominational positions were never discussed or debated. Wouldn't it be spiritually stimulating to turn back history's clock a mere eighty years and re-experience the overwhelming love brothers in Christ had for one another under the banner of interdenominational fundamentalism? Wouldn't it be glorious to fellowship with others of like precious faith without being suspected of committing a traitorous act of compromise?

Today suspicion abounds and condemnatory pronouncements increase against good men and organizations simply because man-made innovations, standards and rules have become the tests of fellowship. The "doctrine of Christ" alone is no longer the standard. Instead, man's misinterpretations of Scripture are. May God allow us to see the situation and deal with such destructive additives before it is too late. The cancer is growing, and it may soon destroy our movement. To understand the situation perfectly, let's look at fundamentalism in detail.

Fundamentalism's Separatist Stance

Dr. Ed Dobson, editor of **The Fundamentalist Journal,** presents us with a brief historical sketch of our movement. He states: "Fundamentalism's war in the '20s was a vibrant demonstration of the church's responsibility to defend the faith from doctrinal heresy. The clear teaching of Scripture mandated a confrontation with heresy and separation from it (I John 4:1-3; II Peter 2:1; Romans 16:17-18; II John 10,11). The war concluded with Fundamentalists withdrawing from the mainline denominations and forming their own fellowships, schools and organizations. Truth had been defended and purity maintained. However, the unity that these early Fundamentalists demonstrated was quickly dissipated as each group set about the task of rebuilding and recuperating from the aftermath of the bloody conflict.

"Over fifty years have elapsed since that controversy. We have continued to defend the truth and have remained loyal recipients of our religious heritage. However, we are not without our extremes and excuses. Like our forefathers, we have a fallible tendency to overreact. In our sincere desire to maintain purity, we sometimes go beyond the guidelines of Scripture and reason. There are these polemic Fundamentalists who have added their own personal convictions to the historic list of fundamentals. They insist on conformity to all THEIR VIEWS and failure to do so means immediate examination by their group. Anyone outside their fold [and there are numerous folds, each with its own standards — JVI] is considered suspect. Their desire for internal purity leaves them critical of everyone else who claims the same Saviour. It is one thing to go to war against heresy. It is another thing to go to war against a Christian brother."

I wholeheartedly agree with our founding fathers in their separatist stance. Liberal theologians denying the deity of Christ, His virgin birth, the substitutionary atoning work of Christ upon the cross, the physical resurrection and the personal, bodily return of the Lord Jesus Christ are definitely apostates. (Webster's dictionary defines an apostate as one who has departed or defected from the faith.) Apostates are also described in I John 2:19: "They went out from us, but they were not of us; for if they had been of us, they would no doubt have continued with us; but they went out, that they might be made manifest that they were not all of us." In defecting and turning away from the doctrine of Christ, they actually renounced the faith, for I John 2:23 declares: "Whosoever denieth the Son, the same hath not the Father; but he that acknowledgeth the Son hath the Father also." Thus, their departure made them false prophets and teachers to be avoided. John warns: "Beloved, believe not every spirit [teacher], but try [test] the spirits [teachers] whether they are of God; because many false prophets are gone out into the world. Hereby know ye the Spirit of God: Every spirit [teacher] that confesseth that Jesus Christ [God] is come in the flesh is of God: And every spirit [teacher] that confesseth not that Jesus Christ is come in the flesh is not of God: and this is that spirit of antichrist, whereof ye have heard that it should come" (I John 4:1-3).

Now since apostates were and are antichrists, and because two cannot walk together unless they be agreed (Amos 3:3), there was only one course of action possible for fundamentalism's founding fathers — total severance and separation from such outrageous unbelief. This position was based upon such scriptural texts as II Corinthians 6:14-18: "Be ye not unequally yoked together with unbelievers: for what fellowship hath righteousness with unrighteousness? and what communion hath light with darkness? And what concord hath Christ with Belial? or what part hath he that believeth with an infidel? And what agreement hath the temple of God with idols? for ye are the temple of the living God; as God hath said, I will dwell in them, and walk in them; and I will be their God, and they shall be my people. Wherefore come out from among them, and be ye separate, saith the Lord, and touch not the unclean thing; and I will receive you, And will be a Father unto you, and ye shall be my sons and daughters, saith the Lord Almighty.''

We see, then, that our separatist stance began as a biblically oriented position against apostasy. We severed religious connections with those who denied the ''five-point'' teaching concerning Christ and the inerrant Bible. This was a good and just platform for fundamentalism since Christ alone was our standard, our rallying point. What one thinks about Christ separates the wheat from the tares, the just from the unjust, the genuine from the false and the apostates from the children of God.

This is the position I embraced as a God-given conviction years ago. I have not changed. The rules have changed, but I have not. In fact, I am still so committed to Christ and His Word, and so opposed to apostasy, that I recently delivered the following message via national television:

> What does the Bible have to say about apostasy? I realize that I shall be called an apostle of discord, a cultist, a hyper-fundamentalist and an extremist but I couldn't care less. I stand with the great Apostle Paul who said in Galatians 1:10 ''...if I yet pleased men, I should not be the servant of Christ.''
>
> Now there are two ways to say it. One is to use such a profound vocabulary that all will be astounded at my intelligence but probably never get the message. The other is to say it with all the simplicity that God meant for it to be given so that everyone gets the plain truth.

For instance, I can say, "In promulgating your esoteric cogitations or articulating your superficial sentimentalities and amicable, philosophical or psychological observations, beware of platitudinous ponderosity." Or, in simpler terms, "Keep your talking simple and to the point." Let me do just that.

First of all, the Bible teaches that apostates will arise within the Christian church. Acts 20:29: "For I know this, that after my departing shall grievous wolves enter in among you, not sparing the flock." II Peter 2:1: " . . . there were false prophets also among the people, even as there shall be [future tense] false teachers among you, who privily [or secretly] shall bring in damnable heresies, even denying the Lord that bought them, and bring upon themselves swift destruction." Jude, verse 4: " . . . there are certain men crept in unawares, who were before of old ordained to this condemnation, ungodly men, turning the grace of our God into lasciviousness, and denying the only Lord God, and our Lord Jesus Christ." Notice carefully — they creep in very secretly, quietly, and slowly, and once they are in they take over and deny the Lord Jesus Christ. This has to do, you see, with the doctrine of Christ: His deity (I Timothy 3:16), His virgin birth (Matthew 1:23), His substitutionary blood atonement (I Corinthians 15:3; Ephesians 1:7), His bodily resurrection (Romans 4:25; 10:9- 10) and His bodily return.

Second, the Bible describes the great damage apostates do. Acts 20:29: "They spare not the flock [God's people]." Romans 16:17: "They cause divisions and offences . . . " Verse 18: " . . . they . . . deceive the hearts of the simple." I Timothy 4:2 — they speak lies in hypocrisy. I Timothy 6:3 — they "consent not to wholesome words, even the words of our Lord Jesus Christ." II Timothy 2:18: " . . . [they] overthrow the faith of some." Oh, how true and how sad! II Peter 2:1: " . . . [They] bring in damnable heresies, even denying the Lord." II Peter 2:10: " . . . they are not afraid to speak evil of dignities." Verse 12: " . . . [They] speak evil of things that they understand not . . . " Verse 14: "[They have] eyes full of adultery, and that cannot cease from sin . . . " They also [beguile] unstable souls. Verse 15: " . . . [They] have forsaken the right way . . . " Verse 18: " . . . they speak great swelling words of vanity . . . " or use a great vocabulary to draw men to themselves. II John, verse 7: " . . . [They] confess not that Jesus Christ is come in the flesh . . . " They abide not in the doctrine of God. Jude, verse 4: " . . . [They turn] the grace of our God into lasciviousness, and [deny] the Lord Jesus Christ." Notice how often the Bible states that they deny Jesus Christ. This is what apostasy is all about. Anyone who says, "I will not accept the doctrine of the virgin birth, His deity, His blood atonement, His bodily resurrection and His second coming" is an apostate, even if he has a collar or a doctorate in religion. Flee from him!

Third, consider the names and titles God gives to apostates. God? Yes, God! Why do I say this? Because II Timothy 3:16 says: "All scripture is given by inspiration of God." So, in Acts 20:29, God calls apostates "grievous wolves." In II Corinthians 6:14, God calls apostates "unbelievers." In II Corinthians 11:13, God calls apostates "false apostles" and "deceitful workers." In Philippians 3:18, God calls apostates "the enemies of the cross of Christ."

In I Timothy 6:5, God calls apostates "men of corrupt minds and destitute of the truth." In II Timothy 2:20, God calls apostates "vessels of dishonour." In II Peter 2:1, God calls apostates "false teachers." In II Peter 2:12, God calls apostates "natural brute beasts." God said it, I didn't. Don't get mad at me. He wrote it, I only quote it. In II Peter 2:19, God calls apostates "servants of corruption." Now here is the one I want you to get: I John 2:18, God calls apostates "antichrists."

Fourth, and finally, consider God's commands to desert these apostates.

I then elaborated on Romans 16:17, II Corinthians 6:14-18 and II John verses 7-11. May I ask you a question? Does this message sound like I am in fellowship with apostates; a bosom buddy to those who mock my Jesus? Someone is undoubtedly wondering if I am still in control of my mental apparatus by asking such an absurd question. I am. Well then, what's behind something so nonsensical? I'll tell you.

Recently the World Congress of Fundamentalists under the Chairmanship of Dr. Bob Jones, Jr. and Dr. Ian Paisley resolved and declared that Dr. W. A. Criswell (Southern Baptist), Dr. George Sweeting (President of Moody Bible Institute), Dr. Jerry Falwell (world famous Christian leader) and Dr. Jack Van Impe were pseudo-fundamentalists, which Webster's dictionary defines as "fake, false or counterfeit."

Concerning men and movements they said:

We believe that it is not enough just to proclaim biblical principles of separation, but that it is further necessary and scriptural to identify men, institutions, and movements that are involved in apostasy or compromise with it. To this end the World Congress of Fundamentlists WARNS BIBLE BELIEVERS AGAINST:

POINT 5: Pseudo-fundamentalism represented by such men as W.A. Criswell, Jerry Falwell, George Sweeting and Jack Van Impe."

May I ask a question in behalf of numerous men and organizations, including myself, who were accused of either being apostates or compromisers with apostates? Dr. Jones, Dr. Paisley and members of the resolutions committee, "who art thou that judgest another man's servant? To his own master he standeth or falleth." And "why dost thou judge thy brother? Or why dost thou set at nought thy brother? For we shall all stand before the judgment seat of Christ" (Romans 14:4,10). Who gave you the right to indiscriminately judge scores of men and movements under various labels, identifying us as fellow travelers with Christ rejectors? As a historic fundamentalist, I protest your prejudiced denunciation of numerous good and godly men in the presence of 4,000 delegates as well as your release of printed materials concerning our alleged defection. My prayer is: "Father forgive them; for they know not what they do" (Luke 23:34).

Has fundamentalism deteriorated to the point where one man or group sets itself up as judge and jury, sentencing innocent victims without a hearing? What a shame when religious leaders operate their organizations in such an unchristlike manner.

I cannot remain silent. I had resolved never to answer my critics. Now I must. I do so in behalf of thousands upon thousands of my precious "babes in Christ," converts who might become utterly confused and disillusioned because of such public pronouncements against me. I cannot allow any man or organization to destroy their faith in the ministry God, in His sovereignty, used to bring them to Christ. Therefore, I speak plainly and boldly.

It's a sad day when men are judged on the basis of the leadership's likes and dislikes. This produces inconsistencies as "compromises" are overlooked among friends but vehemently condemned among adversaries. This double standard is wrong.

Furthermore, such judgment is based on third and fourth generation separation. Dr. John R. Rice predicted this would happen. He said in **The Sword of the Lord**: "Those who teach secondary separation go beyond the scriptural command of II Corinthians 6:14. They not only separate from modernists and liberals, but also from the fundamentalist who won't separate from the fundamentalist who won't separate from the modernist. This kind of separation is not taught in the Bible. In fact, if I had to check out the association of everyone with whom fundamentalists had fellowship, I would need a full-time staff to do nothing else and then it would still be impossible. The situation gets rather silly."

How right Dr. Rice was. How wrong such an espionage system becomes. In one citywide crusade in the West, the chairman called me saying, "I just received a call from a minister informing me that your name is listed as an honorary board member on the stationery of the Detroit Bible College [now William Tyndale College]." He added, "Since the informer also stated that this is not a fundamentalist school, you must have your name removed immediately or the citywide endeavor will be cancelled." Imagine my heartache and embarrassment as I made such a ridiculous request to Dr. Wendell Johnston, the president of my alma mater, the great institution that had always been, and still is, so true to the Word of God. I encountered many such threats, and always from the same crowd.

This group's suspicion of everyone and his brother is thoroughly documented in the book, **A History of Fundamentalism**, released by Bob Jones University Press. Even the staunchest fundamentalist organizations are accused of harboring compromisers, including the "General Association of Regular Baptist Churches" and "The Independent Fundamental Churches of America" (pages 220-225).

Thank God, I am free! For years I was like the Apostle Peter (study Galatians 2:11-14), afraid to fellowship with disapproved brothers in Christ, lest I be called a compromiser. Hallelujah, that's over! Liberty is mine!

What is the root cause of all the present confusion within fundamentalism? Is all this castigation and vilification of men and movements biblically based? In search of the answer, I delved into a major study of every separatory text, studying the writings of sixty-five prominent theologians. Their conclusions are tremendously interesting in our era of confusion. Don't swallow every word — hook, line and sinker — heard at congresses and conferences on fundamentalism. In some instances the interpretations are grossly twisted. Let's analyze the separatist texts as they appear in their New Testament settings.

Fundamentalism's Position On Apostates

1. **AVOID THEM.** "Now I beseech you, brethren, mark them which cause division and offenses contrary to the doctrine which you have learned; and AVOID THEM" (Romans 16:17).

The consensus by multiplied theologians is that the culprits to be avoided in this portion of God's Word are "Antinomian Libertines," purveyors and perpetrators of error about licentious and lewd living. This crowd lived for the complete gratification of every fleshly lust in existence and condoned such lifestyles under the guise of Christian liberty. They said, "If the fulfillment of our sexual and bodily appetites portrays God as a merciful being, then it is for His glory." "For where sin abounds, grace does much more abound." This is also the same group of lust-ridden leeches described as "enemies of the cross of Christ" in Philippians 3:18-19. The doctrine over which they were causing divisions and offences was "liberty" versus "holiness." Because of their abominable practices and their proclamation and promotion of this lifestyle, they were to be avoided. Dr. H.A. Ironside says: "The evil doers here referred to are not Christian teachers. They are ungodly men. In Philippians 3:18, we have the identical wretched division markers." Drs. Richard DeHaan, W. R. Newell, Charles Ellicott, Albert Barnes and Adam Clarke subscribe to the above interpretation.

    2. COME OUT FROM AMONG THEM.
Second Corinthians 6:14-18: "Be ye not unequally yoked together with unbelievers: for what fellowship hath righteousness with unrighteousness? and what communion hath light with darkness? and what concord hath Christ with Belial? or what part hath he that believeth with an infidel? And what agreement hath the temple of God with idols? for ye are the temple of the living God; as God hath said, I will dwell in them, and walk in them; and I will be their God, and they

shall be my people. Wherefore come out from among them, and be ye separate, saith the Lord, and touch not the unclean thing; and I will receive you, And will be a Father unto you, and ye shall be my sons and daughters, saith the Lord Almighty.''

This text is self-explanatory. Believers are not to be yoked together with unbelievers, especially in religious endeavors. Five reasons are listed as to why such a union becomes impossible. Separation, then, is not only logical but compulsory. Should there be a question as to who the unbelievers are, they are not only atheists denying the existence of God but also religious apostates who deny the doctrine of Christ. Genuine believers wholeheartedly accept I John 5:1 which states: ''Whosoever believeth that Jesus is the Christ is born of God.'' When this truth is denied within a group, one is to come out from among them.

3. JUDGE THEM. Galatians 1:8: ''But though we, or an angel from heaven preach any other gospel unto you than that which we have preached unto you, let him be accursed.''

The judged in this portion of Scripture are legalistic teachers. In Paul's day they attempted to bring God's children under bondage as they commanded them to ''observe days, months, times and years'' (Galatians 4:10). Since they were mutilating the message of ''grace'' proclaimed by Paul, the Apostle of Grace, they were to be shunned and accursed.

Dr. W. A. Criswell states: ''The churches founded by the Apostle are in danger of apostascizing, turning aside and back to the beggarly elements of the law''

(Galatians 4:9,10). This is the viewpoint held by Drs. Ramsey, Luther, Ironside, Black and Ellicott.

4. REPROVE THEM. Ephesians 5:11: "And have no fellowship with the unfruitful works of darkness, but rather REPROVE THEM."

The "unfruitful works of darkness" with which believers are not to "fellowship" are undeniably "the children of disobedience" of verse 6. The contextual setting makes it abundantly clear that these evil doers are not brothers in Christ, as verses 3-8, 11, 12 plainly, loudly and clearly prove. Let's investigate. "But fornication, and all uncleanness, or covetousness, let it not be once named among you, as becometh saints; Neither filthiness, nor foolish talking, nor jesting [telling dirty jokes] which are not convenient: but rather giving of thanks. For this ye know, that no whoremonger, nor unclean person, nor covetous man, who is an idolater, hath any inheritance in the kingdom of Christ and of God. Let no man deceive you with vain words: for because of these things cometh the wrath of God upon the children of disobedience. Be not ye therefore partakers with them. For ye were sometimes darkness, but now are ye light in the Lord: walk as children of light: And have no fellowship with the unfruitful works of darkness [the sins and sinners described in the foregoing], but rather 'REPROVE THEM.' For it is a shame even to speak of those things which are done of them in secret."

It is obvious that this crowd had an insatiable appetite for lustful pursuits. Concerning them, Paul tells us in chapter 4, verse 19: "They being past feeling [as far as their consciences are concerned] have given themselves over unto lasciviousness to work all uncleanness with greediness.'' Isn't it shocking that the individuals to be "REPROVED" are not brethren who fellowship with brethren who fellowship with brethren who fellowshipped with a compromiser, but rather those who practice and promote promiscuity in thought, word or deed? How wrong in God's sight to jestfully make sport of acts such as adultery or homosexuality, sinful pursuits outside the bonds of holy matrimony. Brethren, we are to break fellowship with all practitioners of lust as well as covetous personalities, whose lives exemplify a "greedy graspingness" for material things and money.

Are such resolutions passed and practiced at our fundamentalist convocations? Are leaders censured for such wickedness? If not, why not? Recently I saw a "separatist" praised in print for staunchily defending the faith. This man and others in the movement are known to have a repertoire of "smutty jokes" that would make a pirate blush. Why then are such men praised while brothers who fellowship with Jerry Falwell or Jack Van Impe condemned? It is because men obey the commands that suit them and disregard the ones that convict them.

Two dear friends recently told me how their resignation from the board of Bob Jones University was requested because they shared a preaching engagement with Dr. Jerry Falwell. This type of discrimination makes separatism a laughing matter.

What are we to do with religious leaders who love wine, women and song; who live for the flesh; who tell obscene jokes; and who greedily grasp for monetary gain? God says: "Have no fellowship with the unfruitful works of darkness." Oh, but the crowd to be shunned in Ephesians 5:11 are sinners. Yes, but "as a man thinketh in his heart so is he" (Proverbs 23:7), and "out of the abundance of the heart the mouth speaketh" (Matthew 12:34). Could this be why Matthew 7:22 has religious leaders saying at Judgment Day: "Lord, Lord, have we not prophesied in thy name? and in thy name have cast out devils? and in thy name done many wonderful works? And then will I profess unto them, I never knew you: depart from me, ye that work iniquity."

The greatest tragedy of the present situation within fundamentalism is that those who often shout the loudest about "separation" and brand good and godly men as pseudo-fundamentalists and new evangelicals are often guilty of the sins mentioned in Ephesians 5:3-12 and I Corinthians 5:11. In fact, this truth was shockingly impressed upon me as I re-read three hundred articles stored in my filing cabinet under the heading "Fundamentalism." Two "stalwarts" of the faith who mislabeled and blistered good men and movements more vociferously than others are now strangely silent. Never again will their voices or pens proclaim or publish the names of innocent victims. They left their wives and ran off with younger women. A word of warning before you mislabel good men and tell your followers to "have no fellowship with them:" be certain you are worthy to cast the first stone.

5. MARK THEM. Philippians 3:17,18:
"Brethren, be followers together of me,

and mark them which walk so as ye have
us for an example. For many walk, of
whom I have told you often, and now tell
you even weeping, that they are the enemies of the cross of Christ.''

Our theologians again agree totally that this is the
same crowd mentioned in Romans 16:17 — Antinomian libertines who lived for fleshly pleasure.

Dr. Kenneth Wuest says: ''The enemies in this text
are professing Christian Greeks of Epicurean ten-
dencies. They taught that the satisfaction of the
physical appetites was the highest aim of man.'' Dr.
J. B. Lightfoot states: ''The persons here denounced
are the Antinomian reactionists. The view is borne
out in the parallel expression of Romans 16:17-19.
They degraded the true doctrine of liberty so as to
minister to their profligate and worldly living. These
Antinomians refused to conform to the cross by
living a life of self indulgence.''

Dr. H. A. Ironside adds: ''This crowd lived for self
indulgence.'' Interesting, isn't it, that we now have
three texts — Romans 16:17, Ephesians 5:11 and
Philippians 3:17-19 — that command us to ''avoid,''
''reprove,'' and ''mark'' those who live for the flesh.
Perhaps we need to rethink our position. If we separatists practiced the three texts mentioned above in
their entirety, perhaps our religious superiority and
cockiness against others might come to a screeching
halt. At least it would make us think twice before
censuring others.

    6. IDENTIFY THEM. First Timothy 1:20,
      II Timothy 1:15; 4:14.

These texts expose Alexander and Hymenaeus as

blasphemers, and Phygellus and Hermogenes as defectors. Thus they are identified as apostates, for I John 2:19 states: "They went out [or turned away] that it might be made manifest that they were not all of us." Wycliff says: "Alexander opposed the apostolic teaching. Hymenaeus was a heretic, teaching that the resurrection was past already."

Drs. M. R. DeHaan, Ironside, Barnes, and numerous others identify these men as apostates. Let's begin identifying and exposing the right crowd.

7. **WITHDRAW FROM THEM.** First Timothy 6:3-5: "If any man teach otherwise, and consent not to wholesome words, even the words of our Lord Jesus Christ, and to the doctrine which is according to godliness; He is proud, knowing nothing, but doting about questions and strifes of words, whereof cometh envy, strife, railings, evil surmisings, perverse disputings of men of corrupt minds, and destitute of the truth, supposing that gain is godliness: from such withdraw thyself."

The late Dr. Paul R. Jackson, former head of the General Association of Regular Baptist Churches, in his booklet, **The Position, Attitudes and Objective of Biblical Separation**, states: "False doctrine is another basis of separation." I totally agree. Believers are to withdraw from those who propagate doctrinal error.

What specific error existed during Timothy's era that made such a command necessary? Let's investigate. At this point in history, servants were purchased and possessed, even by believers. At times, servants professing to know Christ belittled their Christian masters. Their remarks were so ungracious that sinners blasphemed God as they watched such relationships. They said, "If employees and employers who claim to be saved experience such friction among themselves, don't tell us that Christ meets every need." What caused this problem? The example of Jesus, as found in His teachings, was being ignored. He said: "I am among you as He that serveth" (Luke 22:27) and "Whosoever will be chief among you, let him be your servant: Even as the Son of man came not to be ministered unto, but to minister, and to give his life a ransom for many" (Matthew 20:27,28).

Since these were undoubtedly the wholesome words of Christ mentioned by Paul in I Timothy 6:3-5, those who rejected His teachings were labeled "arrogant ignoramuses." They spent all their time bickering over the interpretation of the words instead of abiding by them. The results of such nonsensical prattling led to jealousy, strife, railings, evil surmising (suspicious, hidden thoughts about others) and perverse disputings (or protracted wranglings and battles) among them. Paul tells us why they reacted as they did. They were "men of corrupt minds, and destitute of the truth" (verse 5). Or more simply: "They were corrupted in mind and had put away the truth they once possessed." Thus they became defectors or apostates according to I John 2:19, and withdrawal from them was necessary.

Drs. Clarke, Hinson, Ellicott, and Vincent concur.

8. TURN AWAY FROM THEM. Second

Timothy 3:5: "Having a form of godliness but denying the power thereof: from such turn away."

These are professors of religion but not possessors of Christ. Jesus described them in Mark 7:6 saying: "Well hath Esaias prophesied of you hypocrites, as it is written, This people honoureth me with their lips, but their heart is far from me." Dr. Albert Barnes says: "This group opposed the real power of religion, not allowing it to exert any influence in their lives. They lived as if they had no religion." Dr. Adam Clarke adds: "These mentioned in the text have all their religion in their creed, confession of faith and catechism but are destitute of the life of God in their souls."

Since their lives made a mockery of the faith they professed, genuine believers were to "turn away" from such counterfeits.

9. REBUKE THEM. Titus 1:10-13: "For there are many unruly and vain talkers and deceivers, specially they of the circumcision: Whose mouths must be stopped, who subvert whole houses, teaching things which they ought not, for filthy lucre's sake. One of themselves, even a prophet of their own, said, The Cretians are always liars, evil beasts, slow bellies. This witness is true. Wherefore rebuke them sharply, that they may be sound in the faith."

The unruly talkers and deceivers described in the text under consideration were Judaizers (the circumcision). As such, they possessed a prejudiced preference for the Law, boasting of their privileges as sons of Moses. Their Jewish fables and commandments of men were proclaimed to turn believers from the truth (vs. 14) as well as to build a base of support for their greedy lifestyles. Paul, in depicting these money-loving propagators of error, quotes Epimenides of Gnossus, a poet who lived in 600 B.C., saying: "The Cretians are always liars, evil beasts and slow bellies." Since Paul states that this witness concerning these loafers was true, what did he mean? The very word "kretizein" or "to Cretize" meant "to deceive" or "to utter a lie." They were also "evil beasts," a description of their brutal natures. Furthermore, they were called "slow bellies," a derogatory term used to describe their laziness created by excessive fleshly practices which drained their energies.

The Holy Spirit, through Paul, demands that such greedy sluggards be rebuked in order that they might become "sound in the faith" (vs. 13), or literally that they might begin proclaiming and practicing pure doctrine which leads to a God-honoring lifestyle (II Corinthians 5:17).

Adam Clarke states: "This crowd was to be rebuked cuttingly and severely because of their crimes which consisted of despising the truth and teaching others to do the same."

While some fundamentalists classify this crowd as brothers, I cannot because verse sixteen, describing them, declares: "They profess that they know God; but in works they deny him, being abominable, and disobedient, and unto every good work reprobate." Since Revelation 21:8 proves that the abominable are eternally incarcerated in the lake of fire, and since the "false teachers" are described as abominable, I classify them as apostates in my listing.

   10. DON'T RECEIVE THEM. Second John 7-11: "For many deceivers are entered into the world, who confess not that Jesus Christ is come in the flesh. This is a deceiver and an antichrist. Look to yourselves, that we [ye] lose not those things which we [you] have wrought, but that we [you] receive a full reward. Whosoever transgresseth, and abideth not in the doctrine of Christ, hath not God. He that abideth in the doctrine of Christ, he hath both the Father and the Son. If there come any unto you, and bring not this doctrine, receive him not into your house, neither bid him God speed; for he that biddeth him God speed is partaker of his evil deeds."

John deals sternly with apostates and apostasy in this text. However, it is important to remember that "all scripture is given by inspiration of God" (II Timothy 3:16). Thus, the Holy Spirit is literally speaking through the beloved apostle. With this in mind, I John 2:22 states: "Who is a liar but he that denieth that Jesus is the Christ? He is an antichrist, that denieth the Father and the Son." Shedding further light on the subject, II John 7 adds: ["Apostates] confess not that Jesus Christ is come in the flesh [that God became man or the God-man.]" Hence they are again called "deceivers and antichrists."

150

Now what should be the believer's relationship to "false teachers," "apostates," "liars," "deceivers" and "antichrists?" Should he enlist their support? Should he allow them to conduct a church service or home Bible study group? Absolutely not. Their transgression and rejection of the "doctrine of Christ" proves that they have not God (vs. 9). Therefore, "receive them not into your house, neither bid them God speed [saying "God bless you" to them]" (vs. 10). Why not? "For he that biddeth him God speed is partaker of his evil deeds" (vs. 11). Since the catastrophic judgment for aiding and abetting apostate teachers is the loss of rewards at the Judgment Seat of Christ (II John 8 and II Corinthians 5:10,11), DON'T RECEIVE THEM. It's not worth it.

The texts presented to this point have been conscientiously interpreted in their contextual settings. Sixty-five of the greatest theological minds have been extremely beneficial in confirming my convictions regarding these texts.

There should not be one iota of doubt as to "separatism's" scriptural base concerning apostasy. However, may I add a note of caution once again. While it is true that we must "come out from," "judge," "identify," "withdraw from," "turn away from," "receive not" and "rebuke" apostates, we must also "avoid," "reprove" and "mark" immoral men whose "eyes are full of adultery" (I Peter 2:14), whose mouths are full of "filthiness, foolish talking [and] jesting" (Ephesians 5:4) and whose hands covetously reach out greedily for gain. They also are defectors from righteousness, having turned away from the doctrine of godliness. Now since no "whoremonger, nor unclean person, nor covetous man, who is an idolater, hath any inheritance in the kingdom of Christ and of God. Be not ye therefore partakers with them" (Ephesians 5:5,7).

Fundamentalism's Separatist Position On Brothers

In concluding this study on separatism, we will analyze three final texts that deal with brothers in Christ. The World Congress of Fundamentalists, meeting on the Bob Jones University Campus, drew up the following listing under the heading: "Separation from disobedient saints and appeasers."

a. "Note that man" (II Thessalonians 3:14)
b. "Withdraw yourself" (II Thessalonians 3:6)
c. "Have no company with" (II Thessalonians 3:14)
d. "Rebuke them sharply" (Titus 1:13)
e. "Count him not an enemy" (II Thessalonians 3:15)
f. "Admonish him as a brother" (II Thessalonians 3:15)
g. "Keep not company" (I Corinthians 5:11)
h. "With such an one no not to eat." (I Corinthians 5:11)

Then they added, "And while adhering to this separatist position, we will 'let brotherly love continue'" (Hebrews 13:1)

Are you impressed by this eight-point numerical listing? Don't be. It amounts to little when analyzed and interpreted. Notice that points A, B, C, E, and F are all from the same portion of Scripture. Points G and H are based upon one verse. Last but not least, point D does not belong in this grouping. Look again under apostasy, point 9 of this message, to understand why.

Basically then, two texts have been used to create the greatest mistrust of brothers in the history of Christendom. This tragedy exists because a platform and position has been built upon an erroneous interpretation of God's Word.

For years I, as a young man, accepted the above guidelines without question. Finally, I saw the inconsistency and inaccuracy of what I had swallowed. All it produces is bigotry, prejudice and a condemnation of numerous innocent brothers. Presently, many fundamentalists are beginning to realize that something drastic is wrong in our movement. The grieved consciences of these brothers will not allow them to remain silent. Even the most stalwart fundamentalist in my area, Dr. James O. Phillips, president of Faithway Baptist College, recently said: "I am a Fundamentalist, but more and more with the passing of time I am forced to add some 'footnotes.' Don't write me off yet. Before you do, check out my doctrine, my position, my associations, fellowship and support. All these things will stand the test. However, regardless of the cost and misunderstanding, I am going to say something that is on my heart and has been for some time. I have seen enough ARROGANCE, PRIDE AND JUDGING in fundamentalism to satisfy me the rest of my life. 'Every tree is known of its fruit.' We need to look into our own fruitbaskets!"

Thank you, Dr. Phillips. You perfectly expressed the feelings of the silent majority within our movement. They, too, are grieved over the "war games" the neo-fundamentalist leadership seemingly enjoys playing. They care not how many of their own troops are wounded or injured. Nor do they mind continuing the battle based upon misunderstood or misinterpreted texts. As long as recruits continue to obediently follow their commands, the fighting must continue.

At this point, I feel compelled to describe the method of operation used to either humiliate or excommunicate fellow brothers in Christ. It is the "trickle down" theory whereby men and movements become guilty by association. If a fundamentalist shares a speaking engagement or time of fellowship with the friend of a friend of a friend of a pseudo-fundamentalist, who fellowshipped with a neo-evangelical, he becomes guilty of compromise. Then all who fellowship with the newly discovered traitor are also placed on an observation list. Thus, the witch-hunt never ceases. Is the situation really that absurd? You be the judge.

In a 35-page release, Dr. Don Jasmin, a Bob Jones University alumnus, attempts to discredit scores of men and movements based upon his opinions and misinterpretations of Scripture. Note his "guilty by association" trickle down theory in all of its splendor. Dr. Jasmin states: "Dr. Van Impe's ties with the new evangelical Trans-World Radio ministry were boldly declared by Dr. Paul Freed, president of Trans-World Radio, when Dr. Van Impe appeared on a nationwide TV special promoting the Trans-World Radio work."

Question: "Why are Dr. Paul Freed and the Trans-World Radio network condemned as new-evangelicals?

Dr. Jasmin: "The Daily Word, the Trans-World Radio devotional guide, contains full page pictures of three well-known religious leaders: Dr. Theodore Epp, Dr. J. Vernon McGee and Dr. Jack Van Impe. Dr. Van Impe permitted his picture to be displayed twice on the same page with two well-known religious new-evangelical leaders."

Question: "Why are Drs. McGee and Epp new-evangelicals?"

[I will only take space to trace Dr. Epp's supposed downfall. JVI]

Dr. Jasmin: "Dr. Theodore Epp allowed Dr. Dave Breese to be a guest speaker on his program. Also, in its publication, "The Good News Broadcaster," Back to the Bible featured a picture of the ideal family. In it the father had mod hair as well as the quartet. Hence, Back to the Bible is certainly turning away from the Bible.

Question: "Why is Dr. David Breese suspect?"

Dr. Jasmin: "Dr. Dave Breese was chairman of the 1977 convention of the National Association of Evangelicals."

Thus Dr. Breese is guilty because of his association with the NAE, and Dr. Epp is guilty because of his friendship with Dr. Breese, and Dr. Freed is guilty because of allowing Dr. Epp to use TWR facilities, and Jack Van Impe is guilty for using the station that airs the programs of Drs. McGee and Epp, as well as permitting his picture to appear in the same brochure with them!

Are you convinced after reading this analysis of "men and movements" by one who practices and promotes the "rules" of the "World Congress of Fundamentalists" that Jack Van Impe is a fellow traveler with apostates? Have I become such because I proclaim Christ to the world via the facilities of Trans-World Radio, a God-honoring ministry led by one of the greatest Christians I have ever known — Dr. Paul Freed? Is he tainted because he allows Dr. Theodore Epp to use TWR facilities to also proclaim "Christ to the World"? Is the honorable Dr. Epp religiously soiled because he allowed Dr. Dave Breese to be guest speaker on his Christ-exalting program? Is Dr. Breese a fellow traveler with apostates because he chaired the 1977 conference of the National Association of Evangelicals? Enough is enough! The witch-hunt must cease.

The situation is heartbreaking, especially when one realizes that such a condemnatory stand against brothers in Christ is based upon two misinterpreted biblical texts.

1. I Corinthians 5:11: **"Keep not company."** But now I have written unto you not to keep company, if any man that is called a brother be a fornicator, or covetous, or an idolater, or a railer, or a drunkard, or an extortioner such an one no not to eat."

There is no doubt as to the fact that God wants "brothers in Christ" to separate from other "brothers in Christ" when this form of withdrawal is beneficial to the erring believer's restoration. However, our congresses and conferences on fundamentalism have failed to see who the fallen are. They are not brothers who sat in the wrong pew at the wrong time but rather:

a. **"Fornicators"** — those who practice pre-marital sex, adultery, homosexuality or any other fleshly deviation.

b. **"The Covetous"** — those whose lives are lived for monetary gain. Greed for materialism depicts them. They attempt to get all they can, any way they can.

c. **"Idolaters"** — those whose souls devotion is given over to any object that usurps the place of God in their lives.

d. **"Railers"** — those who revile or scold in harsh, insolent, or abusive language. Dr. H. A. Ironside states: "A railer is a person who has a tongue loose at both ends and a pivot in the middle, a vicious talker, an evil speaker, one who can destroy the reputation of another just as a murderer drives a dagger into the heart and destroys a life. A character assassin is as wicked in the sight of God as a murderer."

e. **"Drunkards"** (self- explanatory)

f. **"Extortioners"** — those who illegally take things from others. They force their victims to give them objects that are not due them or that are not rightfully theirs.

After studying this text, how in the name of rationality can the command to "keep not company" apply to any brother in Christ who shakes hands with the third cousin of a compromiser?

Dr. M. R. DeHaan, many years ago (perhaps prophetically), had it right when he said: "This Corinthian crowd was so busy fighting, bickering, envying one another, splitting theological hairs, and arguing over personalities, ordinances and doctrines that they paid no attention to the terrible immoral situation in their midst."

Brothers, let's obey God's Word without question, but let's at least base our conviction on what the verse teaches. Then we'll get back to our historic fundamentalist roots.

> 2. II Thessalonians 3:6-15. The Congress of Fundamentalists lists five points under this one text. They are:
>   a. "Note that man" (verse 14).
>   b. "Withdraw yourself" (verse 6).
>   c. "Have no company with" (verse 14).
>   d. "Count him not as an enemy" (verse 15).
>   e. "Admonish him as a brother" (verse 15).

The interpretation by some errant fundamentalists of the inerrant Word of God concerning this text is that the "disorderly" are "brothers," who fellowshipped with brothers, who fellowshipped with disobedient brothers who had been disfellowshipped because of compromise. Not one of my sixty-five theological sources would accept this distorted interpretation. Let's look at the text in context.

"Now we command you, brethren, in the name of our Lord Jesus Christ, that ye withdraw yourselves from every brother that walketh disorderly, and not after the tradition which he received of us. For yourselves know how ye ought to follow us: for we behaved not ourselves disorderly among you: Neither did we eat any man's bread for nought; but wrought with labour and travail night and day, that we might not be chargeable to any of you: Not because we have not power, but to make ourselves an ensample unto you to follow us. For even when we were with you, this we commanded you, that if any would not work, neither should he eat. For we hear that there are some which walk among you disorderly, working not at all, but are busybodies. Now them that are such we command and exhort by our Lord Jesus Christ, that with quietness they work, and eat their own bread. But ye, brethren, be not weary in well doing. And if any man obey not our word by this epistle, note that man, and have no company with him, that he may be ashamed. Yet count him not as an enemy, but admonish him as a brother.''

Who are the disorderly then? The text in context speaks for itself. Nevertheless, let's use quotes from past and present theological giants to enforce the truth.

Dr. Adam Clarke: ''The disorderly were those who were not working. They were either lounging at home or becoming religious gossips. They were busybodies doing everything they should not be doing, impertinent meddlers in other people's business; prying into other people's affairs, magnifying or minifying, mistaking or underrating everything. They were newsmongers and telltales — an abominable race and a curse to every neighborhood they settled.''

Dr. Charles Ellicott: "They worked not at all, but were busybodies. This is what constituted their disorderliness. They also held gossiping discussions."

Dr. Marvin Vincent: "They were idlers. Have no company with them."

Dr. John Walvoord: "Some had adopted the philosophy that the world owed them a living. Well, 'if any would not work, neither should he eat' (II Thessalonians 3:10). The very fact that they were idle led them into all sorts of difficulty. Idleness is fertile ground in which the devil can sow seeds. So Paul's exhortation was 'Get busy. Earn an honest living. Pay your own way. Take care of yourself. You will not have time then to be interfering with other people's business and making a nuisance of yourself.'"

Dr. A. Gabelein: "The disorder defined by the remainder of the context is loafing. This was contrary to the teaching (tradition) that Paul had given them earlier. The reluctant idler was not to be treated as an enemy, cut off from all contacts, but was allowed to continue in a brotherly status. It was social ostracism first, then I Corinthians 5:9-11."

Dr. Albert Barnes: "Paul warned in I Thessalonians 4:11 that believers were to 'study to be quiet, and to do [their] own business, and to work with [their] own hands.' This was the tradition they had learned from Paul, and that they were commanded to keep. If they did not obey this command, they were to be noted and one's company was to be denied them" [II Thessalonians 3:6,14 JVI].

Wycliffe Commentary: "They were disorderly or unruly as described in I Thessalonians 5:14. They did not follow tradition — Paul's personal example concerning work (II Thessalonians 2:15 and I Thessalonians 4:11,12). It was an attack on laziness.''

Dr. H. A. Ironside: ''These men to whom Paul refers were simply ignoring the divine plan for work. When men are not employed properly they busy themselves in matters in which they should not interfere. So they became a nuisance and were used of Satan. The tongue does not offend so seriously when the hands are kept busy.''

If you have not discovered who the ''disorderly'' are at this juncture, you never will. Needless to say, they are not pseudo-fundamentalists. Alleged pseudos don't have time for idleness. Who are they then? Read the text again. Then practice scriptural separation.

As I bring this message to its summation, I must insert a third point that deals with brothers. Usually this portion of Scripture is listed under the heading of ''apostasy'' within fundamentalist ranks. However, I believe it comes under the heading of ''brothers in Christ.''

3. Titus 3:10: **"REJECT THEM."**

"A man that is a heretick after the first and second admonition reject."

A HERETIC CLASSIFIED AS A BROTHER? Yes. Why? Read on.

Dr. Albert Barnes presents us with a startling twist as to the interpretation of this text. He says: ''The word ''Heretic'' is now commonly applied to one who holds to some fundamental error or doctrine (the dictionary definition rather than the original Greek). Originally, then, it meant one who is a prompter of a sect or party; the man who makes division instead of aiming to promote unity. Such a man may form sects and parties on some points of doctrine on which he differs from others or on some custom, religious rite or peculiar practice. He may make some **UNIM-PORTANT MATTER** a ground of distinction from his brethren and may **REFUSE FELLOWSHIP** with them and start a new organization."

If the above interpretation is accurate, and Drs. Jamieson, Faucett, Brown, Black, Rowley, Ellicott, Guthrie, Motyer, Stibbs, Wiseman, Clark, Vine, Ironside, and Henry agree that it is, then **TRUE SEPARATISTS** should **SEPARATE** from **FAC-TIOUS SEPARATISTS** who separate from all those who will not bow to their **MAN-MADE SEP-ARATIST ISSUES!**

How true. Presently we fight and fuss over men, movements and ministries. One can build a following by taking a stand against hair styles, clothing fashions, music preferences, slide presentations, Christian ventriloquists, puppets, gospel magicians, chalk talks, yo-yo demonstrations, karate exhibitions, Bible plays, story tellers, religious talk shows, discussion groups, quiz programs and Sunday school contests — all classified as "GIMMICKS."

Those who lead such anti-demonstrations might just be the "heretics" God tells us to reject. God's aim is UNITY (Ephesians 4:1-3). Let's work at it as we reject those who reject the above gifted men and the diversified ministries God has given them to use for His glory.

When divisive leaders erect organizations on "heretical premises" (New Testament definition) centered around **UNIMPORTANT MATTERS,**

THE RESULTS ARE PREDICTABLE. They soon turn against each other and devour one another. Could this be the reason that **THREE FUNDA-MENTALIST GROUPS** either passed resolutions or censured one another this year? Let's get back to the Scriptures and rebuild a biblical movement.

To help build this unity, may I give you another set of "thems" that God gave to me after spending 100 hours in prayer, meditation and research for this chapter.

One brother, writing an article entitled, "Separation Applied," states: "Any believer who is unfaithful to "the tradition" (all the Scripture given to the Church) is disobedient." This he applies to the separatist texts considered in this message.

FELLOW FUNDAMENTALISTS, WHAT ABOUT OUR OBEDIENCE TO THIS FINAL LISTING OF "THEMS?" THEY TOO ARE IN GOD'S INSPIRED, INERRANT WORD.

1. BE RECONCILED TO THEM (Matthew 5:24).
2. BE KINDLY AFFECTIONED TOWARD THEM (Romans 12:10).
3. PREFER THEM (Romans 12:10).
4. REJOICE WITH THEM (Romans 12:15).
5. WEEP WITH THEM (Romans 12:15).
6. BE OF THE SAME MIND TOWARD THEM (Romans 12:16).
7. LIVE PEACEABLY WITH THEM (Romans 12:18).
8. DON'T JUDGE THEM (Romans 14:10).
9. DESTROY THEM NOT (Romans 14:15).

10. PLEASE THEM (Romans 15:2).
11. BE LIKEMINDED TOWARD THEM (Romans 15:5).
12. RECEIVE THEM (Romans 15:7).
13. ADMONISH THEM (Romans 15:14).
14. SALUTE THEM WITH AN HOLY KISS (Romans 16:16).
15. CARE FOR THEM (I Corinthians 12:25).
16. RESTORE THEM (Galatians 6:1).
17. BEAR THEM AND THEIR BURDENS (Galatians 6:2).
18. DO GOOD TO THEM (Galatians 6:10).
19. FORBEAR THEM (Colossians 3:13).
20. SPEAK NOT EVIL OF THEM (James 4:11,12).
21. PRAY FOR THEM (James 5:16).
22. HAVE COMPASSION FOR THEM (I Peter 3:8).
23. SHOW BROTHERLY KINDNESS TO THEM (II Peter 1:7).
24. LOVE THEM (I John 3:14; 4:7,8).
25. DIE FOR THEM (I John 3:16).

I have but skimmed God's commandments on kindness. There are approximately three hundred additional verses on love described in chapter 13. This is the way, "walk ye in it" (Isaiah 30:12). For "If we walk in the light, as he is in the light, we have fellowship one with another" (I John 1:7).

As we move into chapters 11 and 12, you will understand why I am deeply grieved over judgmental "Neo-fundamentalism" and its leadership.

> "Let us not therefore judge one another any more: but judge this rather, that no man put a stumbling-block or an occasion to fall in his brother's way" (Romans 14:13).

Chapter 11

The Judgment Seat of the Neo-Fundamentalists or Heart Disease in Christ's Body

Every child of God must one day stand before Christ to have his lifetime of service investigated. Second Corinthians 5:10 states: "...we must all appear before the judgment seat of Christ; that every one may receive the things done in his body, according to that he hath done, whether it be good or bad."

This judgment of believers is exclusively the responsibility of the Lord Jesus Christ. No mere mortal is capable of assuming the place of an omniscient, all-knowing God when it comes to judging men and movements. Finite human beings, regardless of their fundamentalist pedigree or position, are incapable of looking into another man's heart.

Only God, who said in Jeremiah 17:10: "I the Lord search the heart, I try the reins, even to give every man according to his ways, and according to the fruit of his doings" can judge righteously. This is why the Holy Spirit emphatically declares in Romans 14:4,10-13: "Who art thou that judgest another man's servant? to his own master he standeth or falleth. Yea, he shall be holden up: for God is able to make him stand...But why dost thou judge thy brother? or why dost thou set at nought thy brother? for we shall all stand before the judgment seat of Christ. For it is written, As I live, saith the Lord, every knee shall bow to me, and every tongue shall confess to God. So then every one of us shall give account of himself to God. Let us not therefore judge one another any more: but judge this rather, that no man put a stumblingblock or an occasion to fall in his brother's way."

Though the Spirit of God has spoken plainly, God's Word is being rejected as a movement (neo-fundamentalism) within a movement has arisen. This group delights in proclaiming and publishing the latest faults of brethren. They have already injured numerous brothers, and will not rest until they have condemned everyone who disagrees with their biased position.

In the **Baptist Bible Tribune**, November 26, 1982, Dr. Wendell Zimmerman states: "Some preachers feel they are ordained of God to sit in judgment on the soundness of doctrine and practice of other preachers. When they find a prime suspect of heterodoxy, some will twist, distort, misquote, misjudge, misconstrue, mislead and falsify to prove their point. Those who resort to such tactics are practicing situation ethics. Fundamental Baptists need to preach against the wickedness of situation ethics and refuse to be duped by the parade of intelligentsia who promote this diabolical teaching.''

I have been attacked often in religious scandal sheets. Until now, I have refrained from mentioning who my accusers and attackers were. Presently, I have the freedom to do so because of the World Congress of Fundamentalists' resolution, making Drs. Jerry Falwell, W. A. Criswell, George Sweeting and myself "pseudo-fundamentalists" (fakes, frauds and counterfeits).

Before we go any further, let's define the terms "World Congress of Fundamentalists," "neo-fundamentalist" and "pseudo-fundamentalist."

The World Congress of Fundamentalists consists of a small group within fundamentalism who, led by Dr. Bob Jones Jr., attempt to speak for the entire movement. More realistically, they are the neo-fundamentalists Dr. Carl McIntyre labeled in 1976. Because they have constantly created additional man-made rules and regulations contrary to the principles laid down by our founding fathers within historic fundamentalism, they are neo or new-fundamentalists. Anyone disagreeing with or opposing their misinterpretations of God's Holy Word are immediately classified as pseudo or fake fundamentalists.

In publishing the voluminous material that follows, I am not violating Christian ethics in any way. I am simply excerpting articles that have oftentimes been **sold** by members of the neo-fundamentalist movement. Since they proudly display their names on their DEFENDING THE FAITH

167

AND DEFAMING THE BRETHREN materials, I am only reporting what they have already publicized nationally. While a few "militant fundamentalists" love such a diet of sour grapes, loving fundamentalists and evangelicals will understand why someone had to speak out against such judgmental releases that have created the greatest divisiveness ever within the body of Christ.

This book, then, was born of necessity. Young men studying for the ministry had to be made aware of the games boys grown tall play with the lifetime ministries of God's choicest servants. Christians had to be shown the nonsensical reasoning that religious leaders proclaim and print about men who have given their blood, sweat, and tears for the cause of Christ. Too many have believed such stories. Perhaps by printing a deluge of materials of condemnatory releases against scores of good men and movements by neo-fundamentalists, the people of God in multipled groups will see that such bigoted remarks are not worthy to be classified under the heading of "defending the faith," but rather as "sowing discord among brothers," a sin God adamantly hates (Proverbs 6:16-19). Until the Lord is allowed to correct this terrible sin through a Holy Spirit-empowered revival of genuine love, our movement will decline and eventually die. A healthy body cannot exist without love.

I remind you again that I am not attacking any of these men. I am simply reprinting their attacks against hundreds of others. Let's begin with an article entitled, "The Most Dangerous Man In America," by Dr. Bob Jones, Jr. It was reported by Dr. J. Harold

Smith and reprinted by E. J. Daniels, a former board member of the Bob Jones University and a Southern Baptist leader:

"The Devil has been doing everything he can over the last thirty years (that is, for a whole generation) to try to break down the lines of ecclesiastical separation as set forth in the Scripture, and he has been using first one means and then another. We are enjoined not to be ignorant of his devices, and it is well to face Falwell's so-called 'Moral Majority' drive as one of Satan's devices to build the world Church of Antichrist. First, the Devil attacked us with cooperative evangelism as exemplified by Dr. Graham. That Dr. Graham has become an apostate is beyond question in view of his praise of the Pope, the World Council of Churches, and almost everything else that is rotten in our world ecclesiastically. Then the Devil came along with the so-called Charismatic Movement, trying to bring together weak, untaught, and disobedient Christians on the basis of an emotional deception. Now he comes along with a moral crusade that incorporates an appeal to patriotism as well. Satan tried 'soulwinning' as a temptation to Biblical disobedience with Graham. Next he tried 'spiritual gifts' and 'love' in the Charismatic heresy. Now, with Falwell, he uses such good things as morality and reform in an attempt to deceive Christians into alliance with apostasy."

Dr. Jones further stated in his letter to the Bob

Jones University Preacher boys: "Falwell is headed down the road of compromise and well along the way. This road, as Billy Graham has proved, leads to complete apostasy. I have observed the downward trends in the spiritual life of America and the falling away of religious organizations now for more than half a century. I observed at close range how Youth For Christ became an efficient tool in the hands of Satan. I have seen the National Association of Evangelicals at close range from its beginning and have followed the course of the rottenness and decay that has wrecked that organization as any strong spiritual force in America. I have watched prominent evangelists make shipwreck concerning the faith and have grieved over the declension and compromise which has destroyed the Biblical testimony of Faith Missions one after the other, but in all my lifetime I have never been as concerned as I am now about Jerry Falwell. I consider him the most dangerous man in America today as far as Biblical Christianity is concerned. He is a man of considerable charm. He is a man who is quite likeable, but he is a man who is either completely lacking in spiritual discernment, or has, like Ahab, sold himself to do evil. He is more personally ambitious than Billy Graham and doubly dangerous because he claims to be a fundamentalist while ignoring in his own life and activity the Scriptural commands to ecclesiastical separation. My own personal opinion is that Falwell thinks he can be President of the United States in 1984, and he is building himself a political party."

Concerning this article, Dr. E. J. Daniels states:

"I can hardly believe that a great man like Dr. Bob Jones, Jr., Chancellor of the great Bob Jones University, could level such charges against a man like Dr. Jerry Falwell, pastor of perhaps the greatest church in the world, the Thomas Road Baptist Church in Lynchburg, Virginia...

" I agree with Dr. Bob Jones, Jr., that Jerry Falwell is the most dangerous man in America when it comes to the ERA, abortion, the so-called rights of the homosexuals, the Bible-denying liberals, the crooked politicians, the sellers of pornography, Communism, and the leaders of crime, and all others who are set on destroying our great Nation. The Devil trembles in the presence and at the preaching of Jerry Falwell.

" I have relatives in my family who have attended Bob Jones University. It is a tragedy that such a statement should come from a great man like Dr. Bob Jones, Jr., about another great man, Dr. Jerry Falwell.

" After really thinking this matter over, I have come to the following conclusion. The Joneses are jealous of Falwell. The Joneses inherited their position in Bob Jones University from their wonderful and great father and grandfather, Dr. Bob Jones, Sr. Dr. Jerry Falwell had to start Liberty Baptist College from ' scratch.' If Christ tarries another 20 years, I predict that Liberty Baptist College will be ten times the size of Bob Jones University.

" I am sure if Dr. Bob Jones, Jr. ...had thought up the idea of the Moral Majority it would have been okay.

" Keep on keeping on, Jerry! We thank God you

have the courage and the avenues to speak to America, and cry aloud for all of us to turn from our wicked ways and to turn back to God.''

In November, 1981, I featured an article entitled, ''A Call For Revival Within Fundamentalism,'' in our **Perhaps Today** magazine. It is presented in its entirety in chapter 7. At that point in time, I refused to mention the names of those who judged others, and named only the victims. I did not want to create any more bias or confusion than already existed. My only desire was to show God's people the bedlam a minority group within fundamentalism was creating.

Today, the situation has changed. The group has now identified themselves by publically labeling Dr. Falwell and me as fakes and ostracizing us. An article concerning their annual international congress appeared in the August 20, 1983, issue of **The Detroit News** and other U.S. newspapers. Therefore, I need no longer remain silent. Instead, I may freely bare my soul to the people of God. Let's consider, then, the scenario which takes place at numerous meetings conducted by members of the Fundamental Baptist Fellowship, a neo-fundamentalist group.

First, a number of ministers come to the platform. Next, names are presented to these ''ecclesiastical judges'' by the audience. In turn, each minister is given the opportunity to critically denouce various men of God. Incidentally, the main leaders of this movement are Bob Jones University alumni.

One such meeting took place in Tempe, Arizona, and featured Dr. Bob Jones, Jr., himself as one of the speakers and participants. The meeting was also attended by Dr. J.C. Joiner, pastor of the New Testament Baptist Church in Tucson. Dr. Joiner was so offended by the proceedings that he wrote a personal letter to Dr. Jones. In it, he stated:

Dear Dr. Jones: Thank you for the two excellent messages you preached in Tempe. God used you to bless and challenge me!

I do have "ought against you," however, and as a brother in Christ, I must bring this to your attention.

I attended the Fundamental Baptist Fellowship meeting in Tempe, Arizona, on November 1, and witnessed the "open" forum held on Wednesday afternoon. Issues and personalities were discussed. In my opinion, the open forum was not "open" at all because no one was allowed to speak from the floor. The forum degenerated into a gossip session!

Important issues and trends were discussed, but I was appalled that men of God can sit on a panel in judgment of others under the pretense of informing the unlearned! You pronounced judgment on Dr. John R. Rice that he was old and senile and that his ministry over the years had been significantly influenced by two frustrated women on his staff who have convinced him that he is perfect. You pronounced judgment on Jack Van Impe, insinuating that he was an egotistical opportunist who would do anything to get a crowd. You pronounced many judgments upon Dr. Jerry Falwell and his motives. Even the mention that Dr. Falwell's recent complimentary article about BJU in his newspaper was ridiculed as his way of putting the "true" fundamentalists off-balance in this controversy. You and

Dave Sproul spoke of Dr. Jack Hyles as a man who is at this time straddling the fence and [said] that he was a compromiser by waiting to decide which side of the controversy to cast his lot.

The hour of the forum was to be given to discussion of issues and problems that face fundamentalists, but sadly most of that hour was ill-spent in ridicule and character assassinations. I was in agreement with the many important issues discussed on the dangers of compromise, but the intense quest to find and identify the "pseudo-fundamentalist" turned into a "Baptist Inquisition" with you and the panel handing down pronouncements and condemnations. I am unalterably opposed to the manner and method of such conduct! Someone has said, "The failure to distinguish between what is fundamental and what is trivial makes 'feudamentalists.' "

To make the Tempe situation even worse, Dr. Jones's comments concerning men and movements were reported by a major Phoenix newspaper the following day. What kind of portrait must such conduct convey to the unsaved world?

Next, let's look in on a statewide conference of the Fundamental Baptist Fellowship which was conducted in Hartford, Connecticut primarily by Bob Jones University graduates. The statements you are about to read were made in the presence of scores of grade school children. Imagine what must have occurred in their young minds as they heard Christian leaders denounced. Drs. Rodney Bell, Wendell Mullens, Mark Dickerson, B. Myron Cedarholm and the Rev. Hopkins composed the "judgment seat" team at this particular meeting. Read carefully their condemnatory statements of multiplied men and movements. They are shocking!

* Q: Where does Bill Gothard stand?

Dr. Cedarholm: "He has his membership in a new evangelical church, the LaGrange [Illinois] Bible Church. All the Bible churches in our area are strong supporters of Billy Graham. Every man on Gothard's Board is a strong new evangelical. They belong to new evangelical churches such as [the one in Downer's Grove]. If one goes to a Gothard seminar, and I have been to one, you seem to be getting a good course in psychology instead of good Bible doctrine."

*Q: What about Hyman Appleman? (now with the Lord — JVI)

Dr. Cedarholm: "I was in Detroit and had a day off and went to hear Hyman Appleman at the Fair Grounds. When he gave the invitation, I got a little suspicious and counted how many questions he asked so that people would raise their hand. Well, there were 38 before he asked number 39 concerning salvation. I thought that was a strange way to give an invitation. I saw him a few weeks later and said, 'Brother Appleman, why did you ask people to raise their hands so many times before asking them to get converted?' He replied, 'Brother Cedarholm, you've got to loosen them up and get their arms and shoulders loosened up. Before long, they will raise their hands to get saved.' "

*Q: What is a "pseudo-fundamentalist?"

Dr. Wendell Mullens: "Dr. Bell, you ought to answer that question since you coined the phrase. Will you explain your phraseology? [Dr. Mullens then continued]: Well, pseudo — I looked it up — is a false fundamentalist. I believe this term fits Jerry Falwell and others. I have two sisters who are really hard-core new evangelicals and they send their kids to Wheaton. Their husbands are new evangelicals. There is nothing in this world I can do except love them and pray for them. New evangelicals are more dangerous than liberals when it comes to the truth. If my father were a pseudo-fundamentalist, I would have to say he was one. My father recently told me that if he had a million dollars he would send it to Jerry's school. I didn't say anything as it wouldn't do any good. I thought secretly to myself, 'Jerry will get the million anyway, whether you send it or not.' Think what Jerry Falwell could have done for the Lord had he kept his standards right, his preaching right and his associations right."

Dr. Mark Dickerson: "Pseudo-fundamentalism is the false claim to fundamentalism. When you think of movements, you think of men: New evangelicalism, Harold Okenga; the Reformation, Martin Luther; and pseudo-fundamentalism, the phrase coined by Dr. Bell, Jerry is the one that comes to mind."

Dr. Rodney Bell: "Pseudo-fundamentalism is the embryonic stage of new evangelicalism, and I believe Jerry Falwell is about eight and one-half months along, and may deliver early. I have more respect for Billy Graham than I do a pseudo-fundamentalist because Billy refused to be called a fundamentalist."

*Q: Why are men like Drs. Jack Hyles, A.V. Henderson and Tom Malone fellowshipping with these pseudo-fundamentalists?

Dr. Cedarholm: "At Normal, Illinois, the most asked questions were concerning Dr. Jack Hyles. Dr. Hyles has never taken a strong stand when it comes to ecclesiastical separation, I mean an out-and-out outspoken stand. This bothers me and has bothered me. I would like to see him come over to our side, not for convenience sake, but for conviction's sake. Some believe he is pulling away from Falwellism and taking a stand. I don't believe he is. I believe he is moving to a middle position just where he said he was going to stand. He wrote me and said, 'I am not going to be against you and I am not going to be against Jerry. I am going to stand in the middle. My position will probably be a harder place to stand than your position, but this is my conviction.' I believe he has taken the middle position and believe it is dangerous. Either we as a fellowship will have to break with Dr. Hyles or he will have to come our way. I hate that. I do not want it to be that way. I would like to see him come our way, but I do not feel he will ever come. I hope and pray that I am wrong."

*Q: What about the California School of Theology, and why do fundamentalists fellowship with this school?

(I refuse to print the statements made about the leadership of this school. God forgive these neo-

177

fundamentalists for such slander against Christian leaders in the presence of grade school children! — JVI)

*Q: Where has Dr. Jack Van Impe gone astray?

Dr. Mullens: "Well, I felt for a long time that Jack got too involved in the Billy Graham type of evangelism, I mean in the sense of large, mass crusades. I talked to a number of preachers in Greensboro, North Carolina. They named a number of Southern Baptists that were on the crusade planning committee. There is no way to excuse wrong. Dr. Cedarholm made the statement to Jack, 'Jack, if you don't shape up you are going to go down the same road as Billy Graham.' Well, Jack has taken the road of least resistance, I am sure."

(Dear reader, get ready for a real shocker. During the return flight from Edinburgh, Scotland, following the 1976 World Congress of Fundamentalists, Dr. Cedarholm came and sat next to me for a moment. He said: "Jack, I am disappointed in you."

"Why," I replied.

"Your sideburns are too long. If you ever want to speak at our chapel service, you will have to have them shortened."

This was the extent of our conversation on separation. Never did he discuss the Graham issue with me as he so emphatically claims when speaking publically. — JVI)

Dr. Mullens (continued): "I listened to the Cobo Hall sermon on tape. I think it showed emotional

weakness and weakness of conviction. Jack grand-
standed to Dr. Rice, Jerry Falwell and all those
headed in that direction. He played up to that crowd. I
believe his course is set and believe that he is going in
that direction as fast as he thinks this crowd will let
him go.''

(Dr. Mullens was referring to the Sword of
the Lord crowd. Some compromise, eh? —
JVI)

Dr. Bell: ''Birds of a feather flock together, and all
dogs sleep in the same bed. I believe Jack is a
pseudo-fundamentalist. I think he is taking the road
of least resistance and is with the weak, soft crowd
[the Sword of the Lord followers — JVI]''

*Q: What about the Conservative Baptist
Association?

Dr. Cedarholm: ''There are several things that we
could observe about the CBA crowd. First, their men
came from the wrong schools — Denver Seminary,
Wheaton College and Fuller Theological Seminary.
Charles Fuller said if he went to the grave tomorrow,
it would be over that seminary. Of course he would
not say that publically, but he said it privately. He also
said that the tragic mistake he made was to bring
Okenga in as president because he was responsible
for ruining the school. Now as the schools go, so does
the movement. That is what happened to the CBA.

''[Talking about schools], I wrote Dr. George
Sweeting, the President of Moody, who said that his
school stands were it always stood. I told him that he
should write a tract that Moody has either changed or

that he will bring it back to where it used to be. That upset him very much. He made the statement that the former President, Dr. Culberson, was too strict. Well, a lot of men are coming out of that school and I think they are of the new evangelical stripe. The school doesn't stand right, so we find history repeating itself."

*Q: Where does Radio Bible Class stand? Give some comments. What is their position on new evangelicalism?

(There was no reply to this question. Instead, Dr. Cedarholm took off on Theodore Epp of the Back to the Bible broadcast. — JVI)

Dr. Cedarholm: "Theodore Epp is not a militant man by any sense of the word. We know that he is a Mennonite. He hides that just a little bit. I believe he is a Godly man, and I believe as far as his finances are concerned he is one of the best — but there has been a change in his music. I have seen some of the posters of his quartet. He will not face issues. When I went to Nebraska to start a church, he would not give me the names of the converts in a revival he conducted in the area. He said if he did they would give their money to my new church and he needed their support for his broadcast. Once I said to Dr. Epp, 'You should change the name of your broadcast to' Back to One-Half of the Bible,' and that really upset him." (I wonder why. — JVI).

*Q: What about Henry Morris of the Institute For

Creation Research. Does anyone know anything about him?

(Again, there was no response. Dr. Morris, you are one of the fortunate ones! — JVI)

*Q: What about the Baptist Bible Fellowship?

Dr. Bell: "I am concerned with the position of the BBF, especially as to questionable associations. I can't speak for the BBF internationally, but I can speak for it on a local level. We have about 50 men who pulled out of the BBF and started their own fellowship and are fellowshipping with the FBF — good men — while the other element went in the other direction. One thing that has bothered me has been the relationship of BBF leaders to the [California] Graduate School of Theology. A lot of ledership has been going out there frequently, such as Dr. Bill Dowell, Dr. Greg Dixon, Dr. A.V. Henderson, Dr. John Rawlings, Dr. Wendell Zimmerman along with Charles Allen, pastor of the large United Methodist church in Houston, Texas, and Dr. [Charles] Stanley, pastor of the largest Southern Baptist church in the Atlanta area — a long-haired preacher — and Dr. Ed Hill. It's a real hodgepodge."

This concluded the question and answer period.

Then, for another hour, Dr. Cedarholm — following other sermons against men and movements — delivered a sermon entitled, "The Devastation of Compromise." I will excerpt just a few of his remarks:

Comments concerning Dr. Falwell, Charismatics and Armenians:

"The Jesuits said it was all right to kill a person as long as one is trying to advance the interest of the Roman Catholic church. In other words, the end justifies the means. Well, we do not believe that, do we? No, the end does not justify the means. If we are using entertainment and arguments that are according to man rather than God's Holy Spirit, we are not going to have people who are really born again, are we? For example, Jerry Falwell made a statement — and I have heard him make this statement many times — 'If you will just keep busy winning souls, you will remain sound in doctrine.' Well, dear friends, there is nothing further from the truth than that. What are you going to say about the charismatics and armenians? Right down the line, some of them are pretty good soulwinners, but they are not sound in doctrine, are they?"

Comments concerning Leighton Ford

"The Word of God speaks about 'another gospel.' Well, Billy Graham's brother-in-law, Leighton Ford, was in Milwaukee — about 45 miles from us — not long ago, and he talked about two Gospels. Well, my dear friends there is only one Gospel."

Comments concerning the Conservative Baptist Association

"I helped in establishing 1,000 CBA churches.

Then we removed the separation clause out of the CBA constitution. We once had over 2,000 churches. Now they have less than 1,000."

Comments concerning Dr. John E. Carnell

"Dr. John Edward Carnell was a strong fundamentalist. In earlier days, he thought that Eastern Baptist Seminary wasn't strong enough so he did not go there. Dr. Carnell died in the Claremont Hotel in Berkeley, California. He died because of an overdose of sleeping pills. He was to speak to a group of Catholic bishops and priests. Well, he took that overdose of sleeping pills. The coroner, when he gave his verdict, did not want to say it was suicide because he did not know the man's motive. Well, dear friend, I do not like to think that John Carnell was not a saved man, because he certainly was a great preacher and soulwinner. But in his earlier days he went after a couple of doctor's degrees, and before long turned against the Word of God."

Comments concerning Swedish, Conservative and American Baptists

"I have been in and out of three different outfits already. I was born and raised in the Swedish Baptist Fellowship. Then I was in the Conservative Baptist group for almost 20 years as one of the founders, and was also in the American Baptist. I left them all and am independent now."

Comments concerning Baptists in general

"I spoke to a Mormon bishop not long ago. He said, 'Out of the 230,000 converts to Mormonism this past year, the largest percentage are former Baptists.' I would not question the validity of that statement. How does it happen? I believe it is because people who claim to be Baptists have not been informed and they compromised. Before long, they had gone down the road. I talked to several charismatic leaders across the nation. They tell us they have more former Baptists than anybody else. Now, why is it that the Lutherans do not fall for the charismatic movement? Why is it that the Presbyterians do not seem to fall for it the way the Baptists do? I believe, my dear friends, that one of the reasons is we just did not take time to preach the whole counsel of God's Word and have not kept our people informed the way we ought to."

Comments concerning the PTL and 700 Clubs

"Lay people have not been reading the right literature or listening to the right programs. They tell us that more Baptists support PTL and the 700 Club than anybody else. We ought not to be even seeing [watching] those things. Above all, we ought not to be sending them our dollars. No, they belong to good, sound, separatist, soulwinning, missionary minded, anti-new evangelical local churches doing the work of God."

Comments concerning the Conservative Baptist Missionary Fellowship

"Today, Conservative Baptist Fellowship foreign missions will appoint missionaries that go to shows and some of the wives wear pantsuits and that sort of thing. Some of the missionaries say, 'Go to the dances and to the shows. If you are going to lead some of your friends to Christ, why not sit down and smoke with them, sit down and have a glass of beer with them, sit down and play a hand of 500 with them. Maybe by joining in with them you will lead them to Christ.' "

Comments concerning Carl Henry

"Carl Henry was once an outstanding fundamentalist. He is well educated, you know. He has his Th.D. degree from Northern Baptist Seminary in Chicago and a Ph.D. from the University of Chicago. He was a separatist and believed that one ought to get out of the American Baptist Convention. But we know what has happened to him today. He founded Key '73 and Expo '76 and worked with Bill Bright. I once wanted to place an ad in his paper. He said he would not take it because, 'we are trying to win the liberals to Christ. If we have a negative emphasis, we will drive them from us and not be able to lead them to Christ.' That has been the attitude of these people."

Comments concerning Dr. Billy Graham

"Billy Graham was preaching down at Times Square. There he was preaching supposedly to 300 thousand people by police count. As the television

185

camera made its circle, it showed the various theatres at Times Square. There were four major so-called 'religious' pictures showing: Samson and Delilah, David and Bathsheba, The Ten Commandments and The King of Kings. I remember the four. I thought to myself, 'Praise the Lord, Billy is now going to take a shot at the Hollywood crowd and remind people what terrible sin these pictures portray.' What did he do? He turned around and used the subjects of those four films as his four-point sermon. This is exactly what happens when one takes the sting out of the Gospel and minimizes the negatives."

Comments concerning the General Association of Regular Baptist Churches and Drs. Joseph Stowell and W. Thomas Younger

"I wrote to Dr. Joseph Stowell and said, 'There are so many cracks right now appearing in the GARB that if they do not do something to shore up their movement they are going down the drain like the Conservative Baptists in just a few years. They have two of their schools that have taken the word 'Bible' out of their title. The last school to do so was Western Baptist Bible College in Salem, Oregon. [Why?] Dr. Younger said, 'When people read the word 'Bible' in our title, we are associated with the Bible institution movement, and that means we have a lower academic level. So let's take the word 'Bible' out and become a liberal arts college. Then we will get more students and have more money and support.' This doesn't sound like a fundamentalist, does it?"

Comments concerning Dr. Wilbert Welch and the GARBC

"Dr. Wilbert Welch once had the college presidents make a survey among all six of their colleges — seven now with Denver. The survey found that only 22 percent of their young people studying planned to go into the Lord's work, Yet those schools were started to train preachers and missionaries. If I had a school that was supposedly preparing ministers and preachers for the Lord's work and had only five percent doing so, I would close up or change the name."

Comments concerning Dr. James T. Jeremiah and the G.A.R.B.C.

"Dr. Mitch Sidler went down to get some teachers for his Christian day school. Dr. Jeremiah said that he had eighteen, but that they all planned to go to public schools. Well, I tell you dear friends, our attitude at Maranatha Baptist College is that if anybody goes to a public school to teach, we will ask for his diploma."

Comments concerning Philadelphia School of the Bible

"Go to some of these new evangelical schools. Go to Providence and Philadelphia College of the Bible. Look at those campuses. My wife was in the dormitory there. Ask her for details. Go and see what is happening in regard to romance and things of that nature."

Comments concerning Liberty Baptist College

"At Liberty Baptist, a young Korean saw boys and girls with hands around each other kissing and hugging. They were dressed in pantsuits. That Korean pastor turned around, got his money back and came to Maranatha and told me the story. Now listen, friends, when you hear a man say he is going to have fifty thousand students by 1990 and he cannot even control the 3,500 he has, what is he going to do when he has 50,000? I don't recommend that school to anybody."

"When I hear a man say like Jerry did that he wants to beat Notre Dame in football and UCLA in basketball, that shows me he has his priorities all mixed up."

(The "grand finale")

Comments concerning Youth For Christ, Campus Crusade, Inter-Varsity Fellowship, The Navigators and Percy Crawford

"There was a time when Youth for Christ was standing right, but no more today. There was a time when Campus Crusade was standing right, a time when Inter-Varsity Fellowship and the Navigators were standing right. There was a time when Percy Crawford was standing right. He compromised by supporting Billy Graham. He said, 'I must. Otherwise my contributors will turn against me.' When Percy Crawford died, his wife married an unsaved Episcopalian and Mountain Brook, Shadow Brook, Pinebrook and all the other brooks fell apart."

Comments concerning Jack Wyrtzen

"I am concerned about Jack Wyrtzen. He has been in and out of Chicago, speaking in new evangelical meetings. I called him on the telephone one time and reminded him about the men with whom he had associated. I think about his music — secular folk music to draw a crowd. Secular — get that — not folk music, but **secular** folk music. My friends, when we resort to that kind of bait we are going in the wrong direction. Pray for Jack."

Comments concerning beards

"I heard a preacher say just the other night that they plucked the beard from Jesus' face. Well Jesus never had a beard. In Isaiah 50:6, they plucked the hair from His face, not His beard. When Jesus went five or six days, not having had a chance to shave, He was bound to have some hair on His face. Now that is what they plucked. Jesus had no beard."

Comments concerning Christian bookstores

"If you visit the average [Christian] bookstore today — Baker, Zondervan or any of the rest of them — you will see more trash than you could ever dream existed. You'll see records by Billy Graham and charismatic material by Corrie Ten Boom. Time after time I have gone to the manager and asked, "Why do you have these things?" He says, "The public demands it." I reply: "Aren't you interested in preaching the Gospel and defending the faith? Are you just interested in making money?"

189

Comments concerning Christian magazines and radio stations

"When you think of Christian magazines like **Christian Life,** we do not allow them in our library because there is so much trash and junk in them contrary to God's Word. You could also probably name on the fingers of your two hands the Christian radio stations that are doing things right. I talked to the owner of the station in our area and asked why they had some of the charismatics on radio and some of the music that is not right. He said, 'The public demands it.' "

Comments concerning Northwestern College

"I believe with Dr. Dickerson, who referred to the **Pilot** magazine, the official release of Northwestern College, that this school has gone completely to the new evangelical, neo-orthodox position today. We played them in football. They entertained us in the dining hall and fed us a dinner, and what do you think they had — a five-piece jazz orchestra trying to entertain us at dinner time. While there, we tried to walk down the 12-foot-wide hall and I want to tell you that the hippies in pantsuits and dungarees were all over the floor. You almost had to step on bodies to get to the dining hall.

"The president, who is a personal friend of mine — Dr. Bill Bersten — had us at his table. I said, 'Bill, what in the world has happened to you?' I tell you, my wife and I could not get out of there quickly enough. I tell you, it pleased me to know that our athletes got out of there too, and didn't want to be identified with that crowd or sort of thing.''

Dr. Cedarholm's final point was that the new evangelicals are populating hell. I quote: "They are populating hell because they are preaching a false gospel. They use gimmicks and entertainment to try to win people to Jesus Christ. What can we do about these things? Paul tells us in the last chapter of Romans that we should 'mark' these men, and also that we should 'avoid them' [Romans 16:17].''

Imagine the devastating effect of this two-hour tirade against men and movements on the minds of the grade-school children who were present! God help all neo-fundamentalists to see that they are **destroying** rather than defending the faith through such sessions. In addition, they are sowing discord among brethren, and this is one of the seven things God hates the most (Proverbs 6:16-19).

In the remainder of this chapter, we will consider written articles opposing men and movements. The following release, entitled, ''Where Does Dr. Jack Van Impe Stand?'' was authored by evangelist Don Jasmin, editor of **The Voice of Fundamentalism** and a graduate of Bob Jones University. It implicates and judges multitudes of brethren, and may even be purchased from Dr. Jasmin at Greenville, South Carolina, or from Dr. Rodney Bell at Virginia Beach, Virginia. This material covers the seven-year period of time during which I battled to find God's answer to such outspoken bitterness. Since it is thirty-five pages

191

long in its entirety, I will use only excerpts.

Comments concerning Drs. John R. Rice, Lee Roberson, Jerry Falwell and myself

"To defend himself after the strong criticism that came from militant fundamentalists, Dr. Van Impe printed the endorsements of 21 well-known preachers concerning his ministry. The list included the names of three men who, by their actions, have clearly indicated their 'bent' toward pseudo-fundamentalism: Dr. John R. Rice, Dr. Lee Roberson and Dr. Jerry Falwell. Dr. Van Impe called these men 'solid fundamentalists.'

"First, Dr. Falwell, in his **Faith Aflame** magazine, indicated that his Liberty Baptist College Chorale and Youth Aflame Singers would be guests of Billy Kim in Korea [who is] working with Far Eastern Broadcasting Company, a well-known new evangelical missionary radio organization. [This] Dr. Billy Kim was an interpreter for Billy Graham.

"The LBC Chorale also appeared at Ripley Boulevard Baptist Church which is affiliated with the new evangelical North American [German] Baptist Conference.

"Dr. Falwell's relationship with compromising preachers in the Southern Baptist Convention also raises considerable questions [since] Dr. W.A. Criswell was a speaker at Liberty Baptist College."

Comments concerning Dr. Falwell and myself

"When a man's ministry is being criticized or

attacked, the men to whom he goes for counsel or sympathy are often a good indicator of that man's position. When Dr. Van Impe faced that problem, he sought the counsel-sympathy of Dr. Jerry Falwell!

"In Dr. Falwell's endorsement of Van Impe's ministry, Falwell stated, 'Presently, most of us are being attacked by the same sources who are attacking you at this time. I have read carefully the letter which was directed to you from one of the leading fundamentalists of our day [Dr. Bob Jones, Jr.]. The same letter took a very cheap swipe at dear Dr. John R. Rice, Dr. Lee Roberson and myself. I simply want to assure you of our confidence in you . . .' "

Comments concerning Dr. Rice and myself

"Secondly, Dr. Rice has aptly been called 'the grandfather of pseudo-fundamentalism.' In Dr. John R. Rice's evaluation of Van Impe's Cobo Hall address, he stated, 'Dr. Van Impe said what I have been saying all along, what Dr. Falwell said in the same meeting ... that he would not allow the radical critics, the **SECONDARY SEPARATISTS** who spend their time slandering good Christians and trying to 'boycott' Dr. Falwell, Dr. Lee Roberson and the Sword of the Lord to control his meetings. Dr. Jack Van Impe has not changed his position ... he has renounced ... those who spend their time running down good Christians' (The Sword of the Lord, 11-25-77)."

Dr. Jasmin continues:

"Dr. John R. Rice, who praised Falwell and Van Impe so highly, criticized militant fundamentalists severely. Some of the terms Dr. Rice used to describe valiant defenders of the faith in his paper are, 'hinderers of soulwinning,' 'hell-raising pharisees,' 'self-righteous pharisees,' 'fundamentalist nuts,' 'horseflies' and 'railers.' "

Comments concerning Dr. Roberson and Dr. Warren Wiersbe

"Thirdly, [consider] Dr. Lee Roberson. The Shield is the alumni publication of Tennessee Temple University. In it was featured the picture of Dr. George Sweeting, president of new evangelical Moody Bible Institute, as an honorary alumnus. Dr. Warren Wiersbe was another honorary alumnus. This is the same Dr. Wiersbe who spoke at Dallas Seminary, Conservative Baptist Theological Seminary and other new evangelical institutions. The new evangelical compromise of Dr. Wiersbe has been documented in **Faith For The Family**, The Bob Jones University magazine.

"This is the same Dr. Roberson who, within a year [1978-79], had Dr. Hyman Appleman, Dr. J. Harold Smith and Dr. Jimmie Johnson as speakers. All are Southern Baptist evangelists!"

"The reason I emphasize Dr. Van Impe's endorsement by these three men — Dr. Falwell, Dr. Roberson and Dr. Rice, is that they are the three key figures in the rapidly developing pseudo-fundamentalist movement."

Others accused as compromisers by Dr. Jasmin include:

Comments concerning Dr. Charles Ryrie

"Dr. Charles Ryrie, professor at new evangelical Dallas Theological Seminary, delivered the commencement addresses at both Detroit Bible College (a new evangelical institution) and Piedmont Bible College (a fundamentalist school)."

Comments concerning Dr. Lehman Strauss

"Dr. Lehman Strauss became sponsored by new evangelical Biola College, thus making Dr. Strauss the radio voice of Biola."

Comments concerning Dr. Charles Jones

"Charles 'Tremendous' Jones returned to speak during the Feminar-Seminar at Tennessee Temple Schools and the Highland Park Baptist Church."

Comments concerning Dr. Douglas Mac Corkle

"Dr. Douglas Mac Corkle, President [since retired] of the new evangelical Philadelphia College of the Bible, was the guest speaker at the Berean Baptist Church, Grand Rapids, Michigan [a GARBC church]."

Comments concerning Drs. E. V. Hill, W. A. Criswell, Paul Smith, A. V. Henderson, Charles Billington and Jerry Falwell

"The fifth annual Pastor's Conference on Church

195

Growth, sponsored by the California Graduate School of Theology, listed as guest speakers such new evangelical leaders as Dr. Ed V. Hill, Dr. W. A. Criswell and Dr. Paul Smith. However, three well-known Baptist Bible Fellowship pastors also were engaged as speakers: Dr. A. V. Henderson, Dr. Charles Billington and Dr. Jerry Falwell."

Comments concerning Dr. Paul Van Gorder

"**The Dallas Seminarian** stated that Dr. Paul Van Gorder, associate teacher of the Radio Bible Class, would 'bring the special Bible lectures for the Spring, 1978, semester' at Dallas Theological Seminary [a new evangelical institution]."

Comments concerning Dr. Paul Freed

"Dr. Paul Freed was the commencement speaker at new evangelical King's College. The editor's file contains various promotional items and copies of **The King's Life,** the publication of Kings College. Many of the male students have long hair, a clear indication of the spiritual direction and lack of Biblical separation in that institution."

Comments concerning Dr. Robert Cook

"Dr. Cook answered a question by a reader concerning charismatics. Dr. Cook stated, 'Don't worry about others who have slightly differing views of these doctrines. Just stay straight on the Gospel, keep your life true to God, win all the souls you can. Who knows? You may find yourself standing next to a charismatic in the by-and-by when we see our blessed Lord and receive His 'well done.' "

Comments concerning Dr. Bruce Melton

"In the summer of 1975, Dr. Van Impe conducted a crusade in Macomb County, Michigan. One reason why some militant brethren [a reference to the Rev. Staley Sorrell, pastor of Van Dyke Baptist Church in Warren, Michigan] would not participate was the presence of pastor Bruce Melton [Ryan Road Baptist Church — a BBF church] who served as chairman of the counseling committee. It was a well-known fact that at the time Melton was participating in the Van Impe crusade, his platform [at Ryan Road] was permeated with long-haired men and questionable music. This was the same basic inconsistency that Dr. Robert Jordan had pointed out when questioning the sponsorship of the Van Impe Philadelphia bicentennial crusade. Some fundamentalists could not participate in good conscience with such a crusade if it involved association with a compromiser."

(My statements that men were excluded on the basis of — not just the pastor's hair length but even that of his members — have finally been confirmed. Many thought I was exaggerating. I was not. This was the chaotic mess under which I had to conduct united crusades. — JVI)

Comments concerning Temple Baptist Church and my pastor, Dr. A. V. Henderson

"Dr. Van Impe's fundamentalist credentials come under further scrutiny when one discovers that his church membership is maintained at the Temple Baptist Church, Detroit, Michigan."

(This is the church pastored by the late Dr. G. B. Vick, a co-founder of the Baptist Bible Fellowship. The present pastor is Dr. A. V. Henderson. Why is this BBF church tainted? Read on — JVI)

Comments concerning Drs. Tim LaHaye, Al Metzger, Ben Armstrong and John W. Peterson

"The promotional brochures for the 2nd and 3rd 'Annual Super Conference' sponsored by Dr. Jerry Falwell included Dr. A. V. Henderson as a guest speaker. Other listed speakers were new evangelicals Dr. Tim LaHaye, Dr. Al Metzger and Dr. Ben Armstrong and John Peterson, well-known new evangelical musician.

"The conclusion [then] is that Dr. Van Impe maintains his church membership where the pastor has identified himself, by his actions, with the pseudo-fundamentalist movement, and who also participates in and associates with new evangelicals who are sympathetic toward and cooperate with ecumenists! The leadership of Dr. Van Impe's campaigns have been heavily sprinkled with leaders of the Baptist Bible Fellowship who are becoming prominent in the pseudo-fundamentalist movement."

Comments on the General Association of Regular Baptist Churches

"The GARBC is as guilty as the BBF. Each year at their annual conferences, the GARBC continues to pass strong resolutions which many pastors place in their 'file 13' wastebaskets when they returned home. Because these resolutions are not being implemented in spirit and action by local GARBC pastors and churches, new evangelicalism continues to permeate and erode the GARBC movement."

Dr. Jasmin's solution to this dilemma

"Evangelism, missions and positive Bible teaching are not sufficient protections against apostasy. They must be coupled with the militant defense of the faith. Over 20 years ago, Bob Jones University recognized the change in emphasis of 'Back to the Bible' and dropped that ministry from its radio station. For years, however, 'Back to the Bible' has continued to operate under the disguise of a fundamentalist cover. Now its compromise has been exposed, and the only answer is separation.

"May God raise up replacements for those radio ministries that are falling from the ranks due to compromise. The great need is for radio ministries that will not only go back to the Bible and through the Bible, but also be true to the Bible!"

Another Bob Jones graduate, evangelist Dave Sproul, wrote to me concerning the men who endorsed my position as a fundamentalist. The following excerpts were taken from his eight-page letter:

Comments concerning Drs. Jerry Falwell and John R. Rice

"In your newsletter, you carry the letters of several men. Let me refer to four of them. First, let's discuss Falwell. You and he are good friends. You have been on his platform several times. Are you going to walk with him? Can two walk together except they be agreed?

"At his pastor's school, Falwell constantly has Southern Baptist preachers who are in good standing with the S.B.C. They speak positively of the S.B.C. without one word of warning. Jack, are you in favor of impressionable preacher boys and many young pastors having the S.B.C. lauded? That is exactly what Falwell does.

"Moreover, Falwell's music leaves much to be desired. Dave Auckland at Sellersville, Pennsylvania, recently preached against Falwell's music and told his folks why Falwell's choir would never be back. Jack, I am not a musician, but I am a radio major. I know his music is filled with the world's methodology. I refer to the beat, the elongated notes, etc.

"Falwell is weak on the length of a man's hair and makes no bones about it. Some months ago he carried an article in his paper on personal separation in which he admitted that the length of hair at his school on boys was convenience and not conviction. Yet in my estimation much of their length is borderline now.

"Falwell's address at the Southwide Baptist Fellowship was one of the most arrogant, foolish and unrealistic messages I have ever read. Jack, we are not having revival today! Any man with a knowledge of church history knows we are not having revival today."

Comments concerning Drs. Warren Wiersbe, S. M. Lockridge and Jack Hudson

"Is it not interesting that Falwell attacks a strong separatist like Dr. Bob Jr. but applauds men like Wiersbe, Lockridge and Jack Hudson? Wiersbe compromised for years in Youth for Christ and had no compunction about working openly with Graham in Chicago. Lockridge and his acts of compromise are legendary on the West Coast. Jack Hudson worked with the 'I Found It' crusade in his city. No less man than Dr. Ed Nelson told me he thought Jack Hudson was lost to the cause of fundamentalism."

Comments concerning Dr. Lee Roberson, Jack Wyrtzen, J. Vernon McGee, Dick Hillis, Dr. Warren Wiersbe, Bill Bright and Dr. George Sweeting

"Let us leave Falwell and turn to a second man. I refer to Dr. Lee Roberson . . . Men have made Roberson and Rice gods. There is danger in that.

"Years after the issue had become clear on Graham, Roberson was still sending buses to Graham's crusade in Nashville.

"Less than two years ago Dr. Roberson asked Dr. Cedarholm to bring the commencement address. When Dr. Cedarholm asked freedom from the platform to warn graduating students about men and movements if the Lord should so lead, Dr. Roberson denied his request. Dr. Roberson later wrote him a hot letter according to Dr. Cedarholm.

"Indeed, at latest report, Dr. [J. R.] Faulkner

[pastor of the Highland Park Baptist Church in Chattanooga and Dr. Roberson's associate at Tennessee Temple] had a big picture of Billy Graham hanging in his office. That says something!"

Comments concerning the late Dr. John R. Rice

"[Dr. Rice's] defense of Criswell, one of the most insidious betrayers in the 20th century, is pathetic. I confronted Dr. Rice with his band-aid from the Psalms ["I am a companion of all them that fear thee ... Psalm 119:63]. I showed him he was completely wrong in his interpretaton of that verse. Like the other hard questions, he simply ignored it."

Comments concerning Dr. A. V. Henderson

"Then I refer, fourthly, to your own pastor, A. V. Henderson. I think he is a great orator and I thoroughly enjoy his preaching. Yet he went to California School of Theology to speak ... When Dr. Bob III heard about it, he wrote Henderson a gracious letter saying they had heard about it. He told Henderson that if he had gone to California not knowing the situation then they would be happy to go ahead and have Dr. Henderson speak at Bob Jones. But if Dr. Henderson had known the situation in advance, then they would have to cancel him. Jack, if I had that kind of pastor, I would withdraw my letter today."

The October, 1977, issue of **Faith for the Family,** published by Bob Jones University, featured an article by Dr. Rodney Bell which announced and examined the "compromise" of the Southwide Baptist Fellowship. The release followed the Fellowship's annual meeting at which Drs. Warren Wiersbe and S. M. Lockridge were featured speakers. Excerpts follow:

"Several developing trends within the Southwide Baptist Fellowship confront the group's leadership and demand action to keep the Fellowship in line with the historic Fundamentalist position.

"The Fellowship is permeated with 'successism' — an outward success measured in numbers and the value of properties . . . But many times behind these figures are records of wild spending, mounting debts, manipulations, and even bankruptcies . . . Many impressionable preachers have been swept away by these visions of success and have patterned themselves after a 'successful pastor' who, in some instances, is a pied piper leading them to compromise and delusion. From such may eventually emerge the same apostasy that is found in the large Baptist conventions, Youth for Christ, and similar movements.

"The Siamese twin to 'successism' is Southwide's separation position. Fundamentalists recognize no distinction between separating from those who reject biblical truth and separating from those who themselves hold correct doctrines but associate with men who do not. [Wrong. See chapter ten — JVI]. . . . This philosophy permeates the Fellowship and is the smoke screen by which to bypass biblical separation. . . .

"A Fundamentalist is not only one who loves the 'common salvation' but is also one who 'earnestly contends for the faith once delivered unto the saints.' When we quit contending, we are no longer Fundamentalists. Merely believing the fundamentals of the Faith does not make one a Fundamentalist. Fundamentalism is a position as well as a doctrine."

Dr. Allen Dickerson's paper, the **Maranatha Baptist Watchman**, also continually seeks out the faults of others as evidenced by the following excerpts:

Comments Concerning Drs. Tom Malone and Bob Gray

"Dr. Tom Malone, pastor of the Emmanuel Baptist Church of Pontiac, Michigan, and member of the class of 1981 of the Fundamental Baptist Fellowship of America, spoke recently in the 25th Anniversary Conference of the Trinity Baptist Church of Jacksonville, Florida [pastored by Dr. Bob Gray] along with Dr. Jerry Falwell and others. It is interesting that Dr. Malone brought the message on 'Scriptural Separation' at the World Congress of Fundamentalists in Edinburgh, Scotland, June 21, 1976."

[This was undoubtedly written to get Drs. Malone and Gray in hot water with Dr. Bob

Jones, Jr. Did it? Soon Dr. Malone and Dr. Gray left the Bob Jones University Board because of demands that they have no further fellowship with Dr. Falwell. — JVI]

Comments concerning Chuck Crabtree

"Chuck Crabtree, on the staff of the South Sheridan Baptist Church of Denver, Colorado [pastored by Dr. Ed Nelson] will be the song-leader and the featured soloist for the 3rd Annual Bible Conference to be held at the Cornerstone Baptist Church of Colorado Springs. One of the featured speakers will be Southern Baptist evangelist Dr. J. Harold Smith."

[This was probably an attempt to get Dr. Nelson in trouble with Bob Jones University and the World Congress of Fundamentalists. Sometimes it works. — JVI]

Comments concerning my call for love and unity among true brethren

Rev. William Barber wrote:

"Dr. Van Impe: Your new appeal for ecumenical evangelism, although evangelical, is unsupportable when many Evangelicals have no standards, approve of social drinking, attend Hollywood movies, have Board-run churches, tolerate charismatics and present a duke's mixture on eschatology. Dr. Van Impe, you have drastically changed. I cannot personally support your new position or lead my church to do so. I hope you will come back to your original position."

[I did not appeal for ecumenical evangelism, sir. However, I like my new position

205

of love for all the family of God. I used to tear God's people to shreds as unkindly and unjustly as the attackers mentioned in this chapter. Thank God He delivered me from such bitterness. — JVI]

Are solid fundamentalists beginning to see the problem?

Dr. James O. Phillips, an outspoken fundamentalist, is beginning to wonder what has happened to the love fundamentalists once manifested. He said in the **Faithway Fundamentalist** of March, 1983:

"As I have traveled extensively the last few months, my encounters with men have not led me to know of this last named virtue — meekness. A few months ago, I asked a leading Fundamentalist if there was something about the word 'LOVE' from which we were to shy away. His response was, 'It seems to me that when men get off on that tangent they wind up in compromise.' TANGENT? If anything, it is the main stream. All else flows into this stream of truth and love. Although I have met some men who truly exemplified this quality of lowliness and meekness, by and large it is a quality needing much attention."

[Dr. Phillips, may God raise up many more fundamentalist leaders such as yourself. God bless you. — JVI]

This final report, in the form of a letter, is but a

sample of what happens when one begins proclaiming and pleading for love among the brethren. It is from Donald E. Sigler of the Reformation Tape Ministry. He states:

> "Dear Jack Van Impe:
>
> Having observed your new stand on love and your apology to anyone whom you may have offended in the past, let me say that many of your fundamentalist brothers and supporters are saddened by this sudden gush of sick sentimentalism you call love. When I think of the high price the Fathers of the Reformation paid to take a stand for truth without compromise, your new position sickens and infuriates me.
>
> If you really loved those to whom you are now apologizing, you would tell them the truth concerning their false doctrine, not remain silent and compromise the precious Word of God. 'Come out from among them and touch not the unclean thing.' Whatever your motives may be for this new theology, we will continue to oppose your strides toward unity because they are not based on sound doctrine."

Do I understand you correctly, Rev. Sigler? Did you say I compromised the Word of God and that I have a new theology not based on sound doctrine? Please, sir, for the sake of your eternal soul, read and reread chapter 13 which lists approximately 300 commands to love all brothers in Christ. This is not new theology. This is the teaching of Jesus. The blessed Holy Spirit also said, "If a man say, I love God, and hateth his brother, he is a liar" (I John 4:20). I pray that you will apologize to the God of love and every man you have indoctrinated against accepting the "fruit of the Spirit" (Galatians 5:22,23).

Summary

Have you read enough? Is there a hate movement within fundamentalism? In 1977, I stated at the Sword of the Lord Conference in Cobo Hall, Detroit, Michigan, that I would no longer conduct crusades that excluded good brothers simply because they had been mislabeled by those who disliked them. I also said that all this name-calling and character assassination is part of a "hate movement" under which I would no longer conduct mass, citywide crusades.

Within weeks, I was bombarded with mail that called me every unkind name imaginable.

I say with every ounce of sincerity I possess that preaching on love has cost me dearly. Unless one is ready to pay an exorbitant price, don't do it. Please believe me. The wounds inflicted by former friends are deep.

This chapter was written to prove that there is indeed a movement within Fundamentalism that sows seeds of discord and distrust, and promotes bitterness. The foregoing excerpts and illustrations are but an infinitesimal sampling of the scores of letters and articles filling my personal files. The facts speak for themselves. By now the point has been proven. You have read documented attacks on men and movements by militant warriors who proudly wound their own troops and rejoicingly destroy some. At Cobo Hall I stated that there was a hate movement within fundamentalism. After reading the preceding remarks against men and movements, what would you call it?

* * *

Who changed the rules . . . ?

Chapter 12

Neo-Fundamentalism's Leadership

Dr. Bob Jones, Sr., was a great man of God. His memory will live forever in the hearts of multitudes because of the indelible impression he left upon them. His sayings, quoted by thousands annually, will also be remembered as the words of a great man of God. Only eternity will reveal all the good this spiritual giant accomplished. Rexella and I are grateful that we had the privilege of being in his presence for one hour before his homegoing. We loved him dearly, and miss his influence tremendously.

A Commitment to True Fundamentalism

Dr. Jones and Dr. John R. Rice felt called of God to lead fundamentalists into a renewed battle against apostasy. Therefore, on December 26, 1958, an emergency conference was called at Chicago, Illinois. Present at this interdenominational gathering of fundamentlists leaders were such stalwarts of the faith as:

*Drs. G. Beauchamp Vick, Lee Roberson and Jack Hyles (Baptists)

*Drs. Ernest Pickering and William McCaroll (Independent Fundamental Churches of America)

*Drs. Charles A. Thigpen and Linton C. Johnson (Free Will Baptists)

*Dr. Henry Grube (Grace movement)

*Dr. Allan MacRae (Presbyterian)

*Dr. W.B. Bedford (Christian and Missionary Alliance)

*Dr. John F. MacArthur (Independent)

*Dr. W.O.H. Garman (Associated Gospel Churches)

These great men, led by Drs. Jones and Rice, passed a resolution against the sponsorship of mass crusades by liberals and apostates. Thus, the tradition of historic fundamentalism repeated itself in that brothers of varying denominations united against a common enemy — modernists who denied the original five points of our founding fathers. These five points, you will recall, are:

1. The inerrancy of Scripture
2. The Deity of Christ
3. The virgin birth of Christ

4. The blood atonement
5. The bodily resurrection

I signed a statement subscribing to that resolution, and have abided by my vow to this present moment.

Since 1958, however, the situation has changed drastically. In fact, it is almost beyond recognition. Presently, the issue is no longer separation from apostasy, but from anyone and everyone the neo-fundamentalist leadership mislabels and bans. The godliest of men are eliminated as sponsors of crusades and as friends under such an unjust system.

Who changed the rules? How have we drifted so far from the position adopted at the Chicago conference? May the Spirit of God guide me as I attempt to share the burden I have carried for many years.

The Beginning and Excesses of Neo-Fundamentalism

Upon the decease of Dr. Bob Jones, Sr., Dr. Bob Jones, Jr., took his father's place as a leader of one particular segment of fundamentalism. He soon created a monopolistic movement, bringing all "preacher boys" (a term used for the school's ministerial students) under complete control. Obedience to every statement regarding any change of rules or philosophy concerning fundamentalism became compulsory, and any questioning of such rules by students or graduates was branded as an act of disloyalty to one's alma mater. Dr. Roland Rasmussen, pastor of Faith Baptist Church in Canoga Park, California, just became the newest alleged "traitor" when he questioned Dr. Bob about his inconsistencies. In a letter written to him by Dr. Bob III, he was designated BJU's "most disloyal alumnus."

Such subservience to every newly created innovation is also forced upon outsiders such as myself. Because Rexella had attended BJU, I became associated with the school's leadership. Although I was unaware of what was actually occurring in earlier years, I now understand how gradually they dictated the terms under which I was to march as a city-wide evangelist. Before long, I found myself trapped. If I ever dared to disagree with the dictates of the leadership, there were numerous "preacher boys" (graduates) in each area who could extensively damage the upcoming united crusade through a release of "rumors" prior to my arrival. If I wanted Dr. Bob's blessing, I simply had to say, "Yes, sir, I'll forsake that man or group," whenever — according to his "convictions" — he felt I had fellowshipped with the wrong person or church. Suspicion reigned, and my life became a nightmare.

At this point I no longer experienced the unity of former days, because of the distrust created by Dr. Bob's rumor mill. Finally, I kept my promise made at Cobo Hall to refuse to conduct crusades where division reigned.

Why did I allow this attempted control over my ministry to continue for such a long period of time? The answer is "fear." Yes, the fear of being ostracized, mislabeled, misjudged and expelled. The worst finally occurred as Dr. Jerry Falwell and I were branded as "fake fundamentalists" at the 1983 World Congress of Fundamentalists. Praise God, they did us a favor. We are free. I can now finish my course of service to God as the Holy Spirit directs me. The long night is ended, the nightmare is over. Never again will I have to defend myself against the charge of "disloyalty" to a system. Never again will I have to answer multiplied letters from Dr. Bob concerning my "shortcomings" according to his opinion. That day is past. Now I can reach millions annually via television without man's disruptive methods to hinder my ministry for Christ.

Neo-Fundamentalist Tactics

The following excerpts from letters verify my statement that many BJU graduates are "informers." They will also serve as a sampling of the constant policing of my associations by Drs. Bob Jones, Jr., and Bob Jones III. Often, their statements and accusations were totally wrong due to misinformation received from their men in the field. When reading these letters, please observe the dates they were written. Notice the criticism covered the years 1970-1978. I began city-wide evangelism in 1970, and by 1978 had become thoroughly discouraged, thus, discontinuing this ministry because of the constant nit-picking produced by the "preacher boys" rumor mill.

Please understand that there are countless numbers of BJU graduates whose hearts are completely in tune with mine on this matter of love. I do not want to give the impression that all their "preacher boys" deal harshly with the lives and reputations of others. In fact, a number of my employees are graduates of Bob

Jones University, and are undoubtedly the kindest, most gracious people who ever worked for me.

Having said that, I must in all honesty confess, "neo-fundamentalism" is primarily composed of BJU "preacher boys" who judge and condemn everything and everyone who disagrees with their leader.

At This Point Let's Look At The Letters.

October 7, 1970

"It is somewhat ironic that in the same mail with your letter there was a copy of the September, 1970, issue of **Christian Life, sent to me by some of our graduate students** [informers — JVI] who were expressing concern that you were speaking at the **Michigan Sunday School Convention** on the same platform with Criswell. In my estimation, Criswell is doing more harm to the cause of Christ than an out-and-out liberal and Christ-denier. Now Jack, I'm your friend and I'm not nit-picking. I know you want to do right."

Dr. Bob III

January 27, 1971

"I'm indebted to you for sending the **Detroit Free Press** article. This will clarify for a lot of people the matter of your stand and the statement is clear with no equivocation; and **you can count on me to spread the word at every opportunity.**

"I'm afraid your speaking at Tremont Temple is going to cause some confusion, however. The pastor is not exactly known as being an aggressive fundamentalist, but one who skirts the issues and flirts with compromise — a fence straddler who preaches a good message but avoids the stigma of contending for the faith."

Dr. Bob III

(We only rented this auditorium for our own Van Impe rally. — JVI)

June 24, 1972

"Once or twice **pastors have come to me** about your alignments in their cities, and in each case I have advised them to write you and find out what the story is. The one I think of in particular had to do with Kalamazoo. I cannot remember the other instance.

"In my heart I believe you want to be Scripturally aligned, and I sincerely believe you would not knowingly get yourself involved in compromise; and I know as your outreach increases, you're doing everything you can to see that slip-ups do not occur as a result of the enlarging scale of your ministry."

Dr. Bob III

(Emphasis mine — JVI)

December 17, 1973

"I have just gotten back from Detroit, and I was distressed about some of the things I heard up there [More informers — JVI]. You know I have been interested in your ministry, and **I feel sort of a fatherly obligation** to talk to you about this kind of thing. If you are going to use Chuck Oldham [The name is Chuck Ohman, Dr. Bob. — JVI], using him on your program and as you plan to use him, I understand, in the Detroit crusade, none of the Fundamental crowd is going to have any respect for you.

"Oldham [Ohman] is known as a 'New Evangelical.' He has in his group girls who wear mini-skirts [This was not so. — JVI] and, I understand, long-haired men. He has sung for Billy Graham.

[Dr. Ohman, one of the dearest friends God ever gave Jack Van Impe, has been associated with the great fundamentalist, Dr. David Allen, and the Calvary Baptist Church for 25 years. Dr. Bob's remarks came as a result of an attack on Chuck Ohman's reputation by the Rev. Staley Sorrell, pastor of the Van Dyke Baptist Church in Warren, Michigan. Chuck played the trumpet for Dr. Graham 25 to 30 years ago — the same time I played the accordion for him! — JVI]

Dr. Jones continues:
"He is known all over the Detroit area as a compromiser, most of whose music is rock and roll religious music. For you to associate yourself with such a man in your crusades discredits everything you preach because it is at variance with the principles you say you stand for and the position you claim to take."

Dr. Bob, Jr.

[It also discredits you, Dr. Bob, for believing a report that is not factual. Rev. Staley Sorrell preached a sermon in his morning service that was taped. In it he made numerous accusations against Mr. Clate Raymond, Dr. Ohman and myself. The three of us requested a meeting in the presence of his Deacon Board to answer the charges he preached publicly. Mr. Jim Girdner, Chairman of the Board, replied on

February 11,1974 — **one year after your letter** — and said the following: "The deacons met on Sunday, February 3, 1974, at 8:45 to consider your request that you, Mr. Clayton Raymond and Mr. Chuck Ohman be allowed to meet with Pastor Sorrell in the presence of the Board. Having discussed your suggestion very carefully and prayerfully, the Deacons voted unanimously to reject the idea, believing that it would serve no useful purpose for the cause of Christ."[Really? It would have helped us clear up all the rumors Pastor Sorrell spread and which many — like you — Dr. Bob — believed. — JVI]

May 28, 1976

"We are getting a lot of flak about the situation concerning your crusade set-up in Philadelphia. **We have gotten reports from students** of a tie-in between the crusade and the Campus Crusade television campaign. We have tried to **check it out with everybody we know** up that way; and it seems to boil down to this, as reported by one of the men who attended the five-hour session of your committee: A number of the churches represented were out-and-out 'New Evangelicals' with long-haired men, rock music, pro-Graham people and the whole mess.

"It was the feeling of **the young man who got this information** for us [another BJU "informer" — JVI] that you were not aware of it but that your advance man is very weak on the issue of separation.

"We are having enough flak from Carl McIntire, as it is, about men on the platform of our Congress who are compromisers. Of course he is right across the river from Philadelphia [our crusade area] and it is going to give him ammunition. Frankly, if the situation is as our friends in Philadelphia tell us it is, then you are sponsored by the wrong people there and your campaign is set up on a soft and non-fundamental basis. I am going to have to answer to people about this, and I would like to know what I am supposed to tell them.

"The material from these churches, including information about mission boards they support, has just come. [The young man went from church to church looking for damaging literature. — JVI] This group of churches and boards certainly includes compromisers, 'New Evangelicals' and all kinds of 'off-brand' things. We would not even permit many of these mission boards to send their material to our Mission Prayer Band on the campus, yet these 'New Evangelical' people are all tied in with your campaign in Philadelphia. Just one example: Faith Community Church and School has long-haired boys, mini-skirted girls, slacks on both women teachers and students, some of the teachers looking like hippies and the pastor [the Rev. George Slavin] and minister of music both mod. The youth pastor states they are entirely involved in 'Here's Life' [Dr. Bill Bright's soulwinning program] and says he sees nothing wrong with Dr. Graham's ministry. They are far outside the Fundamental camp. Are they in your meeting?"

Dr. Bob Jones, Jr.

[After all the disruption the above erroneous information caused, Dr. Bob discovered that the information sent by the 21-year-old alumnus was completely unreliable. He then had his son, Dr. Bob III, blister the young man, John Davis, for listening to one of their enemies, Bob Jordan. Proof? Read the following letter carefully. — JVI]

Dear John:

"It is almost one o'clock in Edinburgh. I am tired, but I might as well go ahead and answer your letter now because I will never be in a better mood for it all week long. I have been irritated by the tone of it.

"John, I know that you want to keep straight and do the right thing, and I admire you for that. I suppose I should be more patient with you. I still do a lot of foolish things, but not nearly so many as I did when I was just starting out, as you are; so I want to be understanding. If you were not mixed up with Bob Jordan, I would have no problem; but you are unduly under this man's influence; and my total lack of confidence in his judgment and in his methods leads me to **discredit the report** you give because I see too much of him and his ethics involved in it. We don't need 'donkeyism' today; we need Fundamentalism. We don't need mean-spirited preachers who delight in isolating themselves from everybody for un-scriptural reasons. Jordan has cut us off because we don't wear his label. There is nothing Scriptural about that; and knowing how shamefully, un-scripturally and unbrotherly he has treated us, I cannot have any confidence in his judgment that leads him to separate us **from this group in Philadelphia.**

"Frankly, John, I am highly disappointed that after the evidence I have presented to you of this man's spirit **toward your alma mater,** you would continue to give him the time of day; and I sincerely hope the rumor I heard to the effect that you are going to attend his fledgling seminary next year is untrue. Knowing Bob Jordan as I do and having revealed the man's character to you, if you do go there, I will lose all confidence in you.

Bob Jones III

[No one ever apologized to me for the grief caused nationally by listening to the rumors of this young man mentioned above. Neither did anyone correct the situation publicly. Four years later I was still answering questions about my alleged defection in Philadelphia. — JVI]

February 22, 1977

"I think you know we are your friends, and that's why I came to you with the report I picked up in Norfolk.

Dr. Bob Jones III

[Another story begun by an informer about supposed compromise that had no foundation. — JVI]."

August 22, 1977

"I had a phone call from a friend.

Dr. Bob Jones, Jr.

[Yet another informer from Florida. — JVI]."

December 14, 1977

"I have no wish to destroy any man's ministry. I have had no wish to destroy your ministry, and I still do not. I wrote you a **personal** letter, and I did not distribute that letter widely. I sent it to perhaps ten to twelve friends [Quite interesting for a **personal** letter. — JVI] who had expressed to me concern about you and whether you were really strongly Fundamental in your conviction and your position. I think in every case the men were told that the letter was not for circulation, and we stamped 'Confidential' across each page."

Dr. Bob Jones, Jr.

[Apparently the "ten to twelve friends" missed seeing the word "Confidential" on each page or were unable to understand its meaning, because they printed it in their publication. — JVI]

January 16, 1978

[The following letter was written by Dr. James Singleton, pastor of Tri-City Baptist Church in Tempe, Arizona, to Dr. Rodney Bell. Both are BJU alumni. — JVI]

"Dear Rod:

Enclosed is a copy of the letter that I have sent to Dr. Van Impe. I understand from Dr. Bob that he has received a number of such letters. [From whom? The multiplied informers across America? — JVI]."

As an hilarious climax to the statements and instructions contained in the foregoing letters, I want to present an excerpt of a letter written to me by Dr. Bob Jones, Jr. on September 2, 1977. In it he states:

"I do not know a single Fundamentalist in America, Jack, who would refuse to go and preach in a church simply because the music was not up to the standard he thought was spiritual or because some man's hair was too long or because some woman wore a pantsuit; yet you make it appear that this is the kind of thing that is dividing the brethren . . . I do not know any man who makes these the basis of fellowship."

[Dr. Bob, look at the carbon copies of your letters to me dated December 17, 1973 concerning Chuck Ohman, and May 28, 1976, referencing Faith Community Church and their involvement in my Philadelphia crusade. Both are included in this chapter. — JVI]

Through ten years of city-wide ministry, I learned to live with such accusations and inconsistencies. At first they crushed my spirit. Many were the nights Rexella and I lay awake talking, praying and aching from all that the rumor mill had created. As a result, I now understand a statement that Dr. Billy Graham made recently. He said, "I am tired and lonely. The prospect of death is so welcome. I would be very happy if the Lord would call me home. I am looking forward to it because of the pressures and attacks of these men. They are too heavy to bear, and I get homesick for heaven."

Never has a statement meant so much to me. No one can appreciate it unless he has gone through the nightmare described in this chapter.

The blame for fundamentalism's divisiveness has often been laid upon a great servant of God, Dr. John R. Rice. In fact, Dr. Norman Marks — a BJU graduate — accuses (as do numerous others) Dr. Rice as the instigator of the present debacle. He states in a letter to Dr. Bob Jones, Jr.:

Dear Dr. Bob:

"Give my regards to all of the Jones' people. You will notice an enclosed letter that I felt I must write to Dr. Jack Van Impe. I hope I have not made you further trouble by it, but I must air my feelings on the matter.

"I am so very sorry that he has played up to John R. Rice. I see it as nothing more than that. He probably thinks that joining John R. Rice's crowd will get the monkey off his back. The problem is he has insulted all the solid men who understand John R. Rice. I think he has made John R. Rice very happy. Rice has a way of manipulating pastors. Those pastors who have an instinct in them that tells them when they have met up with a spoiled brat and an egotist understand him. The rest he just squashes under his thumb. I think until John R. Rice is out of the picture there will be this constant agitation in the Fundamental ranks."

[You're wrong, Norm. The dear saint is with the Lord. Who's causing the friction now? It is worse than ever. — JVI]
Dr. Marks continues:

"Certainly John R. Rice has been a source of testing and trial for you over a long period of time. He knows how to force a good man to bite his lip so that he doesn't have to retaliate. The best way to defeat John R. Rice is to let him keep yodeling. Yodeling goes real well once in a while, but a constant yodel will make the closest friends yell, "shut up!" John R.

Rice is the true hatemonger and you and I know it. He is also a very divisive man. He has a Diotrephes personality. Somehow he has gotten Jack Van Impe on his side. I think neither you nor I should ever guess how he did it, but he did it.''

Was Dr. Rice at fault? Dr. Bob, Jr., made such charges when he printed his booklet entitled, **Facts John R. Rice Will Not Face**. However, Dr. Robert Sumner, a GARBC leader, wrote me September 14, 1977 saying: "Dear Jack, join the club! I was booted from the Board of BJU a couple of months ago when I had the audacity to write to Dr. Bob and tell him that he was 100% wrong in his booklet attacking Dr. John R. Rice, **Facts John R. Rice Will Not Face**. Not only so, but I told him that the booklet proved that Dr. Rice's position and his father's (Bob Jones, Sr.) position were identical."

The truth about Dr. Rice's position is beautifully described by Dr. Tom Malone: "**The Sword of The Lord** has led us into the heart and soul of the greatest Christian I ever knew — John R. Rice. Dr. Rice's position as a fundamentalist in the middle of the right road has been constantly pictured in the periodical. I tremble to think of the spiritual vacuum that might have been in America in recent years had it not been for **The Sword of The Lord**."

Proof That the Terms "Friendship" and "Loyalty" Are Meaningless To Neo-Fundamentalists

"Retirement" from the Board is routine procedure

at BJU. No one disagrees for long and remains Dr. Bob's friend. Allow me to present another example.

Dr. Bob Gray of Jacksonville, Florida, slated Drs. Tom Malone and Jerry Falwell as guests at his church. Since Jerry is "the most dangerous man in America" according to Dr. Jones, this unholy alliance was not permissible in the eyes of neo-fundamentalism's leader. Hence, Dr. Gray received a letter stating: "You were dropped from the Board of BJU at the last meeting because of your association with Jerry Falwell."

Dr. Malone, one of Bob Jones University's most loyal supporters for more than 38 years, told Dr. Jones: "I will not allow you to dictate the terms of God's will for my life. I resign."

In Dr. Jones' eyes, those who obey him are genuine fundamentalists. Those who do not are often demoted to the rank of pseudo-fundamentalists or new evangelicals. Sometimes dissidents are even excluded from the Kingdom of God! At a University chapel service, Dr. Jones made a shocking statement about me. I have a tape of his message. He said: "One can memorize scripture and be lost. In fact, one may even be called 'The Walking Bible' and not be saved." What did I do to lose my salvation? I simply rejected his dictatorial proclamations.

This exclusion of brothers in Christ comes naturally for Dr. Bob Jones, Jr. For years he has declared restaurants, business establishments, churches, men and movements to be "off limits" if they break his rules. As a result, any association with them is forbidden. Stuart Latimore, a BJU instructor and pastor of the The People's Church in Greenville,

South Carolina, experienced this truth. He taught five-point Calvinism and found his church declared "off limits" with students and faculty forbidden to attend such services. Time has passed, and now Dr. Bob and Dr. Ian Paisley (another five-point Calvinist) are dear friends. Such fellowship with five-pointers is now the "in-thing," and no voice of opposition from any friends of those who suffered over this position in past days is permissible. Consistency, thou art a jewel!

This "off limits" policy extends far beyond the environs of Greenville. It includes every state or area of the globe where submissive "preacher boys" are located. In fact, it is their duty to police the ranks of fundamentalism and report every compromise. Many do, and suspicion builds against men and movements wherever the willing informers are found. Soon godly souls are afraid to even attend disapproved churches or to fellowship with mislabeled brethren.

Drs. Bob Gray and Tom Malone are proof that such prejudice is both promoted and practiced by the leaders and followers of neo-fundamentalism. Regardless of what the leadership does or says, one must remain contented with every statement uttered regardless of the pangs of conscience or humiliation he experiences personally. Imagine how Dr. Bob's followers felt when former President Gerald Ford's wife, Betty, was called "a slut" by their leader. How humiliating it also must have been for graduates to read the following release from the **Associated Press**:

"It's a curious call from a Christian, but the Chancellor of Bob Jones University says the Lord should smite Secretary of State Alexander Haig and "destroy him quickly and utterly." "I hope you will pray that the Lord will smite him hip and thigh, bone and marrow, heart and lungs and all there is to him," Chancellor Bob Jones, Jr., told students on the school's Greenville, S.C., campus. He added: "Haig is a monster in human flesh, a demon-possessed instrument to destroy America."

Dr. Bob's statements about Billy Graham, Jerry Falwell, myself and scores of others have been just as vicious. No wonder he did not object to Dr. Ian Paisley's condemnation of Catholics as "papist rats and murdering scum" at the World Congress of Fundamentalists. Since this is his own style of speaking, why censor those of like vocabulary? Incidentally, it is amazing that Dr. Bob, a man considered to be a leading Shakespearean actor of our day, can't seem to refine his language.

Dr. Jones' Comments to Former Friends and Inquirers

Dr. Jones often directs this same crudeness toward former friends who disagree with any of his actions or philosophies. When they observed how I was being attacked by the Chancellor, numerous people sent me kind words of understanding. Often, they would enclose a copy of a letter they had received from Dr. Bob. Read the following and weep:[I have omitted names for obvious reasons, but the actual evidence is in a safe place. — JVI]

Excerpt of a Letter from Dr. Bob to an Inquirer

My dear Mr. —

You are either a simpleton or a liar. I would like to believe you just do not have any sense. What makes you think you have a corner on the truth? . . .

I have never gotten any message out to Bob Jones people to hinder Dr. Jack Van Impe in his citywide meetings or anything else. That is an absolute falsehood, and I challenge you to produce anything over my signature or mailed out on my stationery that indicates any such thing.

I challenge you also to produce any letter sent out from Bob Jones University or any official of this institution saying that Greg Dixon is going "liberal." It certainly does not take any genius to find out you are a liar.

[How about personal statements released to "preacher boys?" They carry out missions well. — JVI]

Perhaps I should not be so harsh with you. Maybe you got gassed or injured somewhere in the war and are not responsible for what you say or do. . . . You talk about love and Christian attitude. Your letter is a perfect example of hate mail, and there is nothing about it to indicate you have any love for truth. Your letter does not even deserve a reply, but I am going to call your bluff. Now, put up or shut up.

Sincerely yours,

Dr. Bob

Excerpt of a Letter Concerning an Article in "Faith for the Family"

My dear Mr. and Mrs. H. M.

I have your letter of January 7th. As you requested, we are removing your name from our mailing list.

I have neither the time nor the desire to go into the situation regarding your children here. I have no doubts that your daughter will make good grades at Liberty Baptist College. That is not very difficult to do. I wish her well. It is unfortunate, however, that she will not get the character training and the strong Biblical foundation that she could have received in Bob Jones University, expecially in view of the fact that there seems to be a strong lack in the home.

With best wishes,
Dr. Bob

Excerpt of a Letter Concerning Dr. Jerry Falwell as well as a former BJU student

My dear Mr. E.

As far as I am concerned, it could not matter less whether you are in total disagreement with me or not.

If ____ has told anybody that he was introduced by one of our guest opera stars to homosexuality, then he is not telling the truth. After ____ was a student here, we found out that he had had that problem for a long time; and we let him go.

All I can say about ____ is that he is a liar and a crook and a rascal who did his best to destroy Bob Jones University and who blighted every life that he touched. It is a strange thing that if the school was underhanded and evil, he remained here until we kicked his tail off the campus.

Very truly yours,
Dr. Bob

[I purposely left the names out in the above letter. We do not want to publish identities under such circumstances. — JVI]

In spite of such a barrage of abusive language, loyal "preacher boys" follow along without question. In fact, they just passed a resolution at the World Congress of Fundamentalists, commending Dr. Bob for his "abounding love." This loyalty is exemplified in a letter written to me by Dr. Phil Shuler:

Dear Jack:

Your mother told my wife Sunday at First Baptist, Troy, that "Jack has completely broken with Bob Jones." Jack, I hope she was just upset and emotional, but wrong! Don't break with that man! . . .

When you break with Bob Jones, you break with the University, the strongest bastion of faith with LONGEVITY left in America! They have been saying the same thing for 50 years.

I hope your mother was wrong, Jack. I can't believe it. I am honest in this statement. If Bob Jones wrote me today, and told me he was "through with me," I would never break with him! If he kicked me off the Board and never allowed me to set foot on campus again, I still would send students there, and support the school. Why? I happen to know God's "mark" on a man.

Another loyal follower, Dr. Wendell Mullens, made the following comments in an open letter which was sold to the public:

Brother Van Impe:

I believe that you sincerely want to honor God, His Word and His people. I believe, however, that you have sinned against God, His Word, the cause of Christ and against Dr. Bob Jones. . . .

Jack, you had an opportunity at Cobo Hall to take the Biblical stand on separation. You could have shown men like Dr. Rice that they are wrong not to obey the Bible on separation. You could have strengthened the brethren who are less informed or weak in biblical separation. Instead you went and "played up" to men like Dr. Rice and Dr. Falwell who are teaching a whole generation of preachers to compromise.

Dr. Lee Roberson has never been strong on Biblical separation. Is Dr. Jones wrong to say so? Many of the preachers who received their training under Dr. Roberson are very weak on separation. Look at what happened at the Southwide Fellowship in Charlotte!

I believe that your Cobo Hall sermon and November Newsletter will haunt you the remainder of your life, like Watergate will haunt Mr. Nixon.

[The report that will "haunt" me for a lifetime is printed in chapter 5. — JVI]

Inconsistencies in the Neo-Fundamentalist Camp

Isn't it strange that these same men who find immeasurable faults in others overlook the inconsistencies within their leadership? What do I mean?

Calvinism vs. Arminianism

First, let's consider the "five-point Calvinist" issue mentioned earlier. Dr. Bob Jones, Jr., placed Rev. Stuart Latimore's People's Church "off limits" because of its Calvinistic teachings. Could the reason have been Dr. Bob's preference of Arminianism over Calvinism? In a letter addressed to me on April 24, 1974, Dr. Bob voiced his distress that one of his graduates, a Free Will Baptist, had been excluded from the sponsorship of our Greater Honolulu Crusade. He stated:

Dear Jack:

I am taking the liberty of sending Luther Sanders, the Free Will Baptist pastor in Honolulu, the last paragraph of your letter. He is, in my opinion, the best man in the whole island and the one for whom I preach when I am there.

If you are going to preach for Baptists, it ought to be announced as a Fundamental Baptist church revival and not as a union meeting. My suggestion is that you let the advance man know that unless you have been invited by a group of Fundamental Baptists and are there for a Fundamental Baptist revival, any good, Bible preaching, Fundamental, separated man is to be included on the committee and his church made a part of the meeting.

[On this point, Dr. Bob and I were in total agreement. However, had I done this, various Baptist groups would have withdrawn all future support because, in their eyes, this constituted compromise or shades of New Evangelicalism. What a tightrope I walked. — JVI]

Dr. Jones continued:

Sanders is not an extreme Arminian at all. I think sometimes that these Baptist briders do not know what Free Will Baptists really believe. They are not Arminian in the sense that they believe a man can lose his salvation and get it back. Their position is that if a man who is saved can go into apostasy, his salvation is lost and lost forever.

They do not believe that every time a fellow sins, he loses salvation as the Wesleyans believe. In fact, the more I study the Bible, the more I am inclined to believe that the Free Will Baptists are right in their interpretation. Strangely enough, I began to wonder about this long before I knew anything about the Free Will Baptist position, and I was inclined to believe I must be the first man who ever considered this possibility of interpretation; and then I found that the Free Will Baptists believed it. I have much more respect for a good, sensible Fundamental, separatist Free Will Baptist than I do for the Baptist briders, because there is nothing in the scripture whatsoever than can even be twisted to support their doctrine on this point any more than anyone can support the

Romanist Purgatory [teaching].
   Bob Jones, Jr.

Please see the situation: After ostracizing a Calvinist (Rev. Latimore) and promoting an Arminian
(Rev. Sanders), Dr. Jones reversed gears and took up
with Ireland's leading five-point Calvinist (Dr. Ian
Paisley) for a union that has been unsurpassed in his
lifetime. When I spoke at the World Congress of
Fundamentalists in Edinburgh, Scotland, in 1976, I
was startled to see "five-pointers" picketing the
facilities where the lectures for the Congress were
being delivered. The signs reprimanded Dr. Paisley
for compromise because of his relationship with
Arminian Bob Jones.

Today, Paisley's followers have established a
church in Greenville, South Carolina, with the blessing of Dr. Bob upon it. How strange that BJU faculty
members and students are urged to join a church
whose doctrine is identical to that condemned by Dr.
Bob just a few short years ago. How true is God's
Word in Romans 2:21: "Thou therefore which teachest another, teachest thou not thyself?" Since I am
unable to understand how "preacher boys" can ignore such inconsistencies, I move on to the next
issue.

Free Masonry

Dr. Roland Rasmussen recently enlightened the
public with respect to his alma mater's inconsistencies regarding Masonry. The following quote is
used by permission:

Dr. Rasmussen states:

In his letter to me dated May 31, 1974, which I have in a safety deposit box with other important documentation, Dr. Bob Jones, Jr., wrote: 'If [Masonry] is a secret order, then I think the best argument opposing it is that Christians ought not to join it because they are unequally yoked together with unbelievers . . .

The issue is that Christians are lined up in an unscriptural alliance with Jews and unbelievers and unsaved men. Oppose it on that basis . . . '

Dr. Bob Jones III held a similar view that was made apparent in his letter to Mr. Thomas Reisinger dated July 5th, 1974: 'It [Masonry] is a Luciferian religion. We are fully aware of its diabolic origin and purpose and expose it and oppose it as such . . . I believe that any born-again Christian, when the facts from the lips of the Masonic writers themselves are presented, showing that Masonry is a religion and is the worship of Satan, will immediately withdraw.'

Then, in Mid-1974, when some Bible believers began asking Dr. Jones, Jr., and Dr. Jones III if it were consistent with the doctrine of biblical separation for BJU to tolerate those who maintained membership in Freemasonry on the Board of Trustees, Dr. Bob Jr. enunciated his newly adopted position. He said in a letter dated May 12, 1975: 'I personally do not see that membership in a secret society violates a scriptural teaching on separation . . . We do not share their [the Bible believer's] concern and alarm that membership is affiliation with apostasy.'

[Dr. Bob, according to your son's letter above, you two agreed in earlier days and then disagreed later. He claims Masonry is the worship of Satan — and if such a harsh statement is true, then according to the Bible, that's apostasy! You'd better get your heads together. — JVI]

Dr. Rasmussen continues:

Was Dr. Bob Jones' positional change the result of newfound biblical conviction or was it the result of pragmatic expediency? If Dr. Bob Jones' positional switch was the result of his following the pathway of expediency, then it was a tragic sacrifice of the permanent on the altar of the immediate.

How true are the words of James 1:8: "A double minded man is unstable in all his ways." Since I am unable to understand how "preacher boys" ignore such inconsistencies, I move on to the next issue.

Moody Founder's Week

In 1972, I received an invitation from Dr. George Sweeting, president of Moody Bible Institute, to speak during the school's Founders Week Conference. My heart was thrilled, and I accepted — elated to be their guest. My joy, however, was short-lived, for I immediately received the following letter (dated December 23, 1972) from Dr. Bob III:

Jack, you know my concern about your participation in Moody's Founders Week. That platform is known throughout the country as a present-day soft, compromising, New Evangelical conference. They are using you there, Jack, to give them some semblance of fundamental dignity. If you go, they will point to you as an indication that they are not as bad as people have been told. You will be helping further the cause of New Evangelicalism, and I cannot believe you want that.

Several weeks ago, you told me on the phone that after the reaction you had gotten about your part in the Moody's Founders Conference [from "preacher boys" — JVI] you would call them and cancel. I wish you had cancelled it on your own initiative without first getting the drift of feeling and then deciding it would be to your advantage to cancel it. It would have been better to cancel it on a matter of principle, but at least you canceled it. Now, however, I understand you are still considering going; that you have reversed yourself. Jack, I beg you, for the sake of the Lord's cause, not to go. If you go to Moody's Founders Week, I will guarantee that a large segment of Fundamentalists will never participate in your crusades again. You will lose their confidence, and Bob Jones University will be among them. I don't tell you that because you owe the University anything, but the New Evangelicals don't have anything to give you; they couldn't care less about you; they have their evangelists. They can, however, destroy you, so that you are no good to the cause of Christ.

I understand there is a crusade being planned for next fall in Chicago. My feeling is that every one of the staunch, fundamental, separatist men who are participating in that meeting will absolutely pull out, without any question asked, if you go to Moody's

Founders Week; however, your decision about whether to go should not be based on what the reaction will be, but on what is right.

I have also heard [from another "informer" — JVI] that you had consulted "several fundamental leaders" who told you that you should go ahead and appear at Moody's Founders Week.

I think a public statement and disavowal of any connection with Moody's Founders Week will do you a world of good. Your name is still apparently on their materials and, for all the public knows, you are going there; if you are not going, you ought to say so in the loudest possible voice.

Merry Christmas,
Bob Jones III

Until now, no one has heard my side of this story. Let me share it with you.

After originally accepting Dr. Sweeting's invitation, "preacher boys" began to threaten the cancellation of crusades, as Dr. Bob III warned. As a result, the fear mentioned earlier in this chapter gripped me and I cancelled my appearance. This decision, however, was of the flesh rather than under the guidance of the Holy Spirit. Within a few days, the Spirit of God broke my heart over the cancellation and I telephoned several fundamental leaders for counsel. Each one, without exception, encouraged me to speak at the conference.

First, I called Dr. G.B. Vick, my pastor and a leader of the Baptist Bible Fellowship movement. I said, "Dr. Vick, I have a problem."

"What is it?" He replied.

"I have been invited to speak at Moody's Founders Week conference," I answered.

Before I could utter another word, Dr. Vick said, "Praise the Lord, what an opportunity." I had my answer.

I then called Dr. Lee Roberson. He wholeheartedly encouraged me to go. Dr. Joseph Stoll of the GARBC was to speak at Moody's graduation exercises, and we agreed that God would have us go. In addition, Dr. John R. Rice wrote me on December 26, 1972, stating: "I am glad to have your letter. I hope you can be a real blessing and help to Moody Bible and an encouragement to Dr. Sweeting. I am sending a copy of your letter to my brother, Dr. Bill Rice. We both understand your position."

Hence, after seeking the advice of God's greatest giants, I called Dr. Sweeting, apologized, and stated that I had changed my mind and would speak after all.

Shortly after doing what I felt was God's will for my life, the Chicago crusade committee — headed up by Dr. Wayne Van Gelderen and two other BJU graduates — sent me a telegram stating that if I were to go to Moody's Founders Week, the crusade would immediately be cancelled. I also received warning from BJU alumnus in other areas of the nation that I would pay the price if I went. Again, in the flesh, I cancelled my appearance. Fear had conquered!

Now even though I finally obeyed the Jones's, Dr. Bob, Jr., repeatedly told others across America that I was a compromiser who had to be forced to take a stand. In writing to me on December 17, 1973, he said:

> I was distressed when I heard that after you
> assured us you were not going to Moody's
> Founders Week, you changed your mind and
> decided to go; and it was only after the pres-
> sure brought to you by the boys who were
> sponsoring your meeting in Chicago that you
> did not go to Moody. I understand from some
> of these fellows that they just "put it to you"
> that if you went to Moody, they would have
> nothing to do with your crusade and that **they
> forced you to take a stand**.

> Dr. Bob Jones, Jr.

Because Dr. Bob circulated this letter widely to
"preacher boys," Dr. James Singleton — six years
after the fact — continued promoting the issue in an
open letter to me saying:

> I have read Dr. Bob's letter to you, and he
> deals with fundamental principles of Biblical
> separatism. As an example, he deals with
> your acceptance of an invitation to speak at
> Moody's Founders Week until pastors in the
> area **"leaned" on you**. Frankly, Jack, I am
> scared of a man who **always has to be leaned
> on** to take the right side in an issue.
> While I am writing this letter, one of my staff
> handed me a brochure on Moody's Founders Week
> for this year [1978]. It looks like a Who's Who of
> New Evangelicals by anybody's definition. And
> right in the midst as a speaker is Jerry Falwell. [Now
> watch the logic at this point. — JVI] Now, either
> you were right in not speaking at Moody or Falwell is

right in speaking.

[Jerry was right and I was wrong, Dr. Singleton. The difference is that my life's ministry was threatened and no one told Jerry that they would burn his church from under him if he went. — JVI]

Guess what! The first thing that happened when I went to Chicago to conduct my mass crusade was that the same men who threatened to cancel the meeting if I went to Moody's Founders Week drove me to WMBI each morning to promote the crusade services over Moody's radio station. Air time was offered without cost or obligation because of the love and kindness of Moody's leaders. Yes, great Christians know how to turn their cheek.

Now guess again! Please sit up and take notice, Drs. Rodney Bell, Mark Dickerson, David Sproule, Phil Shuler, James Singleton and all others who publish papers or send out open letters. Here is a simple fact you "preacher boys" — and Dr. Wayne Van Gelderen who lives in the Chicago area and who had Dr. Bob's "preacher boys" lean on me — overlooked: On the same Founders Week program was a brother I dearly love in the Lord — Dr. Harold Henniger, pastor of the Canton Baptist Temple in Canton, Ohio. He is a graduate of Bob Jones University, and his picture was on the Founders Week advertising brochure. He attended. He spoke. I did not.

Ten years later, Dr. Bob, Jr. still defames me as the compromiser who had to be forced to take a stand. Dr. Henniger, however, was the honored speaker at Bob Jones University's 1983 Bible Conference.

Oh, how wise was Solomon when he said, "It is not good to have respect of persons in judgment" and "To have respect of persons is not good" (Proverbs 24:23; 24:21). Since I am unable to understand how "preacher boys" ignore both such inconsistencies and God's Word, I move on to the next issue.

The Charismatic Debate

Dr. Rod Bell, in his Fundamental Baptist Fellowship paper, recently carried an article written by one of my former employees, the Rev. Ross Davis, pastor of Simi Baptist Temple, Simi Valley, California. In it, he explains why he resigned as Field Director for Jack Van Impe Ministries. He claims that his resignation resulted from the fact that I featured Mr. Sid Roth, a charismatic, on our telecast.

On August 4, 1980, Rev. Davis's father-in-law, Dr. Phil Shuler — a Bob Jones University Board member — wrote to me stating:

> I am very, very concerned about your September program in which you are planning to have Sid Roth, a known charismatic on your show. I understand and believe that you did not know this when you taped the show, but you know it now . . . I beg of you not to do this thing. Money and extra costs involved in taping again, or editing that section out, should not even be considered. There is only one thing to do, stop it before it happens.

[Now comes the threat similar to those concerning my crusades. — JVI]

I am being ethical in also telling you that I owe my friends an explanation of this matter [another informer — JVI]. It will be forthcoming in my next newsletter, set to come out mid-August or there about. I do not want to do this . . . If you will let me know by August 10 or 12 that you are going to pull this show, then I will omit that part about you in my newsletter.

Needless to say, I decided to ignore any further threats by this crowd and did not respond. Thus, Dr. Shuler's article was released as promised. Some of the facts were incorrect, but I decided to refrain from answering my critics.

Until now, the Spirit of God has not allowed me to ever print a word concerning the facts. I have borne the brunt of numerous accusations without ever replying. However, men of God like Dr. Dick Vigneulle, a BJU alumnus and one of numerous graduates who deplore such tactics, wrote me on June 10, 1983, saying:

What a joy to have had you with us here at Shades Mountain Independent Church. Your ministry had a real impact on our people and gave us a lot on which to meditate. I think you could see from the crowd that attended that you have many supporters in Birmingham, Alabama.

Jack, I will be praying with you and for you regarding your new book. I sense a very heavy burden for the responsibility that this places on your shoulders. I know you will do it scripturally and lovingly, but the more we talked the more convinced I became of its necessity. You will never convince certain elements in the Fundamentalist movement, but I do believe that you will be able to unite a great many back to the basics.

Dr. Tom Malone also talked to me and said: "Jack, I prayed often about your book and felt that God wants me to tell you that you should go ahead with your project."

Here, then, is my side of the story. It can be verified by witnesses.

In the summer of 1980, my television director, Mr. Jonathan Byrd, asked Sid Roth to appear on my program. His group attempts to win their Jewish friends to Christ.

On the basis of this information, Mr. Roth was invited to appear on our program. His interview with Rexella was a real blessing to us, and God used the program marvelously. Since our guests have included experts in the field of science, military leaders, computer specialists, senators, congressmen, and Jewish and Lebanese leaders with a variety of religious backgrounds, I could not see the necessity of canceling programs valued at thousands of dollars just because an employee and his BJU father-in-law thought it was compromising to release them.

There is however, more to the story than was told to Dr. Shuler by his son-in-law. Actually, a power struggle between Mr. Byrd and Rev. Davis began developing several months prior to the Sid Roth taping. In fact, by the time Rev. Davis resigned, he had become so antagonistic toward Mr. Byrd that he informed other employees that he was praying for Mr. Byrd's death. When I did not release Mr. Byrd, Rev. Davis submitted his resignation, using the umbrella of separation to become a hero within the neo-fundamentalist camp.

Dr. Shuler then took the situation concerning his son-in-law and exploited it so as to become re-accepted by neo-fundamentalists. They suspected him of compromise because of conducting a crusade for Dr. Tom Berry, whom they had disfellowshipped because he walked out of a meeting where Dr. John R. Rice was being defamed.

Shuler personally told me on two occasions how disgusted he was with the nit-picking of leaders within this movement. He also informed me that he came home sick at heart because of the tirade launched against Jerry Falwell at the World Congress of Fundamentalists, conducted in the Philippines.

Hence, I was shocked when he reversed gears and began exposing my alleged compromise. However, I knew that it was his way of being reinstated as a militant warrior within the movement that so disgusted him previously.

Through it all and afterward, I never printed a word to defend myself. However, since the Fundamental Baptist Fellowship's article concerning Rev. Davis' resignation has again been circulated nationally — three years after its occurrence — I felt that it was time to set the record straight.

This same crowd has also misrepresented Dr. Jerry Falwell. In the June, 1978, issue of his paper, **The Baptist Messenger,** Dr. Rodney Bell said: "For a long time — much too long, in fact — Dr. Falwell featured singer Doug Oldham as a drawing card. All the time Doug Oldham was and still is a Charismatic.''

I have known Doug Oldham for many years, and know that he is a member of the Church of God denomination headquartered in Anderson, Indiana. I am also a neighbor of Dr. Herbert Streeter, who lives three doors from me, and who formerly pastored the Woodlawn Church of God in Royal Oak, Michigan, where Doug Oldham was Minister of Music. Dr. Bell and other ''preacher boys'' failed to do their homework. Because they openly condemned Doug Oldham for his associations, I have them over the proverbial barrel. Why? Dr. Streeter, in whose church Doug Oldham served, was a member of the Bob Jones University Board for a number of years! Again I say, consistency, thou art a jewel.

Furthermore, if Dr. Bell and Dr. Phil Shuler felt that they must publicly expose my alleged compromise as they did simply because of my love and acceptance of a brother in Christ who affiliates with Pentecostal people, then I think it is only fair to turn the tables and ask them a very heart-searching question? ''Why, brethren, did you remain silent when Dr. Bob Jones, Jr. invited and presented a 'tongues speaker' at the 1976 World Congress of Fundamentalists in Edinburgh, Scotland? Dr. Bell, since you were also on the program, and Dr. Shuler, since you are a member of the BJU board, you cannot plead ignorance. Surely you remember the most shocking statement ever made at a fundamental congress when Dr. O. Talmadge Spence, president of Foundations Bible College in North Carolina, said, ''I believe that glossalalia [speaking in tongues] is for today.''

When Dr. Spence made this statement, I wondered if the great "defenders" of the faith were present. They were! Drs. B. Myron Cedarholm, Archer Weniger, Rodney Bell, Dayton Hobbs and Wayne Van Gelderen were not only present, but were also **guest speakers with Dr. Spence**. Did even one of them rebuke their leader for allowing such a situation to occur? Did any of their "defending the faith and defaming the brethren" tabloids print an article concerning this outrageous act of "compromise" (their description if any other fundamentalist had done so)? Of course not. To this day, not a word has been uttered or published. Instead, they waited five years to pour their pent-up anger on Jerry and Jack.

Personally, I felt that Dr. O. Talmadge Spence was a great man who had the blessing and warmth of God's Spirit upon him as he lectured. I was intrigued by his unusual ability to communicate the Word of God in a most brilliant way. I loved him as a dear brother in Christ.

The question, nevertheless, remains. Why the difference? One "tongues" brother is accepted, the other rejected. Why did the event at the World Congress of Fundamentalists go unreported while the Sid Roth issue received national publicity? Some apologists will say that Dr. Spence is a **fundamentalist** tongues practitioner, since he graduated from Bob Jones University. Many others are New Evangelical tongues speakers since they received their training at Oral Roberts University. Yet, knowing fundamentalists as I do, the issue is **tongues** — and regardless of who does the training, tongues is tongues!

There is no way to skirt the issue. Either Dr. Bob compromised or he didn't. If he did, the FBF should publish his fallacies along with Jerry's and Jack's. If he didn't, the FBF should apologize to Jerry and Jack. As far as the World Congress members are concerned, they should remain silent. It happened at their gathering.

Some may be concerned whether or not I have my facts straight regarding Dr. Spence's World Congress statement reported above. Therefore, let's go one step further. In his book entitled, **A Pentecostal Speaks To Pentecostalists** (published by the Bob Jones University Press), Dr. Spence states on page 4: "We should discover the freedom in our worship for audible praise to God sometimes accompanied by utterances [tongues] through us, especially in our closet of prayer."

Wait! There is another principle at stake. Dr. Bob Jones and Fundamental Baptist Fellowship leaders, as well as World Congress supporters, constantly attack Dr. Billy Graham for his association with Roman Catholics and liberals. Sponsorship by either is anathema in their eyes. Then what about the fact that Dr. Spence lectured on tongues at a Catholic university before making his appearance in Scotland? What now, Dr. Rod Bell? What do you have to say about this, Dr. Phil Shuler? Where do we go from here,"preacher boys?" The following quote is taken from page 214 of Dr. Spence's book:

> While pastoring the National Pentecostal Holiness Church in Washington, D.C., I was requested to give lectures on glossalalia

[tongues] at the Roman Catholic University. This invitation was extended to me by the priest-teacher, Father David Bowman. The class that was designated for these lectures was entitled, " our separated brethren." I made it clear to the teacher that I could not come and speak solely on the subject of glossalalia, because I did not believe it was essential to salvation. After considerable discussion by telephone and personal interviews in his office, I agreed to deal with the Biblical phenomena of the glossalalia after I had presented the genuine gospel of Christ and the doctrine taught by Martin Luther.

May I ask another question? Why did Drs. Bob, Jr. and Bob III overlook in Dr. O. Talmadge Spence what they had for years condemned in Dr. Billy Graham concerning sponsorship by Catholics? I am only asking. I hope you have a good answer.

I would also like to ask how it is possible for Bob Jones University to train young people for Christian service and then pass a resolution condemning their own graduates. Approximately ten years ago, Dr. Herb Streeter and I sent a young man I loved dearly in Christ to BJU. I felt that since other fundamentalist schools rejected charismatics, Bob Jones would be a great place for him to receive a good, solid, biblical education.

Dave appreciated the fact that the school allowed him to fellowship with a Pentecostal group on campus every Sunday morning. Soon however, these students were informed that, because of "flak" received over this gathering of Charismatic students (similar to that the school had received over a five-point Calvinist group which also met on campus) they were to disband. They were then encouraged to attend a non-denominational church which would meet their needs.

Since it is a fact that BJU has trained and is training multitudes of charismatic leaders of the past and present, it is shocking to me how BJU as a part of the World Congress of Fundamentalists chaired by Dr. Bob Jones, Jr., can support a resolution which states: "We call upon all born-again believers to come out from this Satanic Charismatic movement and we denouce this wicked hell-inspired Charismatic movement as the devil's masterpiece of camoflage to deceive and destroy the very elect." This is the height of inconsistency, and extends to every "preacher boy" who attended four years of college with Pentecostal friends and then condemned their own friends at their neo-fundamentalist congress. I consider such action the greatest hypocritical act ever perpetrated in the name of fundamentalism! Certainly the words of Matthew 7:3-5 are applicable here: "...why beholdest thou the mote that is in thy brother's eye, but considerest not the beam that is in thine own eye? Or how wilt thou say to thy brother, Let me pull out the mote out of thine eye; and, behold, a beam is in thine own eye? Thou hypocrite, first cast out the beam out of thine own eye; and then shalt thou see clearly to cast out the mote out of thy brother's eye."

Since I am unable to understand how "preacher boys" ignore such inconsistencies, I move on to the next issue.

The Southern Baptist Issue

Dr. Bob Jones, Jr. often criticized and castigated Dr. John R. Rice for publishing the sermons of the great Southern Baptist leaders, such as Dr. W. A. Criswell, in **The Sword of The Lord**. The "preacher boys" are merciless in their attacks on any who fellowship with Southern Baptists. Dr. George Dollar, while instructing ministerial students at BJU, repeatedly crucified me over the Southern Baptist issue — especially regarding my Greensboro, North Carolina and Augusta, Georgia, crusades. I have numerous letters filled with erroneous allegations not worth printing. It is interesting, however, that Dr. Dollar became strangely silent after I sent him copies of letters I received from Canadian pastors who were concerned about the fact that he had spoken in several World Council churches in their nation.

In closing this lengthy chapter, let me ask one more question: Since I am personally acquainted with numerous ex-BJU board members, and since they have verified the fact that the University has had throughout its history (and still has) Southern Baptists on its Board of Trustees, why not stop the attacking of others who fellowship with these brothers in Christ? Since I am unable to understand how "preacher boys" can ignore such inconsistencies, I leave you to ponder Romans 2:1-3: "Therefore thou art inexcusable, O man, whosoever thou art that judgest: for wherein thou judgest thou condemnest thyself; for thou that judgest doest the same things. But we are sure that the judgment of God is according to truth against them that commit such things. And thinkest thou this, O man, that judgest them which do such things, and doest the same, that

thou shalt escape the judgment of God?" You won't!
The law of sowing and reaping never fails.

Perhaps that's why Dr. David Noebel, of Summit
Ministries, recently said in his paper:

> The Third World Congress of Funda-
> mentalism hath spoken and the Rev. Jerry
> Falwell loses. He was painted with a brush
> called "pseudo-fundamentalist." But then
> W. A. Criswell, George Sweeting of Moody,
> Jack Van Impe, Billy Graham, Luis Palou,
> James Robinson, Billy Kim, Leighton Ford,
> and Paul Cho are also referred to as pseudo-
> fundamentalists, apostates, or compromisers.
> One fundamentalist who came out of the Con-
> gress smelling like a rose, however, was Bob
> Jones, Jr. Bob, Jr., was co-chairman of the
> Third Congress which was held on the campus
> of Bob Jones University. Just a few years ago
> the term fundamentalist referred to what one
> believed about the fundamentals of the Chris-
> tian Faith. No longer. How times change. But
> then, watching the Fundamentalists devour
> each other is fascinating sport. Someone did
> observe that fundamentalist Christians are a
> distinct breed in that they shoot their wounded.
> Perhaps by the Fourth Congress the brethren
> will discover Brother Bob, Jr., has a skeleton or
> two in his closet.

There are numerous other issues I could mention, but
will not at this time. The inconsistencies described are
but the tip of the iceberg. May I suggest that all leaders
preach what they practice. Then we will become
consistent.

"Let us therefore follow after the things which make for peace, and things wherewith one may edify another," (Romans 14:19).

Chapter 13

Obeying Man or God

Neo-fundamentalism is deadly. It attempts to destroy the reputation of men and movements. It often succeeds as its propaganda campaign against good men and organizations is believed. In fact, neo-fundamentalism has done more harm than the combined assaults of the secular world, and has created a divisiveness that has no equal within historic fundamentalism. How sad when the foundation is simply sand rather than the rock, Christ Jesus.

In chapter 10, we discovered that neo-fundamentalism's attacks were based on **two misinterpreted texts**. How is it possible that intelligent men, the "silent majority," would allow such error to permeate a movement without raising a voice of objection? Brethren, error is error, and the manipulating of an inerrant Bible is wrong, regardless of who does it. I cannot and will not remain silent any longer.

Neither should you!

In the light of what has already been said, may I appeal to all loving fundamentalists and evangelicals to make a decision this day as to right and wrong. Study once again the two misinterpreted texts. Then consider the scores of verses presented in this chapter. There can be only two courses of action: you must either choose to continue bowing to the two man-made misinterpretations of the Bible or obey approximately three hundred of God's plain commandments to fellowship with and love the brethren. The following verses need no explanation. Simply read, believe, and obey them:

I. Dissention among brothers

* Luke 17:3,4: " . . . If thy brother trespass against thee, rebuke him; and if he repent, forgive him. And if he trespass against thee seven times in a day, and seven times in a day turn again to thee, saying, I repent: thou shalt forgive him."

* Romans 14:19: "Let us therefore follow after the things which make for peace, and things wherewith one may edify another."

* I Corinthians 1:10,11: "Now I beseech you, brethren, by the name of our Lord Jesus Christ, that ye all speak the same thing, and that there be no divisions among you; but that ye be perfectly joined together in the same mind and in the same judgment."

* I Corinthians 3:1-4: "And I, brethren, could not

speak unto you as unto spiritual, but as unto carnal, even as unto babes in Christ. I have fed you with milk, and not with meat: for hitherto ye were not able to bear it, neither yet now are ye able. For ye are yet carnal: for whereas there is among you envying, and strife, and divisions, are ye not carnal, and walk as men? For while one saith, I am of Paul; and another, I am of Apollos; are ye not carnal?"

* I Corinthians 11:17,18: " . . . ye come together not for the better, but for the worse . . . there are divisions among you . . . "

The result of the contentions of I Corinthians 1:11 and 11:17 are described in I Corinthians 11:27-33: "Wherefore whosoever shall eat this bread, and drink this cup of the Lord unworthily, shall be guilty of the body and blood of the Lord. But let a man examine himself, and so let him eat of that bread, and drink of that cup. For he that eateth and drinketh unworthily, eateth and drinketh damnation to himself, not discerning the Lord's body. For this cause many are weak and sickly among you, and many sleep. For if we would judge ourselves, we should not be judged. But when we are judged, we are chastened of the Lord, that we should not be condemned with the world. Wherefore, my brethren, when ye come together to eat, tarry for one another."

* Colossians 3:13: "Forbearing one another, and forgiving one another, if any man have a quarrel against any: even as Christ forgave you, so also do ye."

* Philippians 4:2: " . . . be of the same mind in the Lord."

* I Timothy 3:3: ["A minister is to be] patient, not a brawler, not covetous."

257

* II Timothy 2:24: " . . . the servant of the Lord must not strive; but be gentle unto all men . . . "

* Hebrews 12:14,15: "Follow peace with all men, and holiness, without which no man shall see the Lord: Looking diligently lest any man fail of the grace of God: lest any root of bitterness springing up trouble you, and thereby many be defiled."

* James 1:26: "If any man among you seem to be religious, and bridleth not his tongue, but deceiveth his own heart, this man's religion is vain."

* James 3:2: " . . . If any man offend not in word, the same is a perfect man, and able also to bridle the whole body."

* James 4:1: "From whence come wars and fightings among you? Come they not hence, even of your lusts that war in your members?"

* James 4:11,12: "Speak not evil of one another, brethren . . . who art thou that judgest another?"

II. Fellowship with brothers

* Mark 9:38-42: "And John answered him, saying, Master, we saw one casting out devils in thy name, and he followeth not us: and we forbad him, because he followeth not us. But Jesus said, Forbid him not . . . For he that is not against us is on our part. For whosoever shall give you a cup of cold water to drink in my name, because ye belong to Christ, verily I say unto you, he shall not lose his reward. And whosoever shall offend one of these little ones that believe in me, it is better for him that a millstone were hanged about his neck, and he were cast into the sea."

* Luke 9:49-56: "And John answered and said,

Master, we saw one casting out devils in thy name; and we forbade him, because he followeth not with us. And Jesus said unto him, Forbid him not: for he that is not against us is for us. And it came to pass, when the time was come that he should be received up, he steadfastly set his face to go to Jerusalem. And sent messengers before his face: and they went, and entered into a village of the Samaritans, to make ready for him. And they did not receive him, because his face was as though he would go to Jerusalem. And when his disciples James and John saw this, they said, Lord, wilt thou that we command fire to come down from heaven, and consume them, even as Elias did? But he turned, and rebuked them, and said, Ye know not what manner of spirit ye are of. For the Son of man is not come to destroy men's lives, but to save them.''

* Luke 11:42: '' . . . for ye tithe mint and rue and all manner of herbs, and pass over judgment and the love of God.''

* John 6:37: '' . . . him that cometh to me I will in no wise cast out.''

* John 10:16: ''And other sheep I have, which are not of this fold: them also I must bring, and they shall hear my voice; and there shall be one fold, and one shepherd.''

* John 17:20-24: '' . . . That they all may be one . . . even as we are one . . . that they may be made perfect in one . . . ''

* Galatians 2:4-6, 11-15: '' . . . false brethren . . . came in privily to spy out our liberty which we have in Christ Jesus, that they might bring us into bondage: To whom [give] place by subjection, no,

not for an hour; that the truth of the gospel might continue . . . for they who seemed to be somewhat in conference added nothing . . . But when Peter was come to Antioch, I withstood him to the face, because he was to be blamed. For before that certain came from James, he did eat with the Gentiles: but when they were come, he withdrew and separated himself, fearing them which were of the circumcision. And the other Jews dissembled likewise with him; insomuch that Barnabas also was carried away with their dissimulation. But when I saw that they walked not uprightly according to the truth of the gospel, I said unto Peter before them all, If thou, being a Jew, livest after the manner of the Gentiles, and not as do the Jews, why compellest thou the Gentiles to live as do the Jews?''

* Galatians 5:1: "Stand fast therefore in the liberty wherewith Christ hath made us free, and be not entangled again with the yoke of bondage.''

* Philippians 1:15-18: "Some indeed preach Christ even of envy and strife; and some also of good will: The one preach Christ of contention, not sincerely, supposing to add affliction to my bonds: But the other of love, knowing that I am set for the defense of the gospel. What then? notwithstanding, every way, whether in pretense, or in truth, Christ is preached; and I therein do rejoice, yea, and will rejoice.''

* I John 1:7: "But if we walk in the light, as he is in the light, we have fellowship one with another, and the blood of Jesus Christ his Son cleanseth us from all sin.''

* Revelation 5:9,10: " . . . for Christ wast slain, and hast redeemed us to God by His blood out of every kindred, and tongue, and people, and nation; And hast made us unto our God kings and priests.''

III. A. Love for our brothers

We are not to be angry with our brothers. Why?

*Matthew 5:22: ''. . . whosoever is angry with his brother without a cause shall be in danger of the judgment: and whosoever shall say to his brother, Raca, shall be in danger of the council: but whosoever shall say, Thou fool, shall be in danger of hell fire.''

*John 13:34,35: ''A new commandment I give unto you, That ye love one another; as I have loved you, that ye also love one another. By this shall all men know that ye are my disciples, if ye have love one to another.''

*John 15:9,10,17: ''. . . continue ye in my love. If ye keep my commandments, ye shall abide in my love . . . These things I command you, that ye love one another.''

*Romans 12:10,16,21: ''Be kindly affectioned one to another with brotherly love; in honour preferring one another; Be of the same mind one toward another. Mind not high things, but condescend to men of low estate. Be not wise in your own conceits. Be not overcome of evil, but overcome evil with good.''

*Romans 13:7,8: ''Render therefore to all their dues: tribute to whom tribute is due; custom to whom custom; fear to whom fear; honour to whom honour. Owe no man anything, but to love one another: for he that loveth another hath fulfilled the law.''

In the following texts, charity is synonymous or

another term for love.

*I Corinthians 13:1-7,13: "Though I speak with the tongues of men and of angels, and have not love, I am become as a sounding brass, or a tinkling cymbal. And though I have the gift of prophecy, and understand all mysteries, and all knowledge; and though I have all faith, so that I could remove mountains, and have not charity, I am nothing. And though I bestow all my goods to feed the poor, and though I give my body to be burned, and have not charity, it profiteth me nothing. Charity suffereth long, and is kind; charity envieth not; charity vaunteth not itself, is not puffed up, Doth not behave itself unseemly, seeketh not her own, is not easily provoked, thinketh no evil; Rejoiceth not in iniquity, but rejoiceth in the truth; Beareth all things, believeth all things, hopeth all things, endureth all things. And now abideth faith, hope, love, these three; but the greatest of these is charity."

*I Corinthians 14:1: "Follow after charity, and desire spiritual gifts . . ."

*I Corinthians 16:14: "Let all things be done with charity."

*Galatians 5:13: ". . . use not liberty for an occasion to the flesh, but by love serve one another."

*Ephesians 3:17-19: "[be] rooted and grounded in love [that you] may be able to comprehend with all saints what is the breadth, and length, and depth, and height; And to know the love of Christ . . . that ye might be filled with all the fullness of God."

*Ephesians 4:1-3,15,16: ". . . walk worthy of the vocation wherewith ye are called, with all lowliness and meekness, with longsuffering, forbearing one another in love; endeavoring to keep the unity of the Spirit in the bond of peace. [Speak] the truth in love, [that you] may grow up into him in all things, which is the head, even Christ: From whom the whole body fitly joined together and compacted by that which every joint supplieth, according to the effectual working in the measure of every part, maketh increase of the body unto the edifying of itself in love."

*Ephesians 5:2: ". . . walk in love, as Christ also hath loved us, and hath given himself for us an offering and a sacrifice to God . . ."

*Philippians 1:9: "[Let] your love . . . abound yet more and more in knowledge and in all judgment."

*Philippians 2:2: ". . . be ye likeminded, having the same love, being of one accord, of one mind."

*Colossians 1:4,7,8: ". . . [love] all the saints, [be] a faithful minister of Christ; [declare] your love in the Spirit."

*Colossians 2:2: "[Let your heart] be comforted . . . knit together in love, and unto all riches of the full assurance of understanding . . ."

*Colossians 3:14: ". . . put on love, which is the bond of perfectness."

*I Thessalonians 3:12,13: ". . . increase and abound in love one toward another, and toward all men . . . stablish your hearts unblamable in holiness before God . . ."

*I Thessalonians 4:9: ". . . love one another . . ."

*I Thessalonians 5:8: ". . . [put] on the breastplate of faith and love . . ."

*II Thessalonians 1:3: "[let] the charity of every one of you all toward each other [abound]."

*II Thessalonians 3:5: ". . . direct your hearts into the love of God . . ."

*I Timothy 1:5: "Now the end of the commandment is [love] out of a pure heart, and of a good conscience, and of faith unfeigned."

*I Timothy 4:12: ". . . be thou an example of the believers, in word, in conversation, in [love] . . ."

*I Timothy 6:11: ". . . follow after righteousness, godliness, faith, love, patience, meekness."

*II Timothy 2:22: ". . . follow righteousness, faith, [love], peace, with them that call on the Lord out of a pure heart."

*II Timothy 3:10,14: ". . . fully [know] . . . doctrine . . . purpose, faith, longsuffering, [love], patience, [and] continue thou in the things which thou hast learned and hast been assured of . . ."

*Titus 1:7,8,14: ". . . a bishop must be blameless . . . not selfwilled, not soon angry . . . a lover of good men . . . Not giving heed to . . . commandments of men, that turn from the truth."

Ministers, especially, are to:

*Titus 2:1,2: ". . . speak . . . the things which become sound doctrine: That the aged men be sober, grave, temperate, sound in faith, in [love], in patience."

*Titus 3:1-3: ". . . be subject to principalities and powers . . . obey magistrates . . . ready to every good work . . . speak evil of no man . . . be no [brawler], but gentle, showing all meekness unto all men. For we ourselves also were sometimes foolish, disobedient, deceived, serving divers lusts and pleasures, living in malice and envy, hateful, and hating one another.''

The Spirit of God again admonishes us to:

*Hebrews 13:1: "Let brotherly love continue."

*I Peter 1:22: "[purify our] souls in obeying the truth . . . unto unfeigned love of the brethren [and] love [for] one another with a pure heart . . ."

*I Peter 2:17: "Honour all men. Love the brotherhood."

*I Peter 3:8,9: "be . . . all of one mind, having compassion one of another, love as brethren . . . Not rendering evil for evil, or railing for railing: but contrariwise blessing."

*I Peter 4:8: ". . . above all things have fervent [love] among yourselves: for [love] shall cover the multitude of sins."

*I Peter 5:14: "Greet . . . one another with a kiss of [love]."

*II Peter 1:5-8: ". . . add to your faith virtue; and to virtue knowledge; and to knowledge temperance; and to temperance patience; and to patience god-liness; and to godliness brotherly kindness; and to brotherly kindness [love]. For if these things be in you, and abound, they make you that ye shall neither be barren nor unfruitful . . ."

Further scriptural instruction tells us that:

*I John 2:9-11: "He that saith he is in the light, and hateth his brother, is in darkness even until now [but] he that loveth his brother abideth in the light, and there is none occasion of stumbling in him. But he that hateth his brother is in darkness, and walketh in darkness, and knoweth not wither he goeth, be-cause that darkness hath blinded his eyes."

Heart Disease in Christ's Body

*I John 3:10,11,14-18: "In this the children of God are manifest, and the children of the devil: whosoever doeth not righteousness is not of God, neither he that loveth not his brother. For this is the message that ye have heard from the beginning, that we should love one another. We know that we have passed from death unto life, because we love the brethren. He that loveth not his brother abideth in death. Whosoever hateth his brother is a murderer: and ye know that no murderer hath eternal life abiding in him. Hereby perceive we the love of God, because he laid down his life for us: and we ought to lay down our lives for the brethren. But whoso hath this world's good, and seeth his brother have need, and shutteth up his bowels of compassion from him, how dwelleth the love of God in him? My little children, let us not love in word, neither in tongue; but in deed and in truth."

*I John 3:23: "And this is his commandment, That we should believe on the name of his Son Jesus Christ, and love one another, as he gave us commandment."

*I John 4:7,8: "Beloved, let us love one another: for love is of God; and every one that loveth is born of God, and knoweth God. He that loveth not knoweth not God; for God is love."

*I John 4:10-12,16,20,21: "Herein is love, not that we loved God, but that he loved us, and sent his Son to be the propitiation for our sins. Beloved, if God so loved us, we ought also to love one another . . . If we love one another, God dwelleth in us, and his love is perfected in us . . . God is love; and he that dwelleth in love dwelleth in God, and God in him. If a man say, I love God, and hateth his brother, he is a liar: for he that loveth not his brother whom he hath seen how can he love God whom he hath not seen? And this commandment have we from him, That he who loveth God love his brother also."

*I John 5:2: "By this we know that we love the children of God, when we love God, and keep his commandments."

*II John 5: "And now I beseech thee . . . love one another."

*Jude 21: "Keep yourselves in the love of God . . ."

But who are our brothers we are to love?

*Matthew 12:50: ". . . whosoever shall do the will of my Father which is in heaven, the same is my brother . . ."

*Mark 3:35: ". . . whosoever shall do the will of God, the same is my brother . . ."

B. Love for our neighbors

* Matthew 19:19: ". . . Thou shalt love thy neighbor as thyself."

* Matthew 22:39: ". . . Thou shalt love thy neighbor as thyself."

* Mark 12:30,31: ". . . thou shalt love the Lord thy God with all thy heart, and with all thy soul, and with all thy mind, and with all thy strength: This is the first commandment. And the second is like, namely this, Thou shalt love thy neighbor as thyself. There is none other commandment greater than these."

* Romans 13:9,10: ". . . Thou shalt love thy neighbor as thyself. Love worketh no ill to his neighbor: therefore love is the fulfilling of the law."

* Galatians 5:14: "For all the law is fulfilled in one

word, even in this; Thou shalt love thy neighbor as thyself."

* James 2:8: "If ye fulfill the royal law according to the scripture, Thou shalt love thy neighbor as thyself . . ."

C. Love even for our enemies

* Matthew 5:44-46: ". . . Love your enemies, bless them that hate you, and pray for them which despitefully use you, and persecute you; That ye may be the children of your Father which is in heaven . . . For if ye love them which love you, what reward have ye? do not even the publicans the same?"

* Luke 6:27,28,35: ". . . Love your enemies, do good to them which hate you, Bless them that curse you, and pray for them which despitefully use you . . . love ye your enemies, and do good, and lend, hoping for nothing again; and your reward shall be great, and ye shall be the children of the Highest: for he is kind unto the unthankful and to the evil."

* Romans 12:14,17: "Bless them which persecute you: bless, and curse not. Recompense to no man evil for evil. Provide things honest in the sight of all men."

* Galatians 6:10: "As we have therefore opportunity, let us do good unto all men, especially unto them who are of the household of faith."

* I Thessalonians 5:14,15: ". . . be patient toward all men. See that none render evil for evil unto any man; but ever follow that which is good, both among yourselves, and to all men."

IV. Make peace with our brothers

* Psalm 34:14: ". . . seek peace, and pursue it."

* Matthew 5:9: "Blessed are the peacemakers: for they shall be called the children of God."

* Mark 9:50: ". . . have peace one with another."

* Luke 2:13,14: "And suddenly there was with the angel a multitude of the heavenly host praising God, and saying, Glory to God in the highest, and on earth peace, good will toward men."

* Romans 12:18: ". . . live peaceably with all men."

* Romans 14:19: ". . . follow after the things which make for peace, and things wherewith one may edify another."

* II Corinthians 13:11: ". . . live in peace."

* Galatians 5:22,23,25: ". . . the fruit of the Spirit is love, joy, peace, longsuffering, gentleness, goodness, faith, meekness, temperance . . . If we live in the Spirit, let us also walk in the Spirit."

* Ephesians 4:3: "Endeavoring to keep the unity of the Spirit in the bond of peace."

* Ephesians 6:23: "Peace be to the brethren, and love with faith . . ."

* Colossians 3:15: ". . . let the peace of God rule in your hearts . . ."

* I Thessalonians 5:13: "Be at peace among yourselves."

* Hebrews 12:14: "Follow peace with all men . . ."

* James 3:17,18: ". . . the wisdom that is from above is . . . peaceable . . . And the fruit of righteousness is sown in peace of them that make peace."

* I Peter 3:10-12: ". . . refrain [thy] tongue from evil, and [thy] lips that they speak no guile . . . eschew evil, and do good . . . seek peace, and ensue it. For the eyes of the Lord are over the righteous, and his ears are open unto their prayers: but the face of the Lord is against them that do evil."

* I Peter 5:14: "Greet ye one another with a kiss of charity. Peace be with you all that are in Christ Jesus."

* II Peter 3:14: ". . . be diligent that ye may be found of him in peace, without spot, and blameless."

V. Forgiveness of brothers

Look again at Scripture's clear teaching on this matter:

*Matthew 6:12: ". . . forgive [your] debtors."

*Matthew 18:21,22: ". . . how oft shall my brother sin against me, and I forgive him? till seven times? Jesus saith . . . Until **seventy** times seven."

*Mark 11:25,26: ". . . when ye stand praying, forgive, if ye have ought against any . . . if ye do not forgive, neither will your Father which is in heaven forgive your trespasses."

*Luke 6:37: ". . . forgive, and ye shall be forgiven."

*Luke 11:4: ". . . forgive every one that is indebted to [you]."

*Luke 17:3,4: ". . . If thy brother trespass against thee, rebuke him; and if he repent, forgive him. And if he trespass against thee seven times in a day, and seven times in a day turn again to thee, saying, I repent: thou shalt forgive him."

*II Corinthians 2:7: ". . . ye ought rather to forgive . . ."

*Ephesians 4:30-32: ". . . grieve not the Holy Spirit of God . . . Let all bitterness, and wrath, and anger, and clamour, and evil speaking, be put away from you, with all malice: And be ye kind one to another, tenderhearted, forgiving one another, even as God for Christ's sake hath forgiven you."

*Colossians 3:12-14: "Put on therefore, as the elect of God, holy and beloved, bowels of mercies, kindness, humbleness of mind, meekness, long-suffering; Forbearing one another, and forgiving one another . . ."

VI. Show meekness toward brothers

*Zephaniah 2:3: ". . . seek meekness."

*Matthew 5:5: "Blessed are the meek: for they shall inherit the earth."

*Matthew 11:28-30: "Come unto me, all ye that labor and are heavy laden, and I will give you rest. Take my yoke upon you, and learn of me; for I am meek and lowly in heart: and ye shall find rest unto your souls. For my yoke is easy, and my burden is light."

*I Peter 3:4: "[Put on] the ornament of a meek and quiet spirit, which is in the sight of God of great price."

*Galatians 6:1,2: "Brethren, if a man be overtaken in a fault, ye which are spiritual, restore such an one in the spirit of meekness; considering thyself, lest thou also be tempted. Bear ye one another's burdens, and so fulfill the law of Christ."

*I Timothy 6:11: ". . . follow after righteousness, godliness, faith, love, patience, meekness."

*II Timothy 2:24,25: ". . . the servant of the Lord must not strive; but be gentle unto all men, apt to teach, in meekness instructing those that oppose themselves."

VII. Be longsuffering toward brothers

*II Corinthians 6:3-6: "[Give] no offense in any thing, that the ministry be not blamed: But in all things [approve yourselves] as the ministers of God, in much patience . . . By pureness, by knowledge, by longsuffering, by kindness . . . by love unfeigned."

*Ephesians 4:1,2: ". . . walk worthy of the vocation wherewith ye are called, with all lowliness and meekness, with long-suffering, forbearing one another in love."

*Colossians 1:10,11: ". . . walk worthy of the Lord unto all pleasing, being fruitful in every good work, and increasing in the knowledge of God . . . unto all patience and longsuffering with joyfulness."

*Colossians 3:12,13: "Put on . . . bowels of mercies, kindness, humbleness of mind, meekness, longsuffering; Forbearing one another, and forgiving one another . . ."

*II Timothy 3:10: ". . . fully [know] doctrine . . . purpose, faith, longsuffering, charity, patience."

*II Timothy 4:2: "Preach the word; be instant in season, out of season; reprove, rebuke, exhort with all longsuffering and doctrine."

272

VIII. Do good to all brothers

*Psalm 34:14: "Depart from evil, and do good."

*Psalm 37:27: ". . . do good; and dwell forevermore."

*Matthew 5:44: ". . . Love your enemies, bless them that curse you, do good to them that hate you, and pray for them which despitefully use you, and persecute you."

*Luke 2:14: "[Practice] good will toward men."

*Luke 6:27: ". . . Love your enemies, do good to them which hate you."

*Luke 6:35: ". . . love ye your enemies, and do good . . . and your reward shall be great, and ye shall be the children of the Highest: for he is kind unto the unthankful and to the evil."

*Galatians 6:10: ". . . let us do good unto all men . . ."

*Colossians 1:10: "[Be] fruitful in every good work . . ."

*I Thessalonians 5:15: ". . . follow that which is good, both among yourselves, and to all men."

*Titus 2:7,8: "[Show yourself] a pattern of good works . . . that he that is of the contrary part may be ashamed, having no evil thing to say of you."

*Hebrews 10:24: ". . . consider one another to provoke unto love and to good works."

*James 3:17,18: "[Seek] wisdom that is from above . . . full of mercy and good fruits . . . the fruit of righteousness is sown in peace of them that make peace."

*I Peter 3:10,11: ". . . he that will love life, and see good days . . . Let him eschew evil, and do good . . ."

IX. Be kind to brothers

*Romans 12:10: "Be kindly affectioned one to another with brotherly love."

*I Corinthians 13:4: "Charity suffereth long, and is kind."

*II Corinthians 6:4-6: ". . . in all things [approve yourselves] as the ministers of God . . . In stripes, in imprisonments, in tumults, in labor, in watchings, in fastings, By pureness, by knowledge, by long-suffering, by kindness."

*Ephesians 4:32: ". . . be ye kind one to another . . ."

*Colossians 3:12: "Put on therefore, as the elect of God, holy and beloved, bowels of mercies, kindness . . ."

*II Peter 1:5-7: ". . . add to your faith virtue; and to virtue knowledge; And to knowledge temperance; and to temperance patience; and to patience god-liness; And to godliness brotherly kindness."

X. Be gentle to brothers

*Galatians 5:22,23: ". . . the fruit of the Spirit is love, joy, peace, longsuffering, gentleness, good-ness, faith, meekness, temperance: against such there is no law."

*I Thessalonians 2:7,8: ". . . we were gentle among you . . . because ye were dear to us."

*II Timothy 2:24: ". . . the servant of the Lord must . . . be gentle unto all men . . ."

*Titus 3:2: ". . . speak evil of no man . . . be no brawlers, but gentle . . ."

*James 3:17: ". . . the wisdom that is from above is . . . gentle . . ."

XI. Admonish brothers

*I Thessalonians 5:12: ". . . know them which labor among you, and are over you in the Lord, and admonish you."
*II Thessalonians 3:15: ". . . admonish [your] brother."

XII. Have compassion on brothers

*I Peter 3:8: ". . . be ye all of one mind, having compassion one of another, love as brethren . . . be courteous."

XIII. Pray for brothers

*I Thessalonians 5:25: "Brethren, pray for us."
*James 5:16: ". . . pray one for another . . ."

When these many commands from God's Word have been effectively woven into a Christian life, the result is a tenderness of spirit that immediately identifies that individual as a child of God and a true servant of the Lord Jesus Christ. It reflects the fullness of the Spirit, and speaks of Christian maturity. Frances R. Havergal describes this tenderness of spirit as "October Mellowness," and discusses its nature and work in an article by that title in the October 1983 issue of **Herald of His Coming**. May the following excerpt speak to your heart:

Heart Disease in Christ's Body

"It is much easier to convince a human soul of its natural impurity than to convince it of its natural hardness, and utter destitution of heavenly and divine tenderness of spirit. The very essence of the Gospel is a divinely imparted tenderness and sweetness of spirit. Without this, even the strongest religious life is a misrepresentation of the true Christlife. Even among intensely religious people, nothing is more rare to find than a continuous, all-pervading spirit of tenderness.

"Tenderness of spirit is preeminently divine. It is not the delicacy and soft sensibility of a mere gentle make-up of body and mind, which some persons naturally possess in a high degree. Neither is it the tenderness of mind and manner which results from high culture and beautiful social training, though these are very valuable in life.

"But it is a supernatural work throughout the whole spiritual being. It is an exquisite interior fountain of God's own sweetness and tenderness of nature, opened up in the inner spirit to such a degree that it completely inundates the soul, overflowing all the mental faculties, and saturating with its sweet waters the manners, expressions, words, and tones of the voice: mellowing the will, softening the judgments, melting the affections, refining the manners and moulding the whole being after the image of Him who was infinitely meek and lowly in heart. It cannot be borrowed, or put on for special occasions. It is emphatically supernatural, and must flow out incessantly from the inner fountains of the life, and resembles having every atom of our being soaked in sweet oil.

"Deep tenderness of spirit is the very soul and marrow of the Christlife. Without it, the most vigorous life of righteousness and good works, and rigid purity of morals, and missionary zeal, and profuse liberality, and ascetic self-denial, and the most blameless conduct — utterly fail to measure up to the Christlife unveiled in the New Testament.

"It is impossible to see the infinite excellence and necessity of real heavenly tenderness of spirit unless it is specially revealed to us by the Holy Ghost. It takes a direct revelation from God to enable us to discern what is the very marrow and fatness of Christ's character, the inexpressible tenderness and gentleness of His nature which is always the heart inside of the heart, the soul within the soul, of the Christlife.

"What specific gravity is to the planet, what beauty is to the rainbow, what perfume is to the rose, what marrow is to the bone, what rhythm is to poetry, what sublimity is to the ocean, what the pulse is to the heart, what harmony is to music, what heat is to the human body — all this and much more is what tenderness of spirit is to religion.

"Without tenderness of spirit the most intensely righteous, religious life is like the image of God without His beauty and attractiveness. It is possible to be very religious, and stanch, and persevering in all Christian duties, even to be sanctified, and be a brave defender and preacher of holiness, to be mathematically orthodox, and blameless in outward life, and very zealous in good works — and yet to be greatly lacking in tenderness of spirit, that all-subduing, all melting love, which is the very cream and quintessence of Heaven, and which incessantly streamed out from the eyes and voice of the blessed Jesus.

"Many religious people seem loaded with good fruits, but the fruit tastes green. It lacks flavor and October mellowness. There is a touch of vinegar in their sanctity. Their very purity has an icy coldness to it. They seem to have a baptism on them, but it is not composed of those sweet spices of cinnamon, and calamus, and cassia, which God told Moses to compound as a fragrant type of the real sweetness of the Holy Spirit. Their testimonies are straight and definite, but they lack the melting quality. Their prayers are intelligent, and strong and pointed, but they lack the heart-piercing pathos of the dying Jesus. The summer heat in them is lacking. They preach eloquently and explain with utmost nicety what is actual and original sin, and what is pardon and purity, but they lack the burning flame, that interior furnace of throbbing love that sighs and weeps and breaks down under the shivering heat of all-consuming love.

"This all pervading tenderness of spirit is not a novitiate grace. It is not a product of April but of October.

"No scene in the Bible opens up a greater vista into the tenderness of the spirit of Jesus, than where He stooped and wrote on the ground, as if His modest and loving heart did not want to hear the horrible account of evil. As we gaze on the soul of Jesus at that time, we see infinite politeness, both toward the accused and accusers; not a trace of unkindness or severity to either party. His whole manner and speech and disposition filled the whole air as with a very sea of refinement, gentleness and inexpressive sweetness of spirit.

"This and similar acts of Jesus is like an opening between mountains, through which we look far off on an outspreading silver sea of love, whose every undulation presents a new phase of unspeakable tenderness toward the poor sinner he came to save. Tenderness of spirit makes its home in the bosom of Jesus, and from that holy castle looks out upon all other creatures, good and bad, through the hopeful, pleading medium of the heart that was pierced on the cross. Tenderness of spirit is in divine sympathy with the poor and downtrodden and unfortunate and hated classes of mankind.

"It feels for the poor or any that are the common butt of worldly scorn. Whenever it hears of any of these spoken of in a harsh and bitter way, it feels a dagger pierce its own heart and a tear of sympathy comes to its eye, and a piercing silent prayer ascends from it to that God who hears the sighing of the prisoner and the cries of the unfortunate. It feels all things from God's standpoint, and lives but to receive and transmit the spotless sympathies and affections of Jesus. It understands the words of the Holy Ghost, "Be ye tenderhearted, forgiving one another" (Ephesians 4:32). Tenderness must be in our very nature, and forgiveness is but the behavior of that nature.

What a beautiful description of true Christianity — the outliving of "Christ in you" (Colossians 1:27). The potential of such a life is inherent within every born-again believer, yet few truly allow the blessed Holy Spirit to possess them so completely that the character and attitude of Christ are manifest in them.

Perhaps your heart was convicted as you studied the many instructions of God in this chapter. If so, why not surrender yourself anew to His leadership in your life. Make the following prayer your desire, today and forever:

"Heavenly Father, as your child I have fallen short of the image of Christ in so many ways. Forgive me. I recommit myself to you today, and seek the fulness of your Spirit in my life. Help me put away all bitterness, criticism, envying and selfishness, replacing them with the love, understanding, compassion and tenderness of your Son, my Saviour. I want to know and love others as He does — looking beyond their faults and seeing their needs. In Jesus' name I pray, Amen."

* * *

"Behold, how good and how pleasant
it is for brethren to dwell together in
unity!"

Chapter 14

God's Leaders Respond

In Psalm 133:1, King David expressed the joy of harmonious brotherhood by stating: "Behold, how good and how pleasant it is for brethren to dwell together in unity!" He then noted that such unity is Holy Spirit-induced by comparing it to the oil with which the priests of Israel were anointed into office, and to the life-giving moisture which caused the land itself to burst forth abundantly.

Today, my heart is filled with joy because of the overwhelming response to my article, "That They All May Be One." Since its release, hundreds of Christian leaders and laymen alike have written to express the fact that their hearts and spirits are united with mine in seeking to love and reconcile the brethren. Excerpts of their letters compose the contents of this chapter.

The following comments were received from outstanding **interdenominational** leaders in our nation:

> Dr. Carl McIntire
> Bible Presbyterian Church
> Collingswood, New Jersey

My dear Jack:

I have read your article, "That They All May Be One." I could not agree with it more. If we would all stand for the inerrant Scriptures and focus our guns on the apostates and the sin of communion with them, it would be a different story.

The fingers of the hand which you display mentions us, the Bible Presbyterians. I am going to send you under separate cover a copy of our constitution. It shows that our position is the basis of our worldwide fellowship.

To keep the emphasis where it needs to be is what Satan is seeking to frustrate. There are so many areas where men are confused, and you have described some of these situations in your statement. Be of good courage.

> Faithfully, your friend,
> Carl

* * *

> Paul B. Smith, Co-Pastor
> (Son of Oswald J. Smith)
> The People's Church, Toronto
> Willowdale, Ontario, CANADA

My dear Jack,

Thank you so much for your letter and the copy of your magazine. It was good to hear from you.

Would you give me permission to re-print your article, "That They All May Be One" in **The People's Magazine**? This reaches approximately 10,000 of our adherents in the Metropolitan Toronto area. I think it would be just as great a blessing to them as it has been to me.

We hear you quite often by way of television. Your ministry has been a blessing.

Awaiting word from you at your convenience, I remain,

> Yours faithfully,
> Paul B. Smith

* * *

Dr. Paul Freed, President
Trans World Radio
Chatham, New Jersey

Dear Brother Jack:

Betty Jane and I enjoyed so much being with you and Rexella the other day. How we do thank the Lord for you and the fellowship that is ours, both personally and in reaching so many needy hearts with the Gospel.

We have been thinking about you these days, trusting that the Lord has been with you in a special way. I am sure as you step out in obedience to His most recent workings in your life, He will honor your ministry even more.

I personally want you to know how much I value your fellowship in the Lord and your very great contribution to the task of proclaiming the Gospel to the many millions who need to hear of our Saviour's redeeming love.

> Your friend in Christ,
> Paul

* * *

> Dr. Richard Seume, Chaplain
> Dallas Theological Seminary
> Dallas, Texas

My dear Jack:

Thank you so very much for your gracious letter. I remember the occasions when you and Rexella ministered in Immanuel Baptist Church in Richmond. Those were good days in many ways.

I read your article in the magazine and appreciated the spirit in which it was written. It would be my hope and prayer that the brethren might accept it in the spirit in which it was written. Be assured of my love and appreciation for your continued ministry, Jack.

> Cheerily,
> Dick

* * *

284

Dr. Peter F. Nieuwkoop
Truth Publications
Elk Rapids, Michigan

Dear Brother Jack:

Greetings from northern Michigan. My purpose in writing you is to commend you for your apology to the body of Christ. I admire you for taking this public stand. You will no doubt get a lot of heat for it and even lose some support. But you have done the right thing. I came to this same conclusion thirty years ago.

Greetings to Rexella, and may the Lord continue to bless and use you. If I can be of help, let me know.

Sincerely in Him,
Peter F. Nieuwkoop

* * *

Board of Bishops
Free Methodist Church
of North America
Winona Lake, Indiana

Dear Brother Jack:

Thank you for your article entitled, "That They All May Be One." My heart reverberates with yours in the concern expressed for unity in the body of Christ.

It is my prayer that the Holy Spirit will continue to anoint you in your ministry during these tremendous days of opportunity for the Gospel in our world.

Faithfully yours,
Robert F. Andrews

* * *

E. Brandt Gustavson,
Vice President
Moody Bible Institute
Chicago, Illinois

Dear Jack:

I appreciated receiving a copy of the text, "That They All May Be One."

We will be praying for you in the days ahead, that the Lord will show you His great love. We are appreciative of your standing lovingly, yet firmly, for our Lord Jesus Christ and His blessed Word.

Warmly in His Name,
E. Brandt Gustavson

* * *

Warren W. Wiersbe
Back To The Bible Broadcast
Lincoln, Nebraska

Dear Dr. Van Impe:

Thank you very much for your letter and for the copy of your article, "That They All May Be One."

I came to similar conclusions some years ago and, of course, like you, I have suffered for them.

I trust that God will bless you as you seek to build bridges instead of walls. I know that God's hand is upon those who seek to love and serve Him.

Sincerely, your friend in Christ,
Warren W. Wiersbe

* * *

Dr. Theodore H. Epp
Back To The Bible Broadcast
Lincoln, Nebraska

My dear Brother Van Impe:

I had the joy of reading your article about your stand with reference to separation.

I couldn't help but feel I should write and tell you how much I appreciated the kind, loving way you expressed yourself while taking a definite stand quite opposite of what you have been doing in some areas, yet not condemning those who take such an ultra-separatist stand. I just wanted to commend you and encourage you and thank you for the way you handled this very touchy subject, yet important matter.

Yours in Christ,
Theodore H. Epp

* * *

Rev. Chuck Wagner,
Executive Producer
Moody Broadcasting Network
Chicago, Illinois

Dear Dr. Van Impe:

Thank you for being our guest on Moody Broadcasting Network's OPEN LINE. We had many follow-up calls to the program, expressing thanks for having you on and to commend you for your gracious spirit and willingness to share what you did. It was a good program, and I'm sure we have challenged many people as they have considered their relationship with our Lord and with fellow servants.

Sincerely,

Chuck

* * *

Dr. John C. Whitcomb
Grace Theological Seminary
Winona Lake, Indiana

Dear Dr. Van Impe:

Thank you very much for your fascinating article in the November/December, 1982, issue of **Perhaps Today** on "That They All May Be One."

For a number of years, I have taught a course in Grace Theological Seminary entitled, "Biblical Fundamentalism." In this course, we struggle with many of the issues that you have dealt with in your article. I am enclosing a copy of my paper entitled, "God's Truth Circles," trusting that it may be of some interest to you as you continue to investigate God's Word on the vital subject of unity and separation in Christian ministry.

Sincerely yours in Him,

John C. Whitcomb

* * *

Lawrence Stone, Executive Editor
Thomas Nelson Publishers
Nashville, Tennessee

Dear Dr. Van Impe:

Your article is a truly remarkable one that shows
the love of the Lord Jesus Christ. I am afraid that you
will be criticized and slandered for what you are
saying, and for that reason you are much in my
prayers. But I also feel confident beyond a shadow of
a doubt that you are following what the Lord would
have you do.

    Sincerely yours,
    Larry

* * *

The Staff of the National
Religious Broadcasters
Morristown, New Jersey

Dear Dr. Van Impe:

Your address at the Eastern NRB Convention
touched all of us from the NRB staff for its depth, its
honesty and its courage. We applaud the stand you
are taking, and we will continue to uphold you in our
prayers. Perhaps the Lord is leading many others to
follow your example and to reach out in love to all
who are dedicated to the Gospel.

    Cordially in Christ,
    Audrey Langdon
    Public Relations
    Director

* * *

Dr. Ben Armstrong,
Executive Director
National Religious Broadcasters
Morristown, New Jersey

Dear Jack,

God indeed used your message. In fact, our delegates embraced you unanimously by a rising ovation after your spectacular talk.

It was apparent to all of us that God had given you sufficient courage to make such an incisive presentation. Your thoughts came across sincerely and the results were magnificent.

Everyone, in fact, is delighted with the courage you have displayed, and with the wonderful manner in which it was received by our people. Many are ready to help you in any way possible to implement this very historic decision. **Time Magazine** is considering an article on the subject, and others will follow.

Warm personal regards to you and Rexella from Ruth and myself.

Cordially yours in Christ,
Ben

* * *

Dr. Bill Gothard, President
Institute in Basic Youth Conflicts
Oakbrook, Illinois

Dear Jack and Rexella:

Thank you for taking the time out of your busy schedule to write to me and keep me updated on what the Lord is doing in your ministry.

I want to assure you of my continued prayer for you both, and for what God will be accomplishing through you.

May God give you that inward peace that surpasses human understanding as your hearts and minds are fixed upon the Lord Jesus Christ.

Bill

* * *

Rev. Richard J. McCarrell
(Grandson of Dr. William McCarrell, founder of the Independent Fundamental Churches of America)
Factoryville Bible Church
Athens, Michigan

Dear Dr. Van Impe:

We met a few years back when my grandfather introduced us. Since that time we have had a few bits of correspondence back and forth.

As a young fundamentalist, I have long been bothered and hurt by the backbiting, fighting, and verbal attacks upon brethren. When you spoke to the incident with Moody Bible Institute, I sympathized with you because I know how that bothered you at the time, and how it bothered my grandfather. Though I was still in school at that time, it was an incident which I will long remember as an example of needless fighting within the fundamentalist camp.

What I am saying is that I agree with the basic form

which you are coming from, and I realize that if there was anyone who has ever been attacked needlessly, it's been you. I, as well as many of the people from our church, are on your mailing list, have supported your work, are continuing to pray for you and will continue to pray for you and support you.

Joyfully in Christ,
Rev. Richard J. McCarrell

* * *

Dr. Leonard W. DeWitt,
President
Missionary Church
Fort Wayne, Indiana

Dear Brother Van Impe:

I greet you in the precious name of Jesus Christ. Someone just passed your article on to me concerning your apology to the body of Christ. I just had to write and say, "God bless you."

Jack, you have trumpeted forth what has been a burden on my heart for years. Tragically, it is not just denomination against denomination. From time to time we find the same attitude within a denomination, and even in local churches.

Let me assure you of my love for you, and that you have a brother in Christ in Ft. Wayne. If I can ever be of help or encouragement, please let me know.

In His Love,
Leonard

* * *

Revs. Ralph and Lou Sutera
Sutera Twins Crusade Team
Canadian Revival Fellowship
Mansfield, Ohio

Dear Brother Jack:

Lou and I were interested in your recent article in **Perhaps Today** regarding the way God has been dealing with you. We just wanted you to know that we are praying for you and thank God for the tremendous way in which He has revealed to you a much larger picture of the body of Christ.

We understand your stance on biblical separation, but we also believe that these principles need not be compromised when still seeking to live in the context of the unity of the Body of Christ. The love that God gives us for each other must include all blood-washed children of God.

We are certain that you will receive sharp criticism for your position, but be assured that there will be many who will "gravitate" to what God is doing in your life. Also, we personally believe God will use your voice to minister to many others who delight in their fundamental posture and yet have not seen this truth about the body of Christ. We know that God is already using the article. We appreciate the privilege to share it with others.

Let us believe God together that this will be a real "breakthrough" that God will use for revival in our day.

Yours in the Gospel,
Ralph and Lou Sutera

* * *

Rev. Willis Stitt,
Founder/Director General
Evangelical Enterprises
Topeka, Kansas

Dear Brother Van Impe:
I value your scriptural presentation and your spiritual attitude toward other believers as expressed in a recent issue of your magazine.
Yours in Christ,
Willis Stitt

* * *

Alfred E. Pontious, President
Alfred E. Pontious Ministries, Inc.
DeFuniak Springs, Florida

Dear Brother Van Impe:
I am now 75 years old and spent 42 years of pastoring with the IFCA, the GARBC and the BBF. I have just read your article, "That They All May Be One," and rejoice in the position you have taken.
In His love and fellowship,
Alfred E. Pontious

* * *

Rev. Marc Nelson
Rochester Bible Clubs
Rochester, New York

Dear Mr. Van Impe:

I just read your article and wholeheartedly agree. I am not welcome in most churches because I am a Calvinist.

I read your article and felt your pain, not so much for myself but for these brothers who are not fellow-shipping with anybody other than their own. To them, no one else is right. They only have the truth.

I love you and your wife and I don't care if we disagree over what I believe as compared to you. Be assured that I will continue to pray for you and Rexella.

In Christian love,
Marc Nelson

* * *

"Uncle Charlie" Van Dermeer,
Director Children's Bible Hour
Grand Rapids, Michigan
(Comments received via telephone)

Dear Dr. Van Impe:

Please send me ten copies of your article, "That They All May Be One." I feel this message is excellent and would like to distribute copies at our Board of Directors meeting.

* * *

295

Heart Disease in Christ's Body

Warren Bolthouse, Founder/President
Family Life Radio
Midland, Michigan

Dear Jack and Rexella:

Thank God for your stand! Your article "That They All May Be One" is timely.

While it is true that we must uphold scriptural truth regarding "separation," we've separated the separated, haven't we?

Your telecasts since your stand reflect a warmness that we need.

We love you.
Sincerely in Him,
Warren Bolthouse

* * *

Frank M. Severn, General Director
SEND International
Farmington, Michigan

Dear Brother Van Impe:

Warm greetings in Jesus' name!

I have read with great interest your letter and enclosed article concerning the need to show love in the Body of Christ. I say a hearty "Amen!" Thank you for sharing your heart's concerns.

We will continue to pray for revival. Lord, begin it in me! May God bless you and your ministry.

Warmly,
Frank M. Severn

* * *

Rev. Victor H. Ernest, President
Vital Christian Concerns, Inc.
Anoka, Minnesota

My Dear Brother in Christ:
Recently I received a heartwarming account "Why I discontinued Citywide crusades." Your letter was heartwarming to my heart for in it was only love for the brethren, love for God, humility, conviction and a very heavy heart. I know so very well what you are experiencing.

Continue to pray for our many brethren fallen with pride, envy, jealousy, resentments, anger, rebellion and false love. For many, they **have** their reward, the applause of man, self-glory. Oh what a tragedy!

Thanks again for the evidence of your innermost heart throb. You remind me of the myrr that has been crushed to bring forth an odor of soul sweetness.

In His Love and Victory,
Victor H. Ernest

* * *

G.M. Jones, Director
Visual Word Services
Prudenville, Michigan

Dear Brother Jack:
I so much appreciate your position on "unity of the brethren" in brotherly love according to God's Word!

Heart Disease in Christ's Body

Knowing your background and knowing you for so many years, I'm sure you will never compromise on basic fundamental doctrine. Hang in there, Jack! It surely will not be long now. PERHAPS! TODAY!

Yours in Calvary's bonds,
Glenn Jones

* * *

Rev. Donald Brewer, Youth Pastor
Peoples Church
Truro, Nova Scotia, CANADA

Dear Brother Van Impe:

I just finished reading your article and I want to say a heartwarming AMEN! The carnality and hypocrisy of ultra-separationism should be exposed for what it is.

Thank you so much for the article you wrote in the spirit of love. May God bless you and Rexella as you step out to serve Him afresh and anew.

In Christ,
Pastor Don Brewer

* * *

Rev. Lloyd G. Weidman, Jr.
Evangelical Free Church
Wellsburg, New York

Dear Dr. Van Impe:

What a tremendous testimony to the world your article was.

I have never been a Baptist, but I have always agreed with them in doctrine. I am a pastor at an Evangelical Free Church. In short, I love the Baptists, but there are other churches preaching the truth, too.

I praise God for you, my brother. You have spoken the truth. I forgive you, because your sponsoring pastors excluded me in Elmira, New York. I am sure the article was hard to write, but it shows your Christlikeness. You are dearly loved.

Sincerely,
Lloyd

* * *

Rev. Harold Mortenson
The Family Church
Seattle, Washington

Dear Dr. Van Impe:

Family greetings. I just read your article as you apologized to the body of Christ. It was fantastic. The eternal Spirit, "Our Father," has revealed Himself. You have been very receptive. May we become even greater channels.

Sincerely,
Harold A. Mortenson

* * *

Pastor Charles Williams
Calvary Bible Chapel
Wheaton, Illinois

Dear Jack:

I heard your telephone interview with Dr. Don Cole last night. Congratulations! Love for **all** of God's people with **no** compromise with error is a good path to follow. Please send me a copy of your statement.

Pastor Charlie Williams

* * *

Rev. H. Dalton Myers
Covenant Community Church
Redford, Michigan

Dear Jack:

My wife Wanda and I were privileged to be in attendance when you presented your message and position paper, and we say, "Thank you and God bless you."

Jack, I have a great burden for the unity of believers. There does seem to be many little kingdoms and little of the unity for which our Lord prayed. Maybe He will use you in a very special way to melt and mold, and encourage some of the hearts of the brethren. Please be assured of our prayers for your ministry, and our hopes for some further and enlarged fellowship.

Yours and His,
Dale

* * *

300

Dr. Paul E. Billheimer
(Noted author)

My dear brother:

Several people have written about your quote from my book in your magazine article entitled, "That They All May Be One." Permit me to express my appreciation. God has given me a great burden to get the message of unity to the Body of Christ. Your article will help immensely. May I tell you that I see your program frequently and appreciate immensely your strong conservative emphasis.

Mrs. Billheimer has just gone to be with the Lord. Your prayers will be appreciated.

In Christ,
Paul E. Billheimer

* * *

Gregory Peet, State Director
Upper Michigan
Child Evangelism Fellowship
Sault Ste. Marie, Michigan

Dear Doctor Van Impe:

I have read and re-read your article in the November/Decmeber, 1982, **Perhaps Today** entitled, "That They All May Be One."

It would take a lot of courage to **think** what you said, it would take a Log of courage to **say** what you said, but it would take **lots** of courage to **print** what you said. Praise the Lord for your willingness to say and print what needed to be said. Thank you for being willing to be vulnerable.

The enclosed check is for a year's subscription to **Perhaps Today** magazine.

In Christ,
Gregory Peet

* * *

Philip Yancey, Editorial Director
Campus Life Magazine
Carol Stream, Illinois

Dear Dr. Van Impe:

I received a copy of your article entitled "That They All May Be One." The decision you describe, as well as the courage to write the article, were beautiful examples of Christian character. I commend you on them, and I hope they will be strong examples to others in the body of Christ. I just wanted you to have this word of encouragement because I imagine you get some criticism for the same stand.

Cordially,
Philip Yancey

* * *

Dr. John R. Terry
Japan Journal
Nara Ken, Japan

Dear Brother Van Impe:

A friend (missionary) sent us your article, "That

They All May Be One.'' We read and thought we'd like to publish it in the next **Japan Journal**. It will be published just as you wrote it.

In His nail-pierced Hands,
Jack

* * *

Dr. George Verwer,
International Coordinator
Operation Mobilisation
Bromley, Kent, England

Dear Jack:

A friend and co-worker in Belgium, Mr. Len Brookes, passed on to me a copy of your article, ''That They All May Be One.'' My heart was greatly moved as I read it, and I really do praise God that you had the courage and love to write these greatly needed words.

I also appreciate the permission you gave for the article to be reprinted, and I would very much like to have it reprinted, especially to distribute to some of my co-workers laboring for the Lord all over the world. These same divisions and difficulties face us in an awesome way in many of the mission fields of the world today and greatly hinder the work of evangelism.

I hope and pray that we will have the privilege someday of meeting.

Yours in Christ,
George Verwer

* * *

Heart Disease in Christ's Body

Rev. Bob Beversdorf
Wheaton, Illinois

Dear Brother Jack:

I called WMBI the night you appeared because I wanted to commend you for the courage it took to say the things you said. Today, a co-worker handed me a copy of your article, "That They All May Be One." I was stunned as I read the article and again overwhelmed by the courage it took to publish it and take this stand.

In the course of time, I have discovered that many Christians often wallow in the mud-puddles of primary and secondary separatism while the Spirit of God moves others in a fresh, sparkling river of His blessing. I myself have had to go back and rebuild bridges burned behind, similar to the ones you have, as God has worked in my life using Philippians 1:15-18.

I am convinced that man will ostracize you for the stand you have taken and will continue to do so unless God intervenes. I am also convinced that your stand will have a positive impact for greater oneness in the body of Christ.

I want to thank you and encourage you. I look forward to fellowship with you in glory at the Saviour's feet.

Your brother in Christ,
Bob Beversdorf

* * *

Dr. Torrey Johnson
Wheaton, Illinois

Dear Dr. Van Impe:

I have read with Christian love and joy your article and the further articles on separation. Love, grace, humility and truth were alive in every paragraph. I love you for all of it, and I am in full accord with all you have written.

You will have my continuing support and prayers. Anything I can do to strengthen your ministry I will do. Just let me know if I can lend a hand. The best is yet to come.

Your brother in Christ,
Torrey Johnson

* * *

Dr. Dwight L. Chappell
Middletown Christian School
Middletown, Illinois

Dear Dr. Van Impe:

Truly the Spirit of God sovereignly "blows where it pleases" (John 3:8). I am thankful that He has brought into your heart a fresh appreciation for the breadth of the body of Christ and granted you the courage to take the stand which you have taken.

I know that you will receive much abuse and be called a turncoat by certain militant separatists. Take comfort in the knowledge that you have spoken God's truth and that others have shared your pilgrimage as well. Take courage also to continue speaking out so that others will follow your stand.

Over the years, God has gradually shown me the difference between being a militant separatistic fundamentalist and being truly regenerate. Sometimes a person can be both of these things, but many times it seems that these individuals are the former without being the latter. I am forced to conclude this because their entire personality and "ministry" are characterized entirely by the works of the flesh and show absolutely no evidence of the fruit of the Spirit.

I fear that many of our so-called fundamental churches and schools are filled with people who have found a similar sociopolitical temperament grouping — super patriots, anti-communists, laissez-faire capitalists and pugnacious personalities — all bound together by a "don't change anything" mentality — but who are devoid of the knowledge of God. Their time is spent in a great continual pursuit of empire building and constant debate over "who is the greatest in the kingdom."

Truly, many who are first shall be last.

Sincerely in Christ,
Dwight L. Chappell

* * *

Dr. William R. Bright
Campus Crusade for Christ
San Bernardino, California

Dear Rev. Van Impe:
Thanks for your wonderful ministry and for the

stand you are taking for wholeness in the body of Christ. You are a source of encouragement to me and many others.

Sincerely and cordially,
Bill Bright

***

Dr. Holland B. London, Chancellor
California Graduate School of Theology
Glendale, California

My Good Friend Dr. Van Impe:

I heard you on television on a Sunday night, and want you to know that I have never been so proud of any minister as I was of you that night. You said exactly what I was trying to say for several years.

I will predict that your ministry will become one of the most outstanding ministries in America because of the definite stand you have taken to be your own man under the inspiration of the Holy Spirit.

As ever,
Holland London

* * *

Dr. Roy L. Aldrich, Sr.,
Founder & President Emeritus
Detroit Bible College
    (now William Tyndale College)
and Presbyterian Leader
New Port Richey, Florida

Dear Jack:

Just a note from your old friend to say that I heartily approve of your new and broader stand about Christian fellowship and separation. Also, I appreciate your courage in apologizing to some you had offended by your former stand.

I continue to support your ministry by prayer and as a Video Volunteer.

Love in Him,
Roy

* * *

L.J. Stucky, Editor
Herald of His Coming
Los Angeles, California

Dear Brother in Christ:

We thank the Lord for everything He is doing to prepare His people for His coming. We also thank the Lord for His dealing in your life and your humble response. Cost what it may to obey God, the results are worth it.

Be assured of our prayers for you as you endeavor to get the body of Christ to love one another with a pure heart fervently. God bless you and your wife and increase your ministry more and more.

In His blessed service,
L. J. Stucky

* * *

Edwin D. Palmer, U.S. Director
Worldwide Evangelization Crusade
Fort Washington, Pennsylvania

Dear Brother Jack:

I want to tell you how much I appreciate what you have written, and how fully I identify with you in the

Lord's leading through this time of very great heartache.

This note is just to assure you of our love and support of you by prayer. May God be pleased to give you an even wider and more fruitful ministry than what you have known in the past years. We join you in the heartcry for a "genuine revival" which will sweep across denominational barriers and make us to be what we are meant to be: one body in Christ.

Sincerely in Him we love,
Edwin Palmer

* * *

Rev. Don Christianson,
General Director
United World Mission, Inc.
St. Petersburg, Florida

Dear Rev. Van Impe:

Your article arrived on my desk today. What a refreshment it was.

There is not a one of us who has not made mistakes in our ministries, but few of us are willing to admit them. Instead, we try to justify our actions and build a wall of pride around ourselves. I want to thank you so much for the example that you are allowing yourself to be to the body of Christ in publicly asking forgiveness for past wrongs and actively promoting oneness in the body of Christ.

May God help you as you embark on a great ministry of reconciliation. It is the most needed ministry today. I believe this new phase of your ministry will be even more fruitful than the one which you have just brought to a close.

Loving and Serving Him together,
Don Christianson

* * *

Fritz Ridenour, West Coast
Field Director
Fleming H. Revell Company
Old Tappan, New Jersey

Dear Jack:

I read your pamphlet, "That They All May Be One."

I have a real appreciation for your courage and humility. In the publishing field, I work with the "greats" and "near greats," but I seldom see anyone who exhibits the kind of commitment that translates into action that humbles or that risks being hurt. We evangelicals do a lot of blustering from the sidelines, but we are not always eager to play in the real game.

Thank you for your stand.

Cordially,
Fritz

* * *

Rev. R. Michael Steeves,
General Secretary/Treasurer
The Baptist Federation of Canada
Toronto, Ontario

Dear Dr. Van Impe:

I have just finished reading your article "That They All May Be One." May I commend you for your courageous stand on a vital issue to the Church in these days. Many men criticize you for having compromised or even abandoned the faith, but I would like to strongly endorse your stand and offer you a word of encouragement in what you have done in obedience to our Lord.

Your theme of unity within the body of Christ is one that I have echoed on numerous occasions. By that I do not mean that we should become one super church world-wide (I strongly oppose that approach). But we should stress our oneness in Christ and foster a greater ability to work together for the winning of the world to Him.

God has surely blessed you in your stand, and will certainly enhance and continue to bless your ministry as a result of your obedience to the leading of His Spirit.

Sincerely yours in fellowship and prayers,
R. Michael Steeves

* * *

Dr. Abe C. Van Der Puy,
Chairman of the Board
HCJB/World Radio Missionary Fellowship
Quito, Ecuador

Dear Brother Jack:
Sincerest greetings! You have blessed many with your confession and affirmation of Christian unity. I am one of the many.

I respect, love and appreciate you, Jack, and your dear wife. Our HCJB folks thank God for you, too.

Thank you for your inspiring and biblical example.
Very cordially in Christ,
Abe C. Van Der Puy

* * *

Chaplain Ray
International Prison Ministry
Dallas, Texas

Dear Brother Van Impe:
I had the good fortune to see your telecast yester-
day. You were saying things about the family of God
that need to be declared to the divided body of
believers. Christ is the issue. We are not. All who
belong to Jesus belong to each other.
May our Lord bless your ministry wonderfully.
Keep us in your prayers. You will be in ours.
In Christ our Lord,
Chaplain Ray

* * *

Dennis S. Boel, Pastor
First Church of the Nazarene
Birdsboro, Pennsylvania

Dear Brother Jack,
I want to tell you that I appreciate very much your
ministry. I listen to your message from the Word as
often as I can. The challenge you proclaim from the
Word comes through clearly, and I know it is being
used to touch many for Christ.

Please know that I appreciate your methodology regarding money, for it troubles me when some of my brothers in the ministry spend so much time pushing for money via their media programs. I don't share these remarks to be critical or negative, but to clarify why I appreciate your approach.

I say all this to just add my support for what I observe you are doing for Christ, and your attitude in doing it.

Very sincerely,
Dennis Boel

* * *

John Sholly, Pastor
First Grace Brethren Church
Des Moines, Iowa

Dear Jack:

I've personally always enjoyed your ministries. I was in a group in Western Pennsylvania where one of the crusade reps took a shot at the Grace Brethren Fellowship of Churches. I was serving as Associate Pastor in an I.F.C.A. church and ate those words many times.

When I was in college 21 years ago, I heard you in Kalamazoo, Michigan. You were the "Pastoral Image" I obtained and keep to this day. Obviously I am a Pastor now. (Grace Seminary, 1972)

Thank you for the honesty and openness in your tract "That They All May Be One."

I would like 200 copies of this tract to give to our

church in a "healing" effort.

Much love and respect in Christ,
Pastor John Sholly

* * *

Ronald Creech, Director of Development
Free Will Baptist Bible College
Nashville, Tennessee

Dear Dr. Van Impe:

I think the saddest indictment against funda-mentalism that I have ever read was your article, "That They All May Be One," giving your reasons why you discontinued citywide cursades.

I really do feel that the fracture that has taken place in the ranks of fundamentalism in the last several years has been so unfortunate. I know that as long as we agree on the fundamentals of the faith we can work together if we will be big enough. I know the Lord must grieve as He looks at our in-fighting with a world dying and going to hell.

I do hope that the stand you have taken and the stand of other fundamental leaders in the country will do something to heal the breach in fundamental circles in this country. The bride of Christ certainly embraces more people than just our little group. God help us all to see that.

May God's richest blessing rest upon you and your work.

Sincerely,
Ronald Creech

P.S. Thanks for sending me the extra copies of the article which I would like to send to some of the brethren in our group.

* * *

John A. Cahill
Heritage Christian School
Indianapolis, Indiana

Dear Brother Van Impe:

A friend just handed me your pamphlet entitled, "That They All May Be One." This explains to me some of the deprecatory remarks I read several months ago in one of our well-known Baptist publications concerning some changes in your ministry.

Those who are critical of a brother in Christ usually shout their condemnations from the housetops for all the world to hear. Just as often, those who agree remain approvingly silent. I decided not to be a member of "The Silent Majority" in this instance.

Jack, I just wanted you to know that I couldn't agree more with your sentiments and decisions as expressed in this pamphlet. I agree because I believe that you are on biblically sound grounds in the decisions that you have made. If this be true, is there anything else that really matters at the Bema Seat and in light of eternity? I shall pray for you, that God may continue to encourage you in your ministry and service for Him.

A Fellow Fundamental Baptist,
John A. Cahill

* * *

315

Heart Disease in Christ's Body

My heart has been deeply touched by these tremendous letters from interdenominational Christian leaders. Now may I present excerpts of letters from leaders within my own denomination. Again, I have been overwhelmed by the response. It would take many pages to print all that has been received. Therefore, I will share just a few of the comments from Baptist leaders:

> Dr. Jack Estep, General Director
> Conservative Baptist Home Mission Society
> Wheaton, Illinois

Dear Dr. Van Impe:

Just recently a friend of mine sent a copy of a newsletter article which described some of your thinking in relation to the super-separatist position. I just want to commend you for the graciousness, for the humility, and for the love which you have displayed in speaking on this particular subject.

I am sure you will receive much criticism, some threats and undoubtedly the lessening of some of your support from certain quarters. But I am just as sure that the Lord will honor your efforts and your desire to promote unity within His body. The Lord commanded Joshua to go neither to the right nor to the left of His Word. This means that it is just as wrong to be to the far-right of God's Word — that is making His Word say things that it does not say — as it is to be to the left — that is not accepting what God already had said. On one hand it would seem to be the safe side, on the other hand it would seem to be the soft side.

316

Perhaps the biggest task we have is that of making sure we are standing solidly on what God has said. I trust the Lord will enable you to deal with these issues with great wisdom and that you will enjoy God's blessing on your ministry in an even greater capacity than ever before. Again, I commend you in the name of the Lord.

With Christian love,
Jack

* * *

Rev. Jim W. Baize, Pastor
Midway Baptist Church
San Diego, California

Dear Dr. Van Impe:
I just wanted to write and let you know that I greatly appreciate your article entitled, "That They All May Be One."

Your article greatly touched my heart, and I hope that many other pastors and laymen who will read it will be just as touched as I was.

In His service,
Jim W. Baize

* * *

Rev. Gilbert Seddon, Pastor
Prior Lake Baptist Church
Prior Lake, Minnesota

Dear Dr. and Mrs. Van Impe:
A pastor friend in the area called me earlier this week to ask me if I had your article entitled, "That

317

They All May Be One.'' I did not receive my copy of the article until yesterday and have since read it through carefully.

I would like to say, Brother Van Impe, that the spirit of your article is, in my opinion, the greatest need of true Christians in our nation today. My heart has been grieved, as yours has, over the ''infighting'' among fundamentalists. I was saved in a fundamental Baptist church. I was trained in fundamental Baptist institutions (Pillsbury College and Central Seminary). I say all this to say that your explanation of this point was well presented.

I have followed your ministry through the years, and became a supporter a few months ago.

Yours in His Service,
Gil Seddon

* * *

Rev. Jim C. Lane, Pastor
Open Bible Baptist Church
Pontiac, Michigan

Dear Brother Van Impe:

I am pleased to read of your recent change of heart and new direction for your ministry. God has recently opened my eyes and we are making many changes in our ministry.

Your friend Rudy Schuermann, for one, has been helping me some. I appreciate a man in your position who will admit mistakes. Enclosed please find a small gift for your ministry.

In Christ,
Jim Lane

* * *

318

Rev. Randy A. McKinley, Pastor
Grafton Baptist Church
Grafton, Wisconsin

Dear Dr. Van Impe:

Over the past few years, I have had a very limited contact with your ministry. For some reason, my overall impressions have not been positive. Something caused me to "bristle" at some of your positions.

Just recently, I read your apology to the Body of Christ. The spirit in which it was written and the overall content was something that caused me to shout with joy. Such a concern for the Body of Christ is long overdue by the nationally known leaders of the church.

I do not know what type of response you have received, but be assured that at least one brother is sympathetic and will be in prayer now more fully than ever before.

Blessings on your ministry,
Randy A. McKinley

* * *

Rev. Phil Hulet, Pastor
Gospel Baptist Church
Lowellville, Ohio

Dear Dr. Van Impe,

About a year and a half ago, after graduating from Hyles Anderson College, God led me to Gospel Baptist Church. As the new pastor, I will support you. I believe in your ministry. God is using you to stand in the gap for Him in this day and age.

One of the reasons I believe God is blessing our work here is because we are supporting a ministry such as yours. Keep up the good work.

Sincerely,
Pastor Phil Hulet

* * *

Rev. Dan P. Bowers, Pastor
Hope Baptist Church
Augusta, Maine

Dear Jack:

I am writing to commend you for your apology to the Body of Christ as reported in the **Fundamentalist Journal** April issue. To publicly "bear your soul" as you have was a courageous act. How I wish that more Christian leaders might put aside pride and personal prejudice to pursue "peace with all men" and "the love of the brethren."

Several years ago when I was a teenager attending Calvary Baptist Church in Bristol, PA, you and your wife held a week of meetings. Your ministry helped nurture a desire in my heart to be a man of God and to preach the Word. God has been fulfilling that desire by making me a pastor.

Well brother, I just wanted to encourage you. You've gone "out on a limb," but I believe that the Lord will honor your courage.

Yours in Him,
Dan P. Bowers

* * *

Rev. Mark Grooms, Pastor
Fellowship Baptist Church
Lorton, Virginia

Dear Dr. Van Impe:

Your message, "That They All May Be One," is great and I couldn't agree more. The fundamental movement has suffered terribly in the past 15 years from its discord among the brethren over positions that won't amount to a hill of beans in eternity.

I was thrilled at your position and thankful for your boldness to come out with it. It has really helped me as well as blessed me.

Dr. Van Impe, just in case you have forgotten me, I was saved when you preached a crusade at the Landmark Baptist Temple in Cincinnati, Ohio, in December of 1969.

May God continue to richly bless you and your ministry. I watch you on TV every opportunity I get.

With warmest regards, I am,
Sincerely yours,
Mark Grooms

* * *

James R. Troxel, Pastor
First Baptist Church
Cedar Falls, Iowa

Dear Brethren:

I have read with deep empathy Dr. Van Impe's article, "That They All May Be One" (Why I Discontinued Citywide Crusades). What he has to say is of significant importance to our congregation at this time.

Would it be possible to obtain about 50 copies of the article? Please indicate to us what these would cost so that we might reimburse you for the expense.

The Lord bless you for your courageous stand! I know from experience that it has not been easy. We are praying for you.

Sincerely yours in Christ,
James R. Troxel

* * *

Dr. Ernest C. Hinze, Jr., Pastor
First Southern Baptist Church
Casper, Wyoming

Dear Dr. Van Impe:
I greatly appreciated the article, "That They All May Be One." I have struggled with the fragmentation the body of Christ has experienced, and more recently have been deeply concerned with how we are actually coming across to the unbeliever.

Thank you for the stand you have taken and the encouragement you will be to so many.

In His love,
Ernest C. Hinze, Jr.

* * *

Rev. Harold M. Walsh, Pastor
United Baptist Church
Burton, Michigan

Dear Jack and Rexella:
I wish you well on the public stand you took. It was

necessary step, even though costly. It will do much to heal many a wound in God's family.

Your old friend in Christ,
Harold

* * *

Rev. H.P. Floyd, Pastor
Victory Baptist Church
Central Point, Oregon

Dear Rev. and Mrs. Van Impe:

We are fundamental Baptists with membership in the Baptist Bible Fellowship of Springfield, Missouri.

We just read your article, "That They All May Be One." Thank God for dedicated, God-fearing men like you. Thank God for your courage to write such an article. It has been needed for years. That article has inspired us so very much. Although we realize how hard it was for you to write, we rejoice that you did.

I trust that many preachers and church members will see themselves in it and come to their senses before it is too late.

Sincerely in Christ,
Rev. and Mrs. H.P. Floyd

* * *

Rev. Robert C. Savage
(son of Dr. H.H. Savage)
Baptist General Conference
St. Croix, VIRGIN ISLANDS

Dear Jack:

I sing a doxology of praise for the "new year" in which you are ministering. May the Lord's joy, peace and love be with you moment by moment.

Rejoicing,
Bob

* * *

Rev. Frank Howell, Pastor
Bible Baptist Church
Cagayan de Oro. City, PHILIPPINES

Dear Brother Jack:

I received your magazine. You are exactly right. I am a BBF missionary in the Philippines. I get so tired of fighting over personality conflicts, pride and mainly jealousy. If we could all work together here, we would have had the Philippines evangelized ten years ago. God forgive us and help us to see what He has given to you and others concerning the body of Christ.

Do you mind if I reproduce your letter and give it to the national pastors here in Southern Philippines? They need to know.

You have my prayers and deep appreciation for your stand on this subject of fellowship and unity with the brethren. Keep up the good work.

Yours in Christ,
Frank Howell

* * *

Dr. Emanuel J. Morris, Pastor
Calvary Baptist Church
Jacksonville, Florida

Dear Dr. Van Impe:

I want to express my appreciation for your apology in the **Perhaps Today** magazine. I am sure that it took prayer, courage and boldness, and I just want you to know that I stand with you in this matter of fellowship with our brethren.

Yours in His service,
Emanuel J. Morris

* * *

Rev. Ronald Thacker, Pastor
Danvers Baptist Church
Danvers, Illinois

Dear Dr. Van Impe:

I attended and graduated from Dr. Tom Malone's school, Midwestern Baptist College.

I want to thank you for your stand for Christ in the midst of persecution. My heart was broken as I read your article, "That They All May Be One." I was present when you preached at Cobo Hall in 1977. I have always been blessed by your preaching. Keep it up! Don't quit!

We at Danvers Baptist Church love you and pray for you and give to your ministry because we believe in you. Your work is so Christ-honoring.

In His service for souls,
Rev. Ronald Thacker

* * *

Heart Disease in Christ's Body

> Rev. Joe Pizzino
> First Baptist Church
> Shady Spring, West Virginia

Dear Dr. Van Impe:

After reading the article entitled, "That They All May Be One," I decided that I must write to you. I am sure you have agonized over this many days. I thank God for your courage and honesty. I have always respected and admired you and your ministry, but have withheld full support due to the problem you covered so well in the article.

Again, thanks for the courageous article. Not many of us are willing to admit wrong or accept change, even when we realize we should. I have preached for almost 36 years and have been grieved over the bickering and fighting in recent years among God's people. What a spectacle it must present to the world. Satan is having a field day.

I shall pray for you and your ministry. Though the article will bring controversy, I believe it will heal more wounds than anything done in recent years. God bless you.

> Yours because of Calvary,
> Joe Pizzino

* * *

> Rev. Mark Bredin, Pastor
> Fellowship Baptist Church
> Kingston, Nova Scotia, CANADA

Dear Dr. Van Impe:

I am pastoring a church in Nova Scotia, Canada. I am a fundamentalist and want to tell you about my

326

appreciation for your message entitled, "That They All May Be One."

It grieves me to see Bible-believing brothers and sisters fighting and sowing discord rather than praying and loving. I appreciate your stand for the truth.

Thankfully yours and His,
Mark S. Bredin

* * *

Rev. Harvey R. Peter, Pastor
First Baptist Church, Lloydminster
Saskatoon, Saskatchewan, CANADA

Dear Dr. Van Impe:

The reason for my writing is simply to commend you for the stand that you have taken, and for the sweet and reasonable spirit in which you have expressed it. I sense that God is drawing together born-again believers of all stripes to turn our world upside down. God knows we need it.

Yours in Christ,
H. R. Peters

* * *

Catherine B. Walker, Special
Asst. to the President For Intercessory Prayer
Foreign Mission Board of Southern
Baptist Convention
Richmond, Virginia

Dear Mr. Van Impe:

We rejoice with you in your new-found love for all of God's people. A loving, forgiving spirit can do so much to bring unity in the body of Christ. May God use you richly in the ministry to which He has called you.

Sincerely yours,
Catherine Walker

* * *

In addition to these comments from inter-denominational and Baptist leaders, I have also received numerous letters from outstanding professors affiliated with our leading Bible colleges and Christian universities. However, I am refraining (often by request) from printing their statements in order to protect their job status. Still, I want to publicly say, "Thank you, precious brethren. Your encouragement means so much to me."

Rexella and our entire staff join me in praising the Lord for the great work of love, unity and reconciliation He is performing in the hearts of His people. We give Him all the glory for the fact that, out of a total of 10,000 ministers and 300,000 laymen who received the article, "That They All May Be One," only **two** negative responses were received. Also, three men who were of the neo-fundamentalist movement called or wrote to apologize for the rumors and slander they had propagated about my ministry in the past. Hallelujah! God is at work. Revival is in the air. A new day is approaching.

* * *